1126
J66
2008

CONFLICT
Coaching

LIBRARY
NSCC, LUNENBURG CAMPUS
75 HIGH ST.
BRIDGEWATER, NS B4V 1V8 CANADA

To Marty and Alex, you make it all worthwhile

—T. J.

To Colby, Eshen, and Sagan, my best friends

—R. B.

LIBRARY
NSCC, LUNENBURG CAMPUS
75 HIGH ST.
BRIDGEWATER, NS B4V 1V8 CANADA

CONFLICT Coaching

Conflict Management Strategies and Skills for the Individual

TRICIA S. JONES
Temple University

ROSS BRINKERT
The Pennsylvania State University,
Abington College

SAGE Publications
Los Angeles • London • New Delhi • Singapore

Copyright © 2008 by Sage Publications, Inc.

All rights reserved. No part of this book may be reproduced or utilized in any form or by any means, electronic or mechanical, including photocopying, recording, or by any information storage and retrieval system, without permission in writing from the publisher.

For information:

Sage Publications, Inc.
2455 Teller Road
Thousand Oaks,
    California 91320
E-mail: order@sagepub.com

Sage Publications India Pvt. Ltd.
B 1/I 1 Mohan Cooperative
    Industrial Area
Mathura Road, New Delhi 110 044
India

Sage Publications Ltd.
1 Oliver's Yard
55 City Road
London EC1Y 1SP
United Kingdom

Sage Publications Asia-Pacific Pte. Ltd.
33 Pekin Street #02–01
Far East Square
Singapore 048763

Printed in the United States of America

Library of Congress Cataloging-in-Publication Data

Jones, Tricia S.
Conflict coaching: Conflict management strategies and skills for the individual/
Tricia S. Jones, Ross Brinkert.
        p. cm.
Includes bibliographical references and index.
ISBN 978-1-4129-5082-4 (cloth)
ISBN 978-1-4129-5083-1 (pbk.)
1. Conflict management. 2. Mediation. I. Brinkert, Ross. II. Title.

HM1126.J66 2008
303.6′9—dc22   2007023143

Printed on acid-free paper

07   08   09   10   11   10   9   8   7   6   5   4   3   2   1

Acquiring Editor:	Todd R. Armstrong
Editorial Assistant:	Katie Grim
Production Editor:	Sarah K. Quesenberry
Copy Editor:	Cate Huisman
Proofreader:	Kevin Gleason
Typesetter:	C&M Digitals (P) Ltd.
Cover Designer:	Bryan Fishman
Marketing Manager:	Carmel Withers

Contents

Acknowledgments

We are grateful to all those in the conflict resolution and executive coaching fields who have worked to develop conflict coaching. Their efforts reflect a diverse collection of academic and practitioner disciplines and perspectives. We are particularly grateful to our colleagues John Dimino, Joe Folger, and Denise Walton of Temple University who worked with us in the initial development of the conflict coaching component of the Conflict Education Resource Team at Temple University in the 1990s and from whom we have had the pleasure to learn in a number of ways throughout the years. We are also very grateful to others who have worked to advance conflict coaching and with whom we have had the opportunity to share ideas and progress in our work on coaching, including Cinnie Noble, Brian Polkinghorn, Susan Raines, and Alan Tidwell.

Writing a book is always a little daunting, but it was made much less so for us thanks to our publishing team at Sage—Todd Armstrong, Katie Grim, Deya Saoud, Sarah Quesenberry, Cate Huisman, Kevin Gleason, Bryan Fishman, and Carmel Withers. We appreciate their enthusiasm for the project, high level of expertise, and unwavering professionalism. We are particularly appreciative for their openness to the idea of including the workbook/ancillary materials on CD-ROM. This idea was a little unconventional, but Todd, Katie, and Deya were supportive and helpful as we crafted the best combination of text and supporting materials. Sarah shepherded us through the production process and helped us see the book become a physical reality. Cate Huisman's copy editing was both brisk and precise. We particularly appreciate her willingness to work with us on a tight schedule. We thank Kevin Gleason for providing careful proofreading. And we are grateful to Bryan Fishman for designing a visually appealing cover and to Carmel Withers for valuable support in terms of marketing materials.

One of the most important processes in writing is the ability to receive quality feedback from seasoned scholars and practitioners. We were extremely fortunate to have excellent reviewers at both the proposal and the final draft stages. We would like to thank Scott H. Hughes, University of New Mexico School of Law; Jessica Katz Jameson, North Carolina State University; Roy J. Lewicki, Fisher College of Business, The Ohio State University; Jackie A. Moorhead, Community Mediation Concepts; Brian Polkinghorn, Salisbury University; Susan Raines, Kennesaw State University; Maria R. Volpe, John Jay College of Criminal Justice—City University of New York; and William Warters, Wayne State University for their carefully considered comments and willingness to provide feedback quickly and completely. Their feedback truly strengthened our work. In any instances where the material seems lacking, the flaws are our own.

At Temple University, the faculty of the Adult and Organizational Development Program in the Department of Psychological Studies in Education were, as always, supportive. So, a big thanks to Cynthia Belliveau, Joe Folger, Larry Krafft, and Mel Silberman for making the AOD program one that supports and sustains scholarship and that recognizes the importance of blending theory and practice. And our sincere gratitude to the administration and leadership in the College of Education at Temple University—Dean C. Kent McGuire and his leadership team. Their willingness to support and recognize the work in conflict processes and its significance to a variety of educational arenas is heartening.

We thank the following individuals from Penn State Abington for their strong collegial support: Ellen Murray Brennan, Dinah Geiger, Ellen Knodt, Binh Le, Eleanor Meehl, Janet Mignogno, Jane Owens, Susan Paciolla, Samuel (Sam) Stormont, and Carla Chamberlin Quinlisk. In particular, we are grateful for the steady backing from the senior leadership team at Penn State Abington, including former Arts and Humanities Division Head David Ruth, current Arts and Humanities Division Head Thomas (Tom) Smith, Assistant Dean Samir Ouzomgi, Associate Dean Peter Johnstone, and Chancellor Karen Wiley Sandler. We also thank Penn State Abington for awarding Ross a summer faculty fellowship in order to support his work on the book and CD-ROM.

We appreciate our students' intellectual curiosity and substantive input regarding some of the ideas developed in the book as well as their excitement for the overall project. In particular, we would like to acknowledge the reflections of David Inloes and Denise Pettus of Penn State Abington. We also had the great opportunity to "beta test" the book with the students of our Special Topics Seminar on conflict coaching.

Thanks to all of those students for their insights and suggestions: Quaiser Abdullah, Karen Aves, Brandi Baldwin, Miriam Bowerman, Cynthia Clark, Cristhian Dantagnan, Dawn Davenport, Mary Claire Dismukes, Adrianne Greth, Denise King, Ulicia Lawrence, Debra Mitchell, Eunice Rush-Day, Nicole Savage, and Jeannette Weiss.

Finally, our deepest gratitude goes to our families, as they made tangible sacrifices so that we could commit to and complete this satisfying but time-consuming endeavor. Marty Remland, Tricia's husband, was a sounding board for ideas and approaches as well as a calming influence able to reinforce that it's important to enjoy the process as well as value the product. And Alex, their son, was gracious in giving so many Saturday afternoons watching Mom at her computer, smiling his way through them, and playing piano to help Mom think. Colby Keyser, Ross's partner was especially thrilled with the finish of the book and CD-ROM, in large part because of the many sacrifices she made to support these projects. Eshen and Sagan, their daughters, literally savored the entire journey as they regularly stopped by for M&Ms from Dad's desktop candy dispenser.

Introduction

Although we are both experienced as conflict coaches, it has been in our other roles as conflict communication researchers, teachers, training development professionals, mediators, and consultants that we have been most impressed by the opportunities for conflict coaching. Over the years, we have asked ourselves the following kinds of questions:

- Is there an alternative dispute resolution option for those who are unable or unwilling to engage in mediation or other dyadic and multiparty processes?
- Is it possible to offer a one-on-one conflict intervention and enhance rather than detract from existing alternative dispute resolution practices?
- Is it ever appropriate to directly share theory and research insights as part of a conflict resolution intervention?
- Does it ever make sense to offer conflict communication training for one?
- Are organizations and individuals interested in one-on-one support regarding conflict communication in order to advance strategic objectives?

To each of these questions, we have responded with a definite "Yes."

With others responding similarly, conflict coaching is becoming a widely recognized professional development intervention. Conflict coaching emerged in the 1990s as a priority in executive coaching and as a conflict resolution process supplementing mediation on university campuses. We anticipate that conflict coaching will expand in use within these and other frameworks, because conflict communication is a key feature of the workplace, and conflict coaching offers possibilities not found in more established executive coaching and alternative dispute resolution offerings.

Goals for the Book and Intended Audiences

Scholar-Practitioner Focus. From the outset, we sought to write a book that would be valuable to both scholars and practitioners, one that would present the theoretical understanding of conflict coaching in conjunction with the attention to skills, intervention, and practice of conflict coaching. Compounding the challenge was the realization that we wanted to address scholars from a variety of disciplines as well as practitioners in a variety of conflict contexts. Thus, this book is intended as a blend and a balance to benefit the variety of audiences for whom we believe it is informative and helpful.

This book and accompanying CD-ROM, which we discuss later in this introduction, are designed as instructional materials to be used in upper-level undergraduate and graduate-level courses on conflict coaching, applied conflict communication, executive coaching, negotiation, or human resource management.

This book and accompanying CD-ROM have also been developed for intermediate or advanced professionals who are already active or who plan to become active as conflict coaches or executive coaches. In addition, they are intended as a resource for those referring others to coaching or for those actively managing the areas of organizational dispute systems, organizational change, or workplace performance.

Interdisciplinary Orientation. Conflict coaching has captured the attention of an array of scholars, students, and practitioners. Academic disciplines represented by those interested in the process include, but are by no means limited to, alternative dispute resolution, business, communication, conflict studies, education, law, peace studies, psychology, social psychology, and sociology. Practitioners interested in conflict coaching include executive coaches, facilitators, human resource professionals, mediators, ombudspersons, organizational communication or organizational development consultants, organizational dispute system managers, and training development professionals. During the writing of and the review process for this book, we have included the contributions of a variety of disciplines in terms of conflict theory, research, and practice.

Strong Theory-to-Practice Mix. We see our emphasis on theory to practice as the defining focus of this book. As scholars and practitioners, we believe fervently that there is nothing as valuable to practice as a good theory. Yet, we also know that translation of theory into practice is often overlooked or underemphasized. In this book we adopted an internal structure that highlights theory to practice. Specifically, in all of the chapters that deal with the conflict coaching process, we have included an explicit statement of principles that should guide this stage or element of conflict coaching and a set of approaches for practice. Both the principles and approaches are directly informed by and derived from conflict theory. We believe that this combination will merge the "why" and "how" of conflict coaching for the scholar-practitioner. Further, we provide an elaborated set of approaches, self-assessments, and activities for use by coaches or instructors in the CD-ROM.

Infusion of Issues of Culture. One of the more difficult challenges for any author addressing conflict management theory and practice is how to deal with questions of culture. Should it be discussed in a separate chapter, or should it be infused throughout all discussions? After long consideration, we decided that the latter was truer to our orientation to how culture influences conflict and conflict management. We realize that this approach may leave some readers wanting more about culture on a particular topic than we were able to provide without significantly lengthening the book.

Concentration on Coaching for Interpersonal Conflict in the Workplace. Conflict coaching can be used with clients who are experiencing family, workplace, or community conflicts, and we believe that our conflict coaching model is applicable to these conflict contexts. But in writing the book, we wanted to place emphasis on one context in order to more fully develop the application in that arena. Given our connection to executive coaching and our assumption that the majority of current conflict coaching is being used in workplace and professional contexts, we concentrated on discussions of coaching for interpersonal conflict in the workplace.

An Overview of the Contents

This book is organized into three sections. Section 1, "Introducing Conflict Coaching," introduces the concept of conflict coaching and the Comprehensive Conflict Coaching (CCC) model that forms the basis for the majority of the book's content. Chapter 1, "Conflict Coaching: Conflict Management Strategies and Skills for the Individual," defines conflict coaching, describes its sources of development in the executive coaching and conflict resolution fields, suggests drivers of continued development, proposes principles for conflict coaching, and suggests reasons why conflict coaching should be pursued and supported by the conflict resolution field. Chapter 2, "The Comprehensive Conflict Coaching

Model," acknowledges existing executive coaching and conflict coaching models, introduces the theoretical foundation for the CCC model, overviews the preparation step and four stages of the model, and addresses a number of ways in which the model is adaptable. The basic ideas in both of these chapters were originally presented in an article by Ross Brinkert (2006) published in *Conflict Resolution Quarterly*.

The second section, Section 2, "Conducting Conflict Coaching," provides chapters that go into depth on each of the stages of the CCC model. In some cases, a stage is discussed in more than one chapter. The chapters in this section present methods of enacting the stages of conflict coaching. In each chapter the presentation of information follows a standard format: (1) explanation of the relevance of this stage in light of the overall model, (2) overview of the critical concepts and theories, (3) introduction of principles for conducting this stage, and (4) description of specific coaching approaches used in this stage. Chapter 3, "Stage One: Discovering the Story" focuses on the unfolding of the client's story about the conflict. Before a client can be helped to manage a conflict, he or she may need help understanding what happened and how the context impacted the unfolding of the conflict. The chapter summarizes humanistic and social science approaches to narrative, applies insights from two areas of narrative theory to conflict management, and discusses specific techniques for discovering the story.

The second stage of the CCC model concerns the application of three powerful perspectives—identity, emotion, and power—to help the client and coach clarify goals for the management of conflict. Thus, three of the chapters in Section 2 are devoted to the explication of perspectives of Stage Two. Chapter 4, "Stage Two: The Identity Perspective," focuses on identity needs or "face" in the conflict. Drawing from identity theory in conflict studies, face theory in sociology, and communication goal theory, this chapter overviews assumptions about identity and conflict, offers a model of identity in interpersonal workplace conflict, presents face work tactics as the primary means of managing identity issues, and concludes with stage-related principles and approaches. Chapter 5, "Stage Two: The Emotion Perspective," turns attention to the role of emotion in conflict. Emotion is becoming recognized as an important dimension of conflict, but many conflict practitioners are not well informed about how emotion theory and research informs effective conflict management. This chapter points out the centrality of emotion in conflict, presents theories of emotion, considers the concept of emotional intelligence, and finishes with principles and approaches for applying the material with clients. Chapter 6, "Stage Two: The Power

Perspective," presents the third perspective. An exploration of power relations can make sense of the past and potential movement of a conflict. Social power theory has long been a core analysis tool for conflict practitioners, and we believe it is essential that clients are helped to understand the power relations in their conflict. This chapter presents assumptions about power, offers goals and power sources as a primary step to selecting conflict strategies and tactics, points out undesirable conflict patterns as a caution when selecting strategies and tactics, presents three strategies as a way of making sense of multiple tactics, and explores some of the ways culture and power interrelate.

Once the coach and client have analyzed the conflict through the perspectives of identity, emotion, and power, the next stage in the CCC model focuses on the future. Chapter 7, "Stage Three: Crafting the 'Best' Story," explains a stage that offers clients the opportunity to reappraise their initial conflict story in light of the three perspectives. Most important, this chapter gives coaches techniques for helping clients define what a successful strategy will look like in their conflict. The chapter considers change theories from appreciative inquiry and visioning approaches, revisits narrative theory for insight into narrative coherence and fidelity, and concludes with principles and approaches.

Stage Four in the CCC model concerns the development of strategies and skills that clients need to make their desired future become a reality. This stage is discussed in a series of chapters that each concentrate on specific skill sets. Chapter 8, "Stage Four: Communication Skills: Confrontation, Confirmation, and Comprehension," is the first of four chapters that concern the fourth stage of the coaching model. No matter how well designed a conflict strategy, it may fail if the strategy cannot be put into effect through good communication. The chapter is organized around three sets of skills central to all conflict management: (1) confrontation or assertive communication that announces the need to address the conflict, (2) confirmation or communication that is respectful of the other's identity, and (3) comprehension or communication that aids in understanding content. The chapter also includes an exploration of culture and communication skills.

Chapter 9, "Stage Four: The Conflict Styles Opportunity," concerns conflict styles and how coaches can work with clients to more effectively apply their own style as well as to understand and more effectively react to others' styles. This chapter provides an overview of various conceptions of conflict styles before developing a coaching approach that most closely follows the five-style approach of Thomas and Kilmann. Chapter 10, "Stage Four: The Negotiation Opportunity," gives coaches insight to help clients decide if negotiation is appropriate for them, decide on the best negotiation orientation, and identify negotiation skills that need to be developed. The chapter focuses on coaching clients in bargaining (competitive), principled negotiation (cooperative), and composite (mixed-motive) negotiations. Chapter 11, "Stage Four: Coordinating Coaching With Other Conflict Processes," explains how the conflict coach can guide the client in finding other alternative dispute resolution (ADR) resources and assessing whether they are of use for the specific conflict. In community, workplace, and educational conflict, individuals are usually a part of a larger system of dispute resolution alternatives and resources; they just don't know the systems or how to access and effectively use them. This chapter also helps coaches prepare their clients for participation in various dispute resolution processes like mediation and arbitration.

The final chapter in Section 2 is Chapter 12, "The Parallel Process: Learning Assessment in Conflict Coaching." Learning assessment is a parallel process: that occurs throughout the conflict coaching experience. It consists of four components: needs assessment, goal setting, feedback, and learning transfer.

The third and final section of the book is Section 3, "Integrating Conflict Coaching Into Your Practice." In this section we step outside the coaching process to consider the issues of developing and maintaining a coaching practice and the future of the field of conflict coaching. In Chapter 13, "Needs Assessment and Program Evaluation for Conflict Coaching," we suggest that conflict coaches should conduct needs assessments and program evaluation to decide whether to engage in conflict coaching, how to engage in conflict coaching, and how to prove that they have positive results from conflict coaching. Finally, in Chapter 14, "The Future of Conflict Coaching," we consider where the field of conflict coaching should go in terms of future research, training and delivery mechanisms, and policy implementation.

An Overview of the CD-ROM

Each copy of the text is accompanied by a CD-ROM that includes a variety of ancillary materials useful for the coach and client or for the instructor and student. The CD-ROM contains a number of resources briefly described here:

General Resources. The general resources include a glossary of key concepts throughout the book and a list of hyperlinks to Web sites that contain related information.

Resources for Client and Coach. These resources are for the coach and client in the process of coaching and include self and other evaluation forms, feedback forms, and checklists for accomplishments and steps within each stage.

Resources for Instructor and Student. These resources are for graduate or undergraduate courses devoted to or with sections on conflict coaching. They include sample syllabi for graduate and undergraduate courses in conflict coaching, a list of recommended books related to coaching and conflict, and paper assignments for both graduate and undergraduate students.

Chapter Resources. For each chapter there is a set of resources that we believe are useful for clients, coaches, instructors, and students. These include a PowerPoint presentation, an annotated bibliography, a set of learning objectives, a chapter summary, a chapter outline, a checklist of critical learning points, a set of discussion or reflection questions, specific hyperlinks to Web sites relevant to that chapter, and a list of key concepts in that chapter. (Each concept is also included in the overall glossary.)

An Invitation to Share the Conflict Coaching Journey

Conflict coaching is a developing area of practice, and although we believe it will soon be generally recognized as a professional intervention, it will take longer for it to mature as a solid, research- and theory-driven enterprise. We have tried to be thorough in our efforts in creating a research- and theory-based foundation for conflict coaching and in sketching out an initial structure that will help coaches and clients. Nonetheless, much work remains. We anticipate that possible success for our work may well be charted in terms of the quality and quantity of others' critiques and proposals for advancement as well as in straightforward acceptance for the ideas and applications we have put forth.

We would like to acknowledge the numerous other applications of conflict coaching that are possible. The scope of this book virtually required that we limit ourselves to interpersonal conflict in workplace settings. Conflict coaching may also be used in multiparty situations and to address group conflict or even larger-scale conflict, and it can also be applied in people's personal lives. We look forward to exploring and writing about these applications of coaching in the near future.

If you are already involved in conflict coaching or you are interested in becoming active with respect to any of the ideas and applications shared in this book and CD-ROM, we invite you to contact us through our website www.conflictcoachingmatters.com.

We sincerely hope that these materials support your academic or applied interests. More broadly, we hope that they strengthen conflict coaching as a distinct conflict management process.

—*Tricia S. Jones, West Chester, Pennsylvania*

—*Ross Brinkert, Abington, Pennsylvania*

SECTION 1

Introducing Conflict Coaching

1

Conflict Coaching

Conflict Management Strategies and Skills for the Individual

I am not afraid of storms for I am learning how to sail my ship.

—Louisa May Alcott

Rowan is a conflict resolution practitioner in a small consulting group. Although she originally entered the field as a mediator, most of her time is now spent as a training development professional delivering topics such as dealing with difficult people in the workplace and conflict styles. After a recent seminar, she was approached by a participant named Kathryn who requested one-on-one assistance with more effectively handling the confrontational style of her immediate supervisor, a senior leader in the organization. Kathryn wanted to better manage her day-to-day communications with this person and also develop herself as a viable candidate for a top-level position. Rowan did not immediately know how to structure a service for Kathryn but was confident that she could be of help.

* * *

Mara is the dispute resolution manager in a large federal organization. While the program she heads is widely regarded as a success (mainly because it resolves many employment disputes through voluntary mediation) she feels dissatisfied that her office regularly turns away individual disputants when counterparties are uninterested in trying mediation or another dyadic or multiparty process.

* * *

3

David and Linda are the respective heads of human resources and organizational learning in a national insurance company. They have teamed up to create a positive conflict culture in the organization. They are especially interested in the prospect of strengthening supervisor-supervisee relationships by developing supervisors' conflict management skills.

I t is striking that while the conflict resolution field has numerous processes for two or more clients, offerings for the individual client are relatively underdeveloped. We believe conflict coaching is a promising means of addressing this gap. Conflict coaching is a process of conflict intervention involving one disputant/client and one conflict resolution professional. Given the resonance of one-on-one professional coaching and the fact that it is often not feasible to engage two or more parties simultaneously, there is a need to advance this process. With the body of conflict communication theory and research, there is a bountiful reservoir on which to draw.

Each of the brief opening cases represents an opportunity to introduce the practice of conflict coaching. Rowan could coach Kathryn regarding her current tensions with her supervisor and more broadly as a promising senior-level leader in a particular organizational conflict culture. Mara is in a position to add conflict coaching as an alternative dispute resolution (ADR) process offering within her organization, possibly with internal capacity or with an outside collaborator. David and Linda may find it appealing to train supervisors in a tailored conflict coaching model as a way of strengthening the supervisor-supervisee relationship. Obviously, many other conflict coaching scenarios are also possible.

In this chapter, we offer a general definition of conflict coaching and explore its two main sources of development, namely the executive coaching and conflict resolution communities. We then propose likely drivers of continued development for conflict coaching before presenting some important conflict coaching principles. The current chapter concludes with a number of reasons why the conflict resolution community, in particular, has much to contribute and gain by developing conflict coaching. This sets the stage for the next chapter, which introduces the Comprehensive Conflict Coaching model, elaborated in detail throughout the remainder of the book.

A General Definition of Conflict Coaching

Conflict coaching is a process in which a coach and client communicate one-on-one for the purpose of developing the client's conflict-related understanding, interaction strategies, and interaction skills. The definition is broad in that it encompasses different forms of communication between the coach and client. Conflict coaching, as it is explored and refined here, is primarily understood as a face-to-face interaction with occasional use of print-based activities and resources; however, it can also reasonably take place via the telephone, Internet, or other oral, written, and/or visual media. The definition is also expansive, as it permits different kinds of conflict-related conversations to take place, including but not limited to ways of making sense of conflict, general plans for actively managing conflict, and specific communication behaviors for the client to possibly enact. While contextual issues (including interpersonal, organizational, and cultural factors) are certainly central to any coaching conversation, they are not included in the definition; this allows for the application of conflict coaching in a wide variety of relational circumstances. Finally, this basic definition allows significantly different coaching models to be proposed. For instance, the model proposed in this book takes a moderate position on the use of the coach's expert knowledge base within the coaching session. Some may argue for stronger use of the coach's perspective, while others may argue that it should be more restrained.

Sources of Development: An Overview of *Conflict* and *Coaching* in the Executive Coaching and Conflict Resolution Fields

Over the past two decades, the concepts of *conflict* and *coaching* have been addressed in combination by a number of different scholars and practitioners. These writings can be grouped in two general categories, although it should be emphasized that they basically developed simultaneously and sometimes thematically overlap. The first category is made up of work from the executive coaching field that, usually incidentally, mentions conflict as playing a role in the executive coaching process. The second category captures work from an explicit conflict resolution point of view.

BACKGROUND ON EXECUTIVE COACHING

Executive coaching is usually one-on-one professional development within an organizational setting. Tobias (1996) noted that the term first appeared in business settings in the late 1980s and came about not as a strikingly new concept or practice but as a more appealing label for a practice of consultation offered to managers and senior leaders that had evolved over time. A thorough review of the literature generally supports this view (Kampa-Kokesch, 2001). Berglas (2002) stated that there were 2,000 executive coaches in 1996 and at least 10,000 in 2002, and there are projected to be more than 50,000 by 2007.

Executive coaching can be narrow to expansive in terms of topics and duration. It has been used to teach specific skills, improve job performance, prepare for professional advancement, and assist with broader purposes such as an executive's agenda for major organizational change (Witherspoon & White, 1996).

Diedrich (1996) worked to modify an executive's style, assist executives in adjusting to change, help in developmental efforts, and provide assistance to derailed executives. Kiel, Rimmer, Williams, and Doyle (1996) characterized approximately one-quarter of their clients as needing help preparing for advancement, a second quarter having performance problems, and the remaining half as needing to reinforce their existing areas of strength. Levinson (1996) noted simply that executive coaching largely involves supporting clients as they advance in terms of adaptive work behaviors. Those with a stronger popular emphasis also commonly include life coaching within an executive coaching framework. For instance, Morgan, Harkins, and Goldsmith (2005) make distinctions in terms of coaching leaders and behavioral coaching, career and life coaching, coaching for leadership development, coaching for organizational change, and strategy coaching. Given the topical breadth of executive coaching, it is not surprising that the coaching relationship may be limited to one or two meetings or extend over many years.

CONFLICT AND COACHING IN
THE EXECUTIVE COACHING COMMUNITY

As briefly introduced earlier, the terms *conflict* and *coaching* seem to have been first joined together in 1994 when Stern (1994) commented on the potential importance of addressing the topic of conflict management within executive coaching work. He noted that executive coaching may be relevant in situations where executives trigger conflict ineffectively or perpetuate destructive conflict.

Kilburg (2000), a prominent executive coaching scholar who has written numerous articles for academically grounded consulting psychologists, wrote a book chapter titled "Working with Client Conflicts." The chapter, consistent with the overall book and Kilburg's general perspective, addressed clients' internal and external conflicts as understood in terms of a combined psychodynamic and systems approach. The chapter is a notable contribution to conflict coaching, especially but not exclusively for those working from a therapeutic background. As well as providing general guidelines, Kilburg offered suggestions for coaches working with executives who are effecting change, managing boundaries and limits, dealing with spiritual and moral issues, and valuing diversity.

Kets de Vries (2005), another executive coaching author working from a psychotherapeutic orientation, combined the concepts of conflict and coaching in terms of more broadly addressing group-based leadership coaching. He proposed that there are important benefits to carrying out leadership coaching in a group setting, in part because it allows for effective conflict resolution.

Coaching for conflict is integral to the executive coaching field because conflict permeates the executive's work world. "Coping with internal and external problems forms the foundation of managerial work, and these problems almost always consist of some form of human conflict" (Kilburg, 2000, p. 217).

CONFLICT AND COACHING IN THE CONFLICT RESOLUTION COMMUNITY

The need for a one-on-one conflict resolution process, in cases where only one party was present for mediation, emerged at Macquarie University in Australia in 1993 (Tidwell, 1997). A response to this need was formalized and put into practice on campus three years later and was known as "problem solving for one." This process involved a six-step model based on the generation of multiple solutions and the selection of optimal solutions through a cost-benefit analysis.

Conflict coaching seems to have first been named as such in and actively practiced in North America as of January 1996 at Temple University in Philadelphia, Pennsylvania (Brinkert, 1999). The campus conflict resolution program was experiencing a low demand for mediation and, consequently, conflict coaching was developed under the co-leadership of professors Joseph P. Folger and Tricia S. Jones. Conflict coaching thereafter became one of the conflict-related services promoted (Jameson, 1998) and engaged in by the Temple campus community. While conflict coaching at Temple was limited to conflict styles coaching until spring 2000 (Brinkert, 2000), it was expanded shortly thereafter to include such subtypes as coaching for confrontation, coaching for diversity, and coaching in possible preparation for mediation. Conflict coaching remains a central conflict resolution service offered on Temple's campus and, year-to-year, is consistently put into practice more often than mediation.

In the current decade, conflict and coaching have been addressed in the literature in ways that differ from the definition of conflict coaching presented at the outset of this chapter. Keil (2000) applied the coaching metaphor to intervening with work teams. Blitman and Maes (2004) suggested ways that skills and behaviors associated with sports coaches may be helpful within mediation. An article in *Personnel Today* (NHS Conflict, 2005) noted the need for a massive amount of "conflict coaching training" (or group-based training meant to assist professionals in working through conflict with clients) in Great Britain's National Health Service (NHS). The NHS Counter Fraud and Security Management Service (CFSMS) was instructed to train 750,000 employees in techniques to calm people in potentially violent situations. The training is reportedly behind schedule but is to be carried out by 2008.

Conflict coaching as a one-on-one process has grown in significance over the past 10 years. It is a service marketed by a growing number of for-profit and not-for-profit conflict resolution organizations and individual practitioners. It has visibility on the relatively popular www .mediate.com Web site and appears to be a growing topic of interest at the annual Association for Conflict Resolution conference.

The emergence of conflict coaching as a recognizable and valued intervention process is perhaps most evident given that highly visible organizations are adopting the practice. Cloke and Goldsmith (2000) noted the opportunity to use coaching as one conflict resolution method in organizations. More recently, Weiss and Hughes (2005) recommended, as one of six strategies, that companies use the escalation of conflict as an opportunity for coaching. They went on to describe how IBM executives receive training in conflict management and are provided with online resources to assist them in coaching others. C. Noble (personal communication, April 9, 2007) developed a proprietary conflict coaching model that has been used for the peer conflict coaching program in the Transportation Security Administration, a division of Homeland Security. As Guttman (2005) commented, conflict coaching is relevant for building leadership competency. As such, it is of interest to training development, human resource, and other professionals who regularly facilitate such initiatives.

LIKELY DRIVERS OF CONTINUED DEVELOPMENT FOR CONFLICT COACHING

This section identifies some reasons why conflict coaching is likely to expand in the coming years. Most of these drivers of continued development flow out of the early emergence of conflict coaching as outlined above. Drawing these together arguably demonstrates a promising future for conflict coaching.

The continued concern with conflict management in a complex service economy. Ongoing emphasis on interpersonal, team, and organizational communication in a complex global service economy will likely mean that organizations will make investments in one-on-one assistance as well as other types of professional development for their leaders, managers, and frontline workers. Effective conflict management is an integral part of an economy emphasizing service and communication. The continued growth of the global service sector and ongoing collaboration and competitiveness in the sector seem to suggest growing opportunities to offer conflict coaching. This trend also suggests growth for the conflict management field in general. There will likely be increased demand for conflict coaching theory and research as well as for practice tools as established universities increasingly and visibly develop coaching programs, especially within their business schools (for instance, Georgetown University, INSEAD, the University of Cape Town, and the University of Pennsylvania).

The strong commitment in many areas of society to productively and ethically manage conflict. Again, this is a trend that broadly supports the growth of the conflict management field. Organizations and individuals frequently have expectations that conflicts should be handled appropriately. Even an all-star organizational performer may not be tolerated if he or she drives other important or promising members from the organization or is otherwise significantly out of step with the culture and goals of the organization.

The continued need for a one-on-one ADR process. While ADR may be ideally suited to purely dyadic or group interventions because of the way that it provides insights and tools for improved interaction, there is still a need to make ADR accessible to individuals. Many clients and ADR professionals acknowledge this reality. Dyadic and multiparty options may not be possible, at least not immediately. It is well accepted among mediators that many mediation referrals do not lead to mediation because one or more parties is reluctant to participate in that process. These parties may find it more appealing to try conflict coaching. Conflict coaching may function as a way of increasing awareness of options for addressing the conflict, including the availability of traditional ADR processes. For some, conflict coaching may be more attractive than other processes for reasons of perceived efficiency and/or effectiveness.

The need for a process that has a strong and tailored skills emphasis. While ADR processes such as mediation offer spaces where parties can interact in more productive ways, and while ADR training activities typically introduce new knowledge and skills in a general manner, conflict coaching offers a unique blend of possibilities for clients. Conflict coaching represents a considerable breakthrough as a conflict management process, as it provides clients with strategies and skills customized to their conflict situations in a relationship rich with interaction. In this respect, conflict coaching complements existing ADR process options and training opportunities. It promises something different, for example, than "mediation for one" or "training for one." It is a fundamentally different opportunity for addressing conflict more appropriately and effectively. Further, conflict coaching may put the unused and underused existing talents and abilities of ADR professionals into use.

Increasing market recognition and demand. The term *conflict coaching* and its basic practice have gained common currency, particularly as they have been visibly adopted by large organizations such as IBM (Weiss & Hughes, 2005). The application of conflict coaching within a growing list of organizations has left many with the sense that it is successful. Of course, peer-reviewed research is certainly needed to justify this view. In some cases, individuals have self-initiated a coaching-type relationship with a trusted ADR professional because they perceived the ADR professional as having expertise that would be valuable to access in a one-on-one format. Also, some ADR and executive coaching professionals have observed more generalized demand for these services and have branded their services as executive coaching and/or conflict coaching in order to attract clients. More and more individuals have some awareness of the term *conflict coaching* both inside and outside the conflict management field.

Increasing interest in the use of conflict coaching as a way to integrate and promote existing ADR processes. The fact that there are a number of established ADR processes does not solve the practical challenge of creating visibility, including providing ways for individuals to determine their appropriateness. Given the habit and preference of most individuals to make one-on-one inquiries regarding conflict-related issues, it seems that most would be amenable to an ADR triage process that is individual in nature. Conflict coaching may be used to introduce mediation, as an entry point in the ombuds process, and to make a more robust organizational dispute resolution system. During intake for a mediation, the mediator typically talks to each party to explain the process and, depending on the type of mediation, coaches them so they can interact in a productive manner. Many mediators do not learn this skill in their training. Ombuds offices may be involved in transitioning parties to mediation but often do much more, as these offices attract parties with many different concerns (Warters, 2000). Conflict coaching may be well suited to much of the person-to-person problem solving in which ombudspeople engage. And it may help open up the ombudsperson role to be more systemic in nature, as has been called for in that professional specialty (Wagner, 2000), by incorporating a system of conflict intervention options. This could conceivably result in greater numbers of individuals making use of established ADR processes.

There is evidence that organizational dispute resolution systems that have components in alignment are more effective (Bendersky, 2003). Therefore, it is not unreasonable to suggest that having more components in alignment (i.e., adding conflict coaching to the mix of ADR process offerings) might further enhance effectiveness. The success of existing in-house dispute resolution systems, the best of which resolve up to 90 percent of employee complaints internally (Wexler, 2000), suggests that this is a path worth pursuing.

The likely emergence of conflict coaching as a recognizable executive coaching specialty. Executive coaching continues to have considerable appeal within a wide range of workplace circles. Although some of this appeal may come from the breadth of the process, it is reasonable to assume that there will be increased specialization within executive coaching. Expertise is specialized by nature. Therefore, all other considerations being equal, an individual needing or wanting to work on a conflict-related issue will probably seek out and work with a conflict communication specialist. Conflict communication is central to supervising others, coordinating with peers, influencing upward in the organizational hierarchy, and managing relationships with clients and other external constituencies. Runde and Flanagan (2007) insisted that the ability to handle conflict is a top skill of successful leaders today and is essential to an organization's competitiveness. These authors pointed out that the much talked about need for leaders to be more emotionally competent is intimately linked with their need to be more conflict competent. Runde and Flanagan also emphasize that leaders will themselves admit that there are high costs associated with ineffectively managing conflict.

Continued support and direct involvement from organizational communication professionals who see value as an add-on or alternative to consulting, training, other types of coaching, etc. There are a number of human resource insiders, external consultants, training development professionals, executive coaches, and others who have experienced the need for an allied or alternative intervention in the form of conflict coaching. A human resource specialist or external consultant might not only support a senior leader in defining a strategic message, but he or she might also assist the leader in determining an approach and developing related skills to execute conflict-related aspects of the overall strategy. A training development professional might see the opportunity to assist a participant in developing conflict awareness, strategy, and skills in a more specialized format due to the participant's unique abilities, responsibilities, challenges, and/or opportunities. Some human resource specialists, organizational communication consultants, and training development professionals may want to hone an additional expertise as a conflict coach. Others will want to focus on existing areas of expertise and refer conflict coaching work to colleagues.

Continued development of conflict coaching curricula in graduate and undergraduate programs. When academic programs begin to develop courses and formal curricula in an area, it is a sure sign that the topic has gained a legitimacy. Likewise, the existence of courses and curricula continue to promote and support enhancement of the theory and research in that area. We are fortunate that we have courses on conflict coaching that are already being taught at respected programs in conflict management and dispute resolution (for example, at Columbia University, Kennesaw State University, Salisbury University, and Temple University).

Conflict Coaching Principles

Given the early development of conflict coaching, likely drivers of continued growth for conflict coaching, and broad lessons learned from the introduction of other ADR processes and other consulting and training interventions, we propose the following principles for the practice of conflict coaching. These principles are reflected in the Comprehensive Conflict Coaching model that is introduced in the next chapter and explained in detail throughout the remainder of the book.

A flexible model is vital. While some aspects of the conflict coaching process may always or at least often follow a linear pattern, movement throughout stages or onto and off of thematic touchstones is often flexible. The Comprehensive Conflict Coaching model is presented in stages that have an internal logic. We believe that the logic is compelling enough for the coach and client to follow these stages in many coaching situations. However, we do not believe that coaching is limited to a lockstep application of these stages. The stages could occur in a nonlinear or even simultaneous manner.

Both direct and indirect clients should be considered in the coaching experience. There are organizational or systems participants and stakeholders who may need to be considered in the process of coaching, even though they are not in the room. The organization, in the form of one or more organizational representatives, can play the role of indirect client. Involvement of indirect clients underscores the importance of the organizational context for the disputant. Whether indirect clients are involved in conversations about the coaching process is a case-by-case decision. But all conflict coaching should focus on whether critical indirect clients exist, who they are, and how they might be effectively involved or simply acknowledged.

A relational and systems orientation to conflict coaching is essential. Conflicts must be understood as social constructions of interdependent relationships with normative structures that influence interpretation and action. The Comprehensive Conflict Coaching model is strongly relational in that it assumes a client's conflict only makes sense in terms of his or her relationship to others—his or her web of relationships that define the critical social context. The context of the dispute includes culture in various forms. As such, the conflict coaching conversation never steps out of contextual or cultural concerns. Consequently, within any given coaching session, it is a reasonable expectation that the coach should directly acknowledge this issue, especially if the client does not.

Coaching is a contingent activity. Knowledge is never complete, and coaching should emphasize that there is always another point of view, another way of knowing that might alter the understanding of the conflict. Both the coach and client should be encouraged to take a contingent approach to understanding and approaching conflict. This has deep implications for conflict coaching. In part it means: (a) The coach should express humility even while speaking as an expert; (b) the client should be encouraged to develop his or her understanding and appreciation for the complex and ongoing dance of conflict, particularly given his or her unique circumstances; and (c) coaches and clients should be cautioned about the inherent inability to definitively understand past or present conflict as well as definitively plan future action at strategic or tactical levels.

Conflict coaches should be knowledgeable about conflict theory and research as well as competent in conflict analysis. Conflict coaching requires a knowledge base that not all aspiring coaches have acquired. For the model proposed in this book, the conflict coach needs to be knowledgeable and experienced in conflict research and theory, be knowledgeable and experienced in facilitating adult learning, have considered his or her own cultural background (including perceptions and possible biases), and have some understanding of the context in which the client is experiencing the conflict. Extrapolating from lessons learned from the study of mediator competence (Lieberman, Foux-Levy, & Segal, 2005), conflict coaches should be involved in ongoing training that is both practical and clearly related to theory. Further, coach assessment should combine self-assessment and assessment by others. Finally, coaches' abilities to recognize and respond to clients' emotions may be especially important to develop (Jones, 2005).

Coaching aims to foster client empowerment with the coach combining expert and facilitative approaches. Conflict research and theory can routinely be made accessible and can often be of notable value to individual disputants. Therefore, it is appropriate for coaches to combine expert and facilitative approaches and to share this information. While this model fully embraces the conflict coach as sometimes acting in an expert role, coaches should only assume this stance if they are suitably qualified. Because expertise is limited by its very definition, coaches should expect, not infrequently, to express the limits of their knowledge and/or to recommend outside experts or authoritative resources. Although this model involves the conflict coach occasionally adopting an expert role, this role should not predominate. Any individual conflict coaching session or ongoing conflict coaching relationship should have a general conversational quality. We caution against excessive directiveness by the conflict coach especially, given some practitioner research (Bacon & Spear, 2003) in the executive coaching field, including contrasting findings regarding the coach's role as perceived by the coach and client. However, arguing that any coach directiveness is inappropriate is unwise, given the value of an executive coach's expertise as demonstrated by Wasylyshyn (2003).

Coaching is about helping someone reflect on conflict and possible courses of change; it is not about forcing that reflection or change. Because the client has control and responsibility, his or her point of view is central to the coaching process. The client retains full control about which perspectives to consider as well as which strategies and skills to use outside of the coaching session. While the coach should encourage the client to be aware of multiple perspectives and practical opportunities within the conflict, and the coach can give advice about a particular viewpoint or course of action, the client determines what can be done. We encourage coaches to embrace an active role in providing clients with information and alternatives that will foster client empowerment.

The coach has a responsibility to sufficiently understand the particular client's point of view of the conflict, including the conflict context, prior to offering additional perspectives or specific practical opportunities. The sharing of perspectives and practical opportunities by the coach should always be followed by a clear invitation for the client to respond. This response, even a negative response, should be treated with respect by the coach and integrated into the overall conversation.

Conflict coaching is not appropriate for all cases. There are a variety of reasons why conflict coaching may not be a good alternative. Organizations may advocate coaching as a means of manipulating or silencing. A client may not have the cognitive, emotional, or behavioral competence to participate productively in coaching. There may be a larger social issue that requires an alternative action before or in addition to coaching, but where coaching alone is not appropriate. In some cases, conflict coaching may begin, but the coach or client may realize that the process is flawed and should be discontinued. In Chapter Two we discuss terminating a conflict coaching process and relationship in more detail. Here, it is important to note that such termination can and, when appropriate, should happen.

Conflict coaching should follow a principle of efficiency. A common question about conflict coaching and executive coaching is, "How long will this take?" Of course, there is no definitive answer to that question other than, "It depends." Still, we believe that conflict coaching should attempt to follow a basic principle of efficiency—getting the most benefit with the least amount of time and effort. Some executive coaches describe their coaching relationships as taking months or even years. While there may be some mutually defined conflict coaching relationships of this length, we encourage coaches to think in terms of shorter-term coaching cycles in which the client can move quickly through analysis and action planning to intervention and assessment.

Conflict coaching should follow a high ethical standard. Any discussion of ethics is fraught with disagreement about what is ethical and how one should behave to enact that standard. In the conflict field, ethical codes of conduct are generated and continually debated. This is certainly the case with the practice of mediation despite considerable attention being focused on mediation ethics over the span of many years (McCorkle, 2005). But we believe that no conflict process can be introduced without a consideration of ethics. Even if the frequency with which conflict coaching is used does not grow, a serious examination of conflict coaching ethics is needed within the ADR field.

Whether or not this field-level conversation takes place anytime soon, coaches and organized coaching programs need to be clear with themselves and with potential clients about fundamental ethical matters such as impartiality, conflict of interest, dual roles, and confidentiality. Impartiality would seem to be primarily concerned with ensuring that the coach has no prejudice toward the client. In terms of conflict of interest, the coach has a responsibility to disclose any and all actual or potential dealings or relationships that would result in bias against the client. Likewise dual roles prior to and during the conflict, and those foreseen after conflict coaching, should be directly acknowledged to the client. In order to reasonably safeguard the client and make the process as effective as possible, we strongly advise that, where dual roles exist for coaches, these are put aside within individual coaching sessions. However, we recognize that the complexity of this issue means that it must be more thoroughly considered for each context. The boundaries of confidentiality also need to be made clear to clients prior to engaging in a coaching session. This can be a challenging but vital issue to clarify in some cases, such as those involving an organizational sponsor who insists on some degree of reporting regarding a particular client's coaching involvement or progress. Other matters such as responsibility for the coaching process and outcomes, coach compensation, other coach and client commitments, and the procedure for terminating the coach-client relationship should all be dealt with at the outset of the coaching relationship. Where major ethical compromises exist, the coach should independently withdraw from acting in a coaching capacity.

Conflict coaching requires quality control, assessment, and monitoring. As with any professional human intervention and any business practice, conflict coaching should be introduced only where it can reasonably be considered in alignment with the goals and capacities of those involved and where it can otherwise be executed successfully. Just as important, it should be adopted only in circumstances where there is a commitment from the outset to ensuring quality thresholds, systematic scanning for unanticipated negative and positive outcomes, and a general striving to develop a stronger process through continuous learning on a multitude of levels. Just as the use of other ADR processes tends to be more readily accepted if it is institutionalized before conflicts arise, so too may quality control, assessment, and monitoring be best introduced prior to the start of conflict coaching activities.

Conflict coaching should be seen as part of a larger system of conflict management. Conflict coaching is most powerful if it is offered within a context-specific organizational dispute system, or at least where it is offered within the context of more generally available ADR options. In no respect is conflict coaching meant to supplant more established conflict management options or deemphasize the value of a systemic approach. On the contrary, conflict coaching should be introduced in a manner that strengthens the attractiveness, use, and outcomes of organizational dispute systems and ADR.

Conflict coaching can function as an inflow, parallel, or outflow mechanism for mediation, ombuds processes, and other ADR and organizational dispute system processes. An effective conflict coaching model integrates with a wide range of process options, in the very least, by minimally introducing those options to clients. In this manner, conflict coaching can work well as an initial process for clients and the conflict professionals they engage. Conflict coaching can provide a good setting for the client, and possibly also the coach, to determine the appropriateness and appeal of other conflict processes. Conflict coaching can also be used parallel to or after other processes. In organizational dispute system terms, conflict coaching should be seen as a key loop back process. Conflict coaching is a process to which people can always return as a way of refocusing a conflict at the interest-based level. Of course, the coach must be considerate of potential conflicts in cases where he or she functions in different professional roles with a given client.

Conflict coaching can serve an individual or a group of clients, and the client(s) can likewise be involved in conflict with an individual or group. Although conflict coaching may have gained early appeal and may have primary ongoing appeal as a way to offer conflict management services to individuals who are alone in seeking professional assistance, other client configurations are certainly possible. For instance, two clients in conflict with one another may both opt for conflict coaching prior to, after, or in place of mediation. Conflict coaching may need to be adapted somewhat but is certainly also possible with a client group representing a common party in a conflict. The coaching client(s) may be using the conflict coaching process to explore strategies and skills with another party consisting of one or more individuals or a defined group.

Conflict coaching must be sensitive to various cultural contexts. The direct and indirect parties to conflict coaching are never outside of culture. Cultures relevant to a given coaching interaction may exist at both broad and narrow levels and are likely to be multiple even for a single individual. While most professionals inside and outside of the conflict management field may generally appreciate the importance of relatively universal cultural concerns such as race, ethnicity, gender, and sexual orientation, more local cultural concerns can be just as significant. These can include organizational culture, organization department-level culture, regional differences, industry sector culture, and professional culture. The overall design of a conflict coaching program needs to take prevailing cultural currents into account. Cultural currents also need to be taken into account within specific conflict coaching relationships.

Major Reasons for the Conflict Resolution Field to Develop Conflict Coaching

We are committed to the "big tent" approach to the development of conflict coaching. While we are communication scholars, the approach to conflict coaching detailed in this book draws from multiple disciplines. More broadly, we believe that the continued growth of the conflict coaching process relies on the (loosely) coordinated involvement of currently active professionals representing diverse academic, applied, and personal backgrounds. One such community where we have encountered such productive diversity is in the conflict resolution field. It is our hope that those in this field—together with those from allied fields—become active in the growth of the conflict coaching process. Two main reasons for doing so follow.

The conflict resolution field can enhance the theory, research, and practice of conflict coaching. The range of academic and professional disciplines (including executive coaching) as well as diverse cultural backgrounds represented by those within the conflict resolution field means that conflict coaching could be advanced with increased commitment. Arguably, no scholarly or professional field is better positioned to develop the practice theoretically, facilitate clients' involvement with the process, conduct research, and use research findings to further the process. One of the most exciting opportunities for the conflict resolution field might be increasing access to what many would reasonably see as a desirable, tailored, professional development intervention. As Wasylyshyn (2003) noted, executive coaching tends to be highly valued by clients but seems largely to be limited in access to those in positions of privilege. Conflict coaching may be of benefit to those not only in many reaches of an organization but also in many reaches of broader society. Of course, conflict coaching needs to be developed with a certain degree of restraint as indicated by evidence of the use of executive coaching in situations that warranted other change interventions, most notably systemic or structural change (Murphy, 2005). The conflict resolution field can reasonably take on this responsibility given its history of using multiple means of intervention.

Conflict coaching can support the advancement of the conflict resolution field. Just as the conflict resolution field may grow the conflict coaching process, so too may the opposite be true. Conflict coaching is an opportunity for the field to develop at the scholarly and practitioner levels. Conflict coaching can support core conflict resolution processes. For instance, mediation can get increased visibility as it is introduced through the coaching process. Overall, conflict coaching can act as a vehicle for raising the visibility of the conflict resolution community with various individuals and organizations, including current executive coaches, life coaches, and those administering such services.

Developing conflict coaching related to mediation is perhaps the most obvious move, but developing conflict coaching in a larger sense, in relation to substantive areas of conflict communication theory and research, could arguably offer the deepest and broadest breakthroughs. Conflict coaching can incorporate and reinforce substantive areas of the conflict communication literature that have not been broadly or deeply recognized by the conflict resolution community.

Conflict coaching may have additional appeal to conflict resolution practitioners as it allows them to market an additional service, one that is increasingly seen as cost effective from both supply and demand standpoints. With an increasing push for credentialing within the executive coaching field (Natale & Diamante, 2005), the issue of the conflict resolution community's stake in the larger professional coaching field merits attention.

Conclusion

This chapter began with a definition of conflict coaching, charted sources of development, indicated some likely drivers of continued development, provided general conflict coaching principles, and offered some major reasons for the conflict resolution field to develop this new process. We now turn toward an introduction of the Comprehensive Conflict Coaching model and lead into this introduction with a consideration of existing coaching models in the executive coaching and conflict coaching arenas.

Chapter Summary

Conflict coaching is the process in which a coach and client communicate one-on-one for the purpose of developing the client's conflict-related understanding, interaction strategies, and interaction skills.

LIKELY DRIVERS OF CONTINUED DEVELOPMENT FOR CONFLICT COACHING

- The ongoing emphasis on conflict management in a complex service economy
- The strong commitment in many areas of society to productively and ethically manage conflict
- The continued need for a one-on-one ADR process
- The need for a process that has a strong and tailored skills emphasis
- Increasing market recognition and demand
- Increasing interest in the use of conflict coaching as a way to integrate and promote existing ADR processes
- The likely emergence of conflict coaching as a recognizable executive coaching specialty
- Continued support and direct involvement from organizational communication professionals who see value as an add-on or alternative to consulting, training, other types of coaching, etc.
- Continued development of conflict coaching curricula in graduate and undergraduate programs

(Continued)

(Continued)

CONFLICT COACHING PRINCIPLES

- A flexible model is vital.
- Both direct and indirect clients should be considered in the coaching experience.
- A relational and systems orientation to conflict coaching is essential.
- Coaching is a contingent activity.
- Conflict coaches should be knowledgeable about conflict theory and research as well as competent in conflict analysis.
- Coaching aims to foster client empowerment with the coach combining expert and facilitative approaches.
- Conflict coaching is not appropriate for all cases.
- Conflict coaching should follow a principle of efficiency.
- Conflict coaching should follow a high ethical standard.
- Conflict coaching requires quality control, assessment, and monitoring.
- Conflict coaching should be seen as part of a larger system of conflict management.
- Conflict coaching can function as an inflow, parallel, or outflow mechanism for mediation, ombuds processes, and other ADR and organizational dispute system processes.
- Conflict coaching can serve an individual or a group of clients, and the client(s) can likewise be involved in conflict with an individual or group.
- Conflict coaching must be sensitive to various cultural contexts.

2

The Comprehensive Conflict Coaching Model

Every path serves a purpose.

—Gene Oliver

Jim is the chair of the Department of Communication Studies and has just received word that the College of Liberal Arts (CLA), in which the department is housed, will be undergoing a major reorganization process beginning in the upcoming semester. The college has suffered a serious loss of enrollment in the past three years and has been consistently denied replacement positions and new hires as a result. The dean of CLA is a historian and does not accept the legitimacy of the "newer social sciences" like communication studies. He has remarked that he only understands and values the rhetoricians in the communication studies faculty because of their humanistic and historical approach to the study of communication.

The dean wants to make CLA an elite college with strong, but small, departments with graduate programs and undergraduate honors programs. Many in the college blame the dean for low enrollment; they suspect he has planned the streamlining to allow for his more "elite" college to emerge. The communication studies department has large credit-hour generation from two general education courses, Interpersonal Communication and Public Speaking. The dean values neither and would like to remove them from the general education course list. He sees them as "simple skills courses" unworthy of an elite liberal arts college. Until recently, only the provost's demand for a certain amount of credit-hour generation per college has protected these courses and their home department, Communication Studies.

Jim learned the news of the impending reorganization from the dean this afternoon. Jim and the dean have been at odds since Jim became chair—actually since Jim was elected chair by his faculty over the objection of the dean. While they have remained civil, it is an open secret in the college that the dean dislikes Jim and would prefer to have Jim and his department, especially the social scientists, leave the college and find a new home in the business school or some other professional or preprofessional college. When Jim got the dean's call, the dean made a point of telling Jim he was the last chair to hear about the reorganization.

Jim needs to tell the faculty of the Department of Communication Studies about the reorganization, but Jim is aware that they will not see this as an opportunity to create a united front. The humanistic/scientific split in the department reflects the split in the field of communication, and the department has been operating as two factions for the last several years, with the leaders of the two factions at serious odds. Walter is a nationally respected scholar of speech pathology and audiology, a branch of the discipline related to physical sciences and one that rigorously embraces the scientific method and orientation. Richard is a nationally respected scholar of rhetoric with an emphasis on critical, interpretive, and deconstructionist analysis of texts. Walter and Richard dislike each other personally and professionally; faculty meetings often degenerate to shouting matches and ad hominem attacks. Jim jokes with colleagues in other colleges that he spends most of his time as chair refereeing fights between Walter and Richard. Jim knows he was elected chair because of his perceived ability to mediate the tensions in the department. He knows that the upcoming reorganization will manifest in several very contentious and potentially destructive conflicts.

Richard has been arguing for the past year that the department should split and send the "applied folks" (as he calls the communication scientists) elsewhere. He has garnered strong support for this idea from rhetoricians and faculty in other CLA departments. Jim knows about Richard's behind-the-scenes maneuvering, but has not confronted him for fear that confrontation would lead to tension that would further complicate his job as chair. Jim is aware that Richard has been campaigning to be chair of a newly and exclusively "humanistic" department of rhetoric and that the reorganization may give Richard the opportunity to push for that reality. As Jim contemplates the recent news from the dean, he realizes that his first conflict will be with Richard and that he must consider the best strategy for managing that conflict or he will not be able to lead the department during the reorganization.

Never having been good at handling his own conflicts, Jim wants some help. A good friend who teaches in the conflict studies program in a neighboring university has suggested that Jim talk to a conflict coach to get a better handle on the dynamics of this situation and to plan a strategy for handling it. Jim takes the advice and hires you as his conflict coach.

J im, like most clients who work with a conflict coach, enters this process largely ignorant of what it is or how it will unfold. As a client, he wants to understand the basic logic of conflict coaching, the actions and activities that will improve his abilities, and the underlying principles that guide the work. What he wants and needs to hear is an explanation of the process of conflict coaching.

A model or a framework is important as a way of making sense of something. For conflict practitioners, models are a common and useful tool. We have models of mediation, arbitration, facilitation, etc. Here we present a model of conflict coaching that we believe is important for three reasons. First, the model helps us see the critical assumptions about conflict coaching—the theory bases for our work and the internal logic that guides process and content decisions. Second, the model acts as an action map or stage approach to how to proceed in conflict coaching. It choreographs the conflict coaching as a series of related steps that build upon each other. Third, because all models are necessarily incomplete, a coaching model provides conflict coaches a place from which to start and expand. Our intention in articulating this model is to give coaches a framework they can modify and adapt to suit their style, preference, and clients.

However, models have risks. As noted, they are necessarily incomplete, which means that a component of conflict that some believe is important may not be included. No model will be able to address all factors that influence conflict, but the test of a good model is whether it includes elements that most practitioners see as essential. A more significant danger is the tendency to treat a model as inviolate, as something that must be followed without alteration. We encourage you to think of the model as flexible rather than unyielding.

Before we present our model, we will ground this work in what has come before; we introduce the process models that dominate coaching approaches. Executive coaching, the area producing most coaching models, has given little attention to developing processes that are conflict specific. Although dispute resolution practitioners have begun to use conflict coaching, there are few substantive models of conflict coaching from alternative dispute resolution (ADR) practitioners. After reviewing the existing coaching models, we will present our model, its theoretical foundations, and some important areas of adaptability.

An Overview of Coaching Models

Most coaching models come from the executive coaching literature, a young but increasingly popular area of work, as we discussed in Chapter 1.

EXECUTIVE COACHING MODELS

In executive coaching, the nature of the coaching model depends on the philosophy of coaching, whether "coach-as-expert," "person-centered," or "blended" (Campbell, 2001). *Coach-as-expert* approaches assume that the coach is the diagnostician and directs prescriptive change. In this coaching process, the coach assesses the client, diagnoses deficiencies, and develops strategic interventions that the client is expected to follow. The *person-centered* coaching approach places the client in the driver's seat, with the coach facilitating reflection and discussion of potential strategies. But, as Sperry (2005) argues, most coaching probably follows the *blended* model in which both coach and client see themselves as partners in the discovery of desired change and the best ways to accomplish that.

The generic executive coaching model is exemplified by Valerio and Lee (2005) who identify five common steps that most coaching models contain: contracting, initial goal setting, assessment, implementation and action planning, and evaluation. A similar but more behavioral coaching template is provided by Goldsmith (2004) who suggests eight steps: (1) Include the client in determining the desired behaviors in his or her role, (2) involve the client in determining key stakeholders in the change process, (3) collect feedback, (4) determine key behavior for change, (5) encourage client response to key stakeholders, (6) review what has been learned and help the client develop an action plan, (7) develop an ongoing follow-up process, and (8) review results and start again. Different models place more or less emphasis on these common components, but the similarities are much greater than the differences.

In many executive coaching models, there is more attention given to the contracting and assessment stages than to the analysis, intervention, and evaluation stages. For example, Winum (2005) suggests key questions for the contracting stage to determine what kind of coaching and reporting relationship should be expected and enforced. Those questions include

- Whose budget will pay for this?
- Who will notice if the coaching work is successful?
- What specifically will be noticed?
- How will the environment/culture be improved?
- How will the results of the business unit be impacted?
- If coaching is successful, might there be an impact on retention or morale of the employees who work with the coached individual, productivity of anyone involved, customer experience and retention, extent of any litigation exposure, or time expended by you and others in dealing with the coached individual?
- What would be the impact if there were no change in this situation?
- Can you arrange access to the client's supervisor?

※ What information do you want about progress—when and how?
※ By when do you expect tangible results?

Natale and Diamante (2005) have a similar focus on contracting, insisting that there should always be a written contract that defines the terms of the performance, has a clear confidentiality provision, and specifies length of service, a minimum amount of coaching per day, method of communication between coach and executive, fees, expenses, and a method of billing.

Assessment is a critical stage, usually given great weight in coaching models (Keil, 2000; Kilburg, 2004; Weller & Weller, 2004). Winum (2005) argues that coaches should assess the context of the conflict by interviewing the sponsor (the person who hired the coach) and developing a success profile for the position of the person being coached. Assessment of the client involves interviews, self-assessment instruments, and 360-degree feedback as standard tools.

Some coaching models, like that of Natale and Diamante (2005), emphasize establishing a good coach-client relationship. Their model includes assessment of the coach and the coaching relationship as well as assessment of the client. They start with an "alliance check" in which clients are helped to understand why coaching has been requested. Next is a credibility assessment in which clients test the knowledge and ability of the coach. And then there is a "likability link" in which clients determine whether they are comfortable with the style of the coach and like the coach enough to continue the coaching process.

Implementation and action planning—basically the discussion of what needs to be done, what can be done, and how the client accomplishes this—usually receives the least explication in the coaching literature. Many executive coaching models talk about this aspect of coaching in vague ways that do little more than reify the notion of change as a goal (Cope, 2004). Some models, usually those that are therapeutic in orientation, more explicitly detail the nature of the change process. For example, Chapman, Best, and Casteren (2003), who specialize in career development executive coaching, base their coaching on a transition curve model that begins with a client's initial shock (the client is faced with a realization that there is a gap between performance and expectation), which is followed by denial (the client denies that any change is necessary, withdraws from facts, and tries to block alternate perceptions and information), which is ultimately shattered by awareness (the client comes to understand that change is necessary and begins to focus on his own competence issues), which leads to an acceptance of reality (the client accepts the need for change), which opens the door to experimentation/praxis (the client tries new approaches) that culminates in integration (when the client applies the new skills and behaviors in everyday functioning). Anderson and Anderson (2005) use an insight model that helps clients work through four levels of insight: reflective, emotional, intuitive, and inspirational. Reflective insight is the ability to step back from the experience and note what went well and what did not. Emotional insight is the ability to detect and decipher the information received through emotions. Intuitive insight is the ability to detect dynamics and information that lie just below the surface. And inspirational insight occurs when all the pieces come together, and something is seen in a new light.

Some models of executive coaching vary depending on the coaching task. For example, Stephenson's book (2000) presents a series of coaching models that can be used depending on whether the coaching task is enhancing leadership, career consultation and development, assimilation for new appointees, career transitioning, professional selling, or professional presentation and speaking. Some authors, like Sperry (2005) distinguish between skill-focused, performance-focused, and development-focused coaching—each of which uses variations on his basic model of engagement and contact, initial assessment, coaching plan and implementation, and evaluation of progress and outcome.

PREVIOUS CONFLICT COACHING MODELS

In Chapter 1 we reviewed the coaching field and argued for its value and expansion. It is valuable to revisit the models of conflict coaching that have been presented in the conflict literature, specifically the ones at Macquarie University and Temple University. Both models were developed and initially applied within the context of campus mediation programs in response to a low interest in mediation but a high incidence of single party demand for help.

The Macquarie University Problem Solving for One Model. Tidwell (1997) documented the Problem Solving for One (PS1) model that originated at Macquarie University in Australia as a tool for the mediation agency created for university faculty, students, and staff. This model was the first published model of conflict coaching. Tidwell contrasts PS1 with mediation: "Unlike mediation, PS1 is person focused, and starts (as we put it) 'where the person is not where they should be.'" (Tidwell, 1997, p. 311). The PS1 model is influenced by brief therapy and assumes that coaching is an efficient, short-term process.

The PS1 model rests on three basic activities: problem analysis, option costing, and communication skills development. Problem analysis focuses on helping the client analyze the conflict through various mapping procedures. Option costing involves both the generation of possible options for solution and the analysis of the costs and benefits of each, so the client can be guided in selecting the most beneficial and least costly alternative. Once a decision for action has been made, the coach concentrates on skill development to ensure that the client has the necessary communication skills to enact the option for solution. The PS1 process has six stages:

- *Preamble and introduction.* The facilitator describes the PS1 process and clarifies expectations, much like the opening statements in most mediation sessions.
- *Storytelling.* The facilitator asks the disputant to tell the story of the conflict, presenting the essential facts and details.
- *Conflict analysis.* The facilitator helps the client dissect the conflict using tools like conflict mapping, which attempt to articulate the origins, nature, dynamics, and possibilities for resolution.
- *Alternative generation and costing.* The facilitator and client work together to generate a variety of options for resolution and to forecast the possible costs and benefits of each.
- *Communication strategy development.* The facilitator provides the client with effective communication strategies and skill enhancement necessary to make the selected intervention work.
- *Restatement of the conflict handling plan.* The facilitator and client develop a plan for future action.

The PS1 model has several elements that we believe are critical. Philosophically, the model embraces a blended approach to coaching that empowers the disputant. Beginning with clarifying expectations about the process, PS1 builds alignment and gives the client a choice about whether to participate in the process. Encouraging the client to "tell the story" is critical, and the emphasis on communication strategy development is a strength of the model.

Temple University CERT Model of Conflict Coaching. Conflict coaching also moved forward in the late 1990s with the institution of the Conflict Education Resource Team (CERT) at Temple University in Philadelphia. Combined efforts, principally involving Ross Brinkert and Denise Walton, resulted in the development and use of a basic conflict coaching model (Brinkert, 1999, 2000). The model shared much in common with the basic framework of PS1, but it placed a greater emphasis on conflict styles. Temple's conflict styles coaching model involved the following basic stages:

- *Explanation of the coaching process.* The coach introduces the coaching process, and the coach and client discuss expectations for participation.
- *Introduction to conflict styles.* The client completes a standard conflict styles self-assessment instrument. The coach and client score the instrument.

The coach explains each style and invites the client to share an example of using the particular style.

※ *Developing choices in a particular conflict.* Here the client is invited to describe a past, present, or anticipated future conflict and apply each of the conflict styles. The client is then encouraged to evaluate the various choices represented by the respective styles in order to determine optimal choices and next steps.

※ *Closing.* Again, much as in mediation, the coach explains additional opportunities for dispute resolution, including coming back for mediation, coming back for additional coaching, or being referred to other resources for skill development, etc.

The Temple model of coaching was intended as a brief, one-session intervention with individual client-disputants who were experiencing roommate conflicts, conflicts with student team members in class, or other such student-student campus conflicts. The goal was to develop a process that would be helpful in the specific conflict but also educational, a process that would help students see possible patterns in their handling of conflict and consider developing additional styles and response options. Since its inception, the Temple model has been expanded to include additional conflict coaching modules and more emphasis on emotional awareness in conflict.

The Comprehensive Conflict Coaching (CCC) Model

In this section we present the CCC model of conflict coaching and explain its assumptions and processes in relation to the conflict case introduced at the beginning of the chapter. Initially, we provide a brief explanation of some underlying theoretical assumptions that guide the model. This reminds us that all models, whether for practice or theory building, involve assumptions that should be made explicit in order for readers and potential users to reflect on whether they share the assumptions. Then, we articulate the various stages of the model. These stages serve as the bases for the remaining chapters. We provide an overview and rationale but leave the detailed coverage of related literature, practice approaches, and principles for delineation for those chapters. And finally, we end this chapter with a consideration of ways that the CCC model can be adapted.

THEORETICAL UNDERPINNINGS OF THE CCC MODEL

Most conflict analysis is interdisciplinary. The phenomenon of conflict is simply too complex to be adequately understood by one discipline of study or by one theoretical perspective. Yet, to acknowledge this does not mean that our model is not more influenced by some intellectual traditions than others. We believe that to be explicit about our adherence to a communication perspective is key to understanding conflict and the practice of conflict coaching. Similarly, within that communication perspective, we accept the assumptions of a constructionist orientation to conflict. And finally, we see any process of change, including that constituted in conflict coaching, as necessitating a systems orientation in analysis.

What does it mean to have a communication perspective on conflict? Communication scholars see conflict as a social construction that is influenced by context and that creates a foundation for current and continuing relationships. As noted by Folger and Jones (1994, p. ix), "Central to a communication perspective is the realization that conflict is a socially created and communicatively managed reality occurring within a sociohistorical context." In the case of Jim, the conflict is something that Jim and Richard have created through their social interaction. The meaning of their fields of study, their presumed differences as humanists or scientists, their identities as friends or enemies, are all meanings they have given to actions and elements in their situations. Similarly, they have the power, as a constructionist orientation indicates, to reconstruct or deconstruct any of these meanings and, by so doing, completely redefine the conflict, their relationship, or their roles in the conflict.

As Gergen's (1999) work suggests, seeing conflict as socially constructed through communication requires us to be attentive to the communication or social interaction to which meaning is attached. And from this perspective we see conflict coaching as a process of understanding interpretations that lead to conflict and possible reinterpretations (and accompanying actions) that can reduce or manage conflict. Jim and Richard are probably not keenly aware of the communication behaviors they are using that influence the way they and others understand this conflict. But, their level of awareness does not alter the fact that their conflict is only knowable through their communication.

A very powerful form of social construction is narrative, or the development of a coherent story that explains the experience of the conflict. Stories are created and recreated throughout a conflict episode. For example, many conflict scholars argue that conflict is the production and management of narrative (Cobb, 1994) even if they do not subscribe to a specific "narrative approach" to mediation or dispute resolution (for example, Winslade & Monk, 2000). Jim and Richard probably have different narratives of what has happened and what is happening with the department and the reorganization. Part of their conflict management is the ability to create a coherent narrative and the ability to share that narrative with others. If Jim can't tell his story in a way that can be comprehended by others, he will not be able to influence them to support his efforts to maintain the current department.

A communication perspective focuses on the enactment of conflict, the analysis of verbal and nonverbal communication to identify patterns of process over time. Operating from a communication perspective means the conflict coach will be concerned with patterns of interaction and how those patterns of interaction are linked to social context. Can the coach help Jim recognize his patterns of avoiding conflict that trigger more aggressive or territorial response from his colleagues? Is Jim's repeated tendency to mediate between Richard and Walter creating the impression that Jim does not have his own interests in this conflict or would rather be a mediator than a party to the process? Is Jim's interaction with the dean constrained by the decision-making processes of the university; would the interaction have different meaning and effect if it occurred in another workplace context?

A communication perspective privileges communication behavior, but it does not dismiss information that can be obtained from other perspectives, such as sociological or psychological approaches to understanding conflict. Insights from other perspectives are valued and are blended in an interaction frame to understand how psychological and sociological processes inform and influence the social construction of meaning through communication.

For a coach, a communication perspective places discursive structures and features (the who, what, and how of conversational interactions) front and center as primary skills for intervention and conflict management as well as analysis. A conflict coach is ultimately interested in helping Jim understand what to do and how to do it as well as understand why it is a good choice for conflict management. Thus, a conflict coaching model from a communication perspective assumes that the coach is competent in communication skill development. A coach will do Jim little good if he can only tell Jim to negotiate but not tell Jim how to negotiate.

An important way that clients and coaches orient toward the coaching process is in terms of clarifying and advancing client goals. A goal strategy combines the basic striving to be effective with the need to be situationally appropriate (Cody et al., 1986; Marwell & Schmidt, 1967). Dillard, Segrin, and Harden (1989) have shown that a primary influence objective is always accompanied by a number of related situational objectives. Notably, these related objectives may be below the level of awareness for the source or the target. The primary goal is the "what" of conflict, the basic aim regarding changed behavior or changed circumstances. The secondary goals represent general motivations that shape the communication in terms of the primary goal. There cannot be communication without them. We loosely incorporate the Dillard, Segrin, and Harden (1989) approach into a goal model that highlights the following goal types: content goals, identity goals, emotion goals, and power goals. Most notably, we elevate the importance of identity, emotion, and power for making sense of how clients can best understand and accomplish their primary objectives.

Finally, adopting a systems orientation as part of a communication perspective means three practical things for the conflict coach. Two of these have already been mentioned—the importance of patterns and the importance of context. The systems perspective reinforces attention to patterns of communication rather than random acts (Fisher, 1976). While a single behavior may be very important, the client's strengths and weaknesses as a conflict manager are usually found in recurring patterns of behavior that need to be surfaced and broken. A systems perspective continually reminds the coach of the importance of context in determining meaning of communication (Jones, Remland, & Sanford, 2007). The layers of context—relational, social, organizational, cultural, institutional, etc.— all color the meaning and appropriateness of any communication. Thus, a coach must help the client to recognize and analyze the impact and interplay of relevant contexts. The third practical aspect of a systems orientation is that it reminds us that all parts of the system are interrelated and that change in one part of a system will ultimately affect other parts of the system. This is an extremely valuable insight when considering and planning change interventions. The strategy that Jim adopts for dealing with Richard will not simply affect Jim and Richard. As members of a system, their actions will directly and indirectly affect others in the system—other communication faculty, other CLA faculty, communication students, etc.

STAGES OF THE CCC MODEL

Jim has just called you to inquire about the nature of conflict coaching and to gather information about your process and orientation. To gain his confidence and demonstrate that you have a solid analytic approach and effective strategy for intervention, you need to articulate your model of practice.

In conflict coaching there is preparatory interaction and then the coaching process, just as in mediation there is an intake process followed by the mediation. In this chapter we discuss considerations for the preparation, but we concentrate on the stages of the coaching process. For readers interested in a more thorough treatment of preparation for coaching, we have included a variety of check sheets and explanatory aids on the accompanying CD-ROM.

Preparation for Coaching: Ensuring That Conflict Coaching Is Appropriate.
In our earlier review of the executive coaching models, preparation is what executive coaching scholars discuss as "contracting" (Valerio & Lee, 2005) or the "alliance check" (Natale & Diamante, 2005). Preparation involves determining whether the client understands and desires

coaching, whether the client is able to profitably engage in coaching, and whether the coach is an appropriate choice for the client. We see this preparation as involving three conversations (although they may take place in one interaction or be separate). We also acknowledge that content in the preparation discussions may need to be restated and revisited later in the coaching process. In this manner, "preparation" covers the broader function of managing the coach-client relationship on an ongoing basis.

Initial Conversation. The initial conversation or contact is about managing expectations. This initial interaction allows the coach to provide a basic overview of coaching, a brief discussion of process and principles, and a sense of time and resource commitment. For example, in your initial conversation with Jim, you would want to provide a basic definition of coaching, explain how coaching can be advantageous and what needs to be included to make it effective, present your model of coaching and what will be expected of Jim and of you, and give a sense of how long it will take and what it will cost. Basically, Jim should leave this initial conversation having received answers to the following questions (even if Jim didn't ask these questions):

- What is conflict coaching?
- How can conflict coaching help me?
- What will I get out of conflict coaching?
- What do I need to do to participate effectively in coaching?
- What are some limitations of coaching?
- When is coaching appropriate and when is it inappropriate or maybe even counterproductive?
- What is the coaching process?
  - What will happen?
  - How long will it take?
  - How much time will it take?
- How much control do I have over the process?
- How will we know if coaching is helping?
- What happens when coaching is over?
- Who will know about the coaching?
  - Who can know?
  - Who must know?
  - How much is confidential?
- Who pays for the coaching? And how much?

Assessing the Client's "Coachability." There is always a possibility that a client is not mentally competent or otherwise able to participate in coaching. A coach needs an interaction with the client or with others that enables the coach to decide whether the client can effectively participate. Through initial conversation, questionnaires, or data collection, the coach may determine that this client is not ready for or able to participate in coaching. For example, in executive coaching, Frisch (2005) assesses client characteristics to determine whether someone is a good candidate for coaching. He argues that a client with very significant personal or familial problems (for example, substance abuse or psychological impairment) should be automatically rejected as a candidate for coaching. Beyond that, additional factors such as the client's tolerance for risk, the client's willingness to try new approaches, the client's emotional resilience, and the client's motivation to change should all be considered by the coach before committing to a coaching relationship. Usually, if a client like Jim is referring himself to coaching, the coach can determine whether Jim is a good candidate for coaching by interviewing him on his history, concerns, and motivations for the process. If Jim was referred to coaching by the dean or the provost of the university, the coach may ask about basic employment information and the sponsor's perceptions of Jim's suitability for coaching. If there is serious concern about Jim's competence, the coach could ask Jim to complete psychological assessment instruments or talk first with a counselor before beginning the coaching process. Finally, it is important to point out that from the coach's standpoint, Jim retains the choice about whether or not to proceed and, once he has started, to continue with coaching, even if he is mandated to participate by his workplace.

Assessing the Coach's Ability. There are also questions about the coach's fit with the situation. In most cases, these are not questions of competence as much as questions of potential bias or conflict of interest. If a coach were good friends with Richard or sought to gain prominence for his department or university if Jim's department were disbanded, there are obvious conflicts of interest, and that coach should not enter into this coaching relationship. We know all too well that conflict practitioners are only human and have biases that can interfere with their work. Perhaps a coach has a very strong humanistic orientation and is biased against social science. The bias may be strong enough to dissuade the coach from working with Jim.

Stages of the CCC Model—The Coaching Process. Let us assume that the preparation conversations with Jim went well, and Jim has decided to start conflict coaching. The conflict coaching process consists of four stages, with some stages involving a variety of options (see Figure 2.1). Prior to conflict coaching, the coach has preparatory conversations with the client. During conflict coaching, the four stages are Discovering the Story; Exploring Three Perspectives—Identity, Emotion, and Power; Crafting the Best Story; and Enacting the Best Story. In addition, there is a parallel process of Learning Assessment

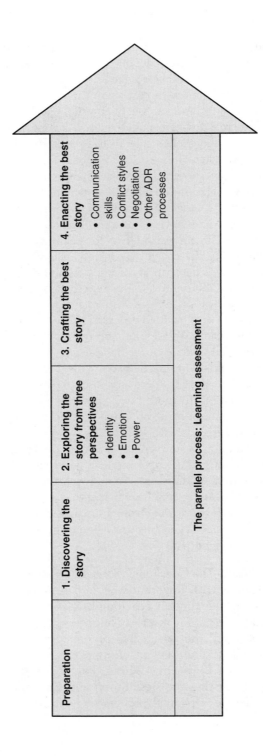

Figure 2.1 The Comprehensive Conflict Coaching Model

NOTE: While stage-to-stage movement can be nonlinear and even simultaneous, this figure represents the overall flow of a typical coach and client conflict coaching relationship. It is also a good way to initially learn the model.

that extends throughout the conflict coaching experience. Each of these stages is discussed in more detail.

Stage One: Discovering the Story. The first stage helps clients construct a coherent narrative of their experience of the conflict and engage in perspective taking about the possible narratives of other parties in the conflict. In this stage, the coach concentrates on discovering as much of the story as possible in order to have an adequate understanding of the conflict, the parties, and the context. Clients usually express content goals during this stage for both themselves and others, although, notably, these content goals may be changed, refined, or understood more fully later in the coaching process. This stage is discussed in much greater detail in Chapter 3. The discovery process is intended to increase coherence. Most coaching will involve at least the following three levels of clarification:

Initial Story. This is the client's story that comes with little urging from the coach. The conversation begins with the coach asking very general questions about the conflict and listening as the client tells the story for the first time to the coach. The initial story provides information about how the client sees important issues, persons, and opportunities in the conflict. The initial story often presents characterizations of other parties and assumptions about information and actions. When the coach asks Jim, "What's going on?" in his conflict, Jim may tell an initial story that sounds very similar to the one presented at the beginning of this chapter. The initial story paints a particular picture that represents Jim's current view of the conflict but that may change considerably with more discussion and refinement.

Refine Story. After the client presents the initial story, the coach helps the client refine that story. The story is expanded through some basic questions that ask the client to add information or detail. Part of the refinement process is encouraging the client to provide more information pertinent to how other parties in the conflict may be communicating and experiencing the conflict and talking more about how the conflict is affecting others in the system. Whereas the initial story is the outline, the refined story is the essay. A key aspect of refinement is that the coach is not challenging the narrative of the client, but is encouraging the client to provide the most comprehensive and coherent version of that narrative. Working with Jim, the refinement may go more deeply into the dynamics of the department and the dynamics of the field that have resulted in the bifurcation of humanistic and scientific communication scholars. The refinement could also go to explaining how the dean's vision for the college is reinforced or sanctioned by other organizational academic changes at the university. The story refining comes to closure when there does not seem to be more important information for the client to add.

Testing the Story. At this point the coach becomes more assertive by "testing" the refined narrative. The coach can ask questions to challenge the client's understanding of facts or information. Or, the coach can test assumptions that the client is making about the situation or the people involved. In this way, testing can lead to challenges of hostile attributions the client is making about the other party and can increase the client's ability to consider alternative explanations for a person's actions. A common consequence of testing is increasing the client's ability to take the perspective of the other party. Through the testing process, the coach can help identify information that the client does not have and needs to have to make strategic decisions. The process of testing allows the coach to raise questions about what doesn't make sense, or about what a person hearing this story may question. In Jim's case, the testing of the story may lead to a variety of important insights. For example, the coach may test whether the reorganization is really imminent or whether the process of the reorganization will take two or three years to complete. This insight could help Jim strategize about longer-term actions, because the demise of the department is not likely to happen as soon as he had thought. Similarly, the coach may help Jim test his assumptions about how resistant Walter might be to accommodating Richard in order to keep the department together. Perhaps Jim has been assuming Walter's noncooperation without considering the alternative, or perhaps Jim has assumed that his best role in this conflict is as mediator/chair. Perhaps the coach can help Jim think about how this conflict would unfold for him if he stepped out of the chair's position. The testing could raise questions about whether the provost supports the dean's reorganization and the dean's evaluation of the Department of Communication Studies. Jim may be encouraged to identify information that would convince his department they are seen much more favorably in the university than the dean would want them to think. All of these tests do not lead to a "true" story, but they help create a more complex and coherent story that serves as a better foundation for analysis and action.

Stage Two: Exploring Three Perspectives—Identity, Emotion, and Power. Once the client's story has been told, refined, and tested, the client has a description of the current situation. How does the coach help the client move from the understanding of the present to the orchestration of the desired future? The coach has to help the client understand the forces or drivers in the conflict in order to understand what to change and how to change it. We believe that there are three essential analytic elements in any conflict: issues of identity, issues of emotion, and issues of power. In Chapter 4 we begin by explaining the role of identity in conflict and how the identity perspective can inform the client's preferred actions and outcomes in the conflict. In Chapter 5 we discuss emotion and emotional communication in conflict, again focusing on how the coach helps the client see his or her emotions as a diagnostic and analytic tool. And in Chapter 6 we consider power dynamics in conflict. The power perspective helps clients see how they are able to influence the development of the preferred conflict outcome.

It is very important to emphasize that we see identity, emotion, and power as the perspectives through which we define all of our relationships with others. It is the merging of these three perspectives that clarifies the nature of a relationship, the experience of conflict in the relationship, and the means of recognizing necessary change and redefinition in the relationship. Thus, these three perspectives are all essential in order to have a relational orientation to conflict (Jones, 1994; Wilmot & Hocker, 2007).

The topics of identity, emotion, and power can take volumes to fully explain. Our goal in these chapters is to help the conflict coach understand how each of these elements functions as a strategic perspective that a client should engage before making decisions about "what to do" in the conflict. Think of these three perspectives as three lenses through which the coach will ask the client to view the conflict. Each lens highlights certain critical insights. Together, the lenses help the client see clearly what future situation is best for him or her. As you will see in the chapters, identity, emotion, and power are intricately linked. Understanding one helps you understand the others. Impacting one will impact others. Thus, effective strategic action is most likely when the client understands the congruence of the perspectives and how specific action will affect each component.

The Identity Perspective. Desired and damaged identity lies at the heart of the experience of conflict. Most people are in conflict because they believe someone or something is preventing them from "being who they are" or "who they want to be." Likewise, people in conflict are often ignorant of how their actions are negatively impacting the identity of the other. The conflict coach helps the client clarify current identity and desired identity. The coach helps the client see how the client can protect his or her identity and affect the other's identity. And the coach can help the client appreciate the consequences of these influences on identity. In working with Jim, the coach can help Jim clarify how the current conflict is damaging his identity as a leader, a scholar, and an influential member of the field. The coach can help Jim reflect on whether he has conflict between his own identities—perhaps maintaining the chair role is making it difficult for him to be the scholar he'd like to be. If Jim's identity has been damaged or is not what he would like, the coach can help Jim think about what his preferred identity is and how best he can create and protect that identity. The coach should also encourage Jim to think about the identities of other parties in the conflict and the things that might damage their identities and escalate the conflict.

The Emotion Perspective. Emotions are central to conflict. Our emotions help us understand when we are in conflict, they serve as a metric of how important the conflict is to us, and they provide a way of understanding what needs to change in order for us to feel better about the situation. As we discuss in Chapter 5, many clients and coaches are not well versed in the nature of emotion and the role of emotion in conflict. Many are uncomfortable with emotion and are unwilling to use it as an analytic tool. But coaches should help clients be more emotionally aware and appreciate the strategic value of emotions in conflict. Emotions are strongly linked to identity and power. Emotions are motivation and, as such, help us understand why people act in certain ways. One of the roles of the emotion perspective in conflict coaching is to help clients understand why they are motivated to do something but also to understand why another party may be motivated to behave in a certain way. What is Jim's emotional experience of this conflict? Is he angry, sad, depressed, afraid, or amused? How are these emotions affecting what he sees as possible options for action? How are these emotions preventing him from being comfortable with the status quo? What needs to happen for him to have a more positive emotional experience of this department and the reorganization?

The Power Perspective. What is the client's ability to influence the current situation in a way that is favorable to him? That's the bottom line of power. Assuming that Jim knows what he wants (e.g., he knows his identity needs, and he understands his emotional needs), can he make changes to the current situation that will increase his ability to create the desired identity and the more positive emotion? What factors are in his way? What resources are needed to increase his influence? What are the consequences of changing the power in his relationship with Richard, with the dean, etc.? The conflict coach can help Jim appreciate all of these aspects of power and can help Jim understand how the larger system restricts power or provides power that can affect Jim's conflict.

Stage Three: Crafting the Best Story (discussed in Chapter 7). At this stage in the conflict coaching, the client has constructed a coherent story of the conflict and has looked at that conflict through the three perspectives of identity, emotion, and power. The coach has facilitated the client's analysis of the conflict and now encourages the client to envision what the situation would be like if the conflict were managed most effectively. Granted, the coach and client understand that attaining an ideal outcome may be unlikely. But, the coach knows that attaining the ideal outcome is impossible if the client can't even articulate what that is. Using insights from the three perspectives, the coach assists the client in crafting a story of success, a journey with clear milestones that would meet the identity, emotion, and power interests of the client.

Stage Four: Enacting the Best Story. Knowing what you want is the first step to getting it. But, you must also know what needs to happen to move you toward that end. In this stage, the coach helps the client consider the best approach for dealing with the conflict to ensure the optimum outcome. Part of this will be to identify basic strategies for conflict management. Should Jim avoid the situation with Richard altogether, or collaboratively negotiate with Richard, or seek mediation? Part will be assessing whether Jim has the skills to enact the preferred strategy or tactic. If Jim needs to have effective communication skills to interact with the dean more effectively, can the coach provide skills training for Jim? And part of the challenge is helping Jim to understand how to leverage the larger system of conflict management opportunities available in the university and the community. Because Stage Four includes a variety of strategic and tactical opportunities, we have devoted four chapters to it. Chapter 8 presents advice on improving the three critical communication skills in conflict—confronting, confirming, and comprehending. Chapter 9 explains how coaches can instruct clients in conflict styles and the appropriate style for the conflict. Chapter 10 concentrates on negotiation skill, looking at the client's ability to negotiate effectively in a collaborative, competitive, or mixed-motive situation. Chapter 11 focuses on developing clients' awareness of other dispute resolution systems and processes to enhance their success.

The Parallel Process of Learning Assessment. Assessment and evaluation are essential components of conflict coaching and tend to occur throughout the process. We describe assessment of the client's learning and successful implementation of the conflict strategy as a parallel process to the first four stages. Once clients have a vision and an action plan for managing the conflict, they should develop benchmarks of success to determine progress along the way. In this stage, covered in Chapter 12, we discuss learning assessment in an adult learning context. The coach can help Jim define what he will see if his conflict management strategy is successful. In a more general sense, the coach can help Jim to reflect on and assess what he has learned through the conflict coaching process.

Some Areas of Adaptability for the CCC Model

In Chapter 1, we proposed principles that apply to the variety of forms of conflict coaching that have emerged. The Comprehensive Conflict Coaching model is consonant with these principles. However, given that the CCC model is a particular kind of conflict coaching, it is useful to detail some considerations specific to this model.

Again, as noted in Chapter 1, any conflict coaching process needs to be flexible in terms of the stages or touchstones that it proposes. While these may have a general logic and a degree of practical regularity, they also need to show capacity for repetition, reordering, and simultaneous activity. The CCC model is premised on the basic flow of preparing for coaching, discovering the client's initial conflict story, taking some important perspectives on the story, determining a best story, working on ways of actively creating the best story, and, throughout this process, considering overall goals of the coaching relationship. The CCC has been designed with the understanding that the coaching conversation may be extremely fluid and find itself appropriately and effectively shifting from this basic pattern. Nonetheless, the basic pattern remains useful for purposes such as describing the model to potential clients and others, for teaching the model to potential coaches, as a tentative map at the beginning of a conflict coaching relationship, and as a way of generally making sense of most conflict coaching relationships.

Beyond some flexibility in the stages of the CCC model, it is meant to be broadly adaptable in various respects, including the following: (1) making conflict coaching fit with different coach-practitioner business/organizational approaches, (2) using the model with different client audiences, (3) recognizing that different coaches and coaching programs may have different capacities and established limits for the length of coaching sessions and overall coaching relationship, and (4) allowing for some variability in the requirements for the breadth and depth of coach knowledge and skill. These areas of adaptability can interrelate in important ways, as will be noted below.

Different Coach-Practitioner Business/Organizational Approaches. Most individuals and organizations currently offering conflict coaching also offer other ADR, executive coaching, consulting, and/or training development services. There are a variety of ways that conflict coaching can be institutionalized (e.g., for-profit vs. nonprofit, corporate vs. community, fee-for-service vs. volunteer staffing, as a stand-alone service vs. as a part of a system of ADR alternatives). Given the endless varieties of current and hypothetical business/organizational configurations for the coach, we expect and welcome thoughtful and often unique approaches to blending conflict coaching with other service offerings and handling the practical constraints and possibilities of making the coach's larger organization successful.

Different Client Audiences. Although this book primarily addresses conflict coaching within the workplace, there are many other settings in which it can be applied. (Of course, there is plenty of audience diversity even when confining ourselves to the workplace.) Whether within the world of work or beyond, conflict coaching seems to offer real promise but only if it is made relevant and accessible. The model can be shaped in these respects by determining the primary needs for coaching within a specific setting as well as systematically considering related basic issues such as prospective coaches, clients, and coaching sponsors as well as the most effective ways to engage these groups in making the program successful. Some major audiences beyond the workplace include schools (K-12 and institutions of higher education), communities, and faith-based organizations.

The Length of Coaching Sessions and the Overall Coaching Relationship. While a moderately extensive conflict coaching relationship may include 8 to 12 one-hour sessions and span over 2 to 3 months, other options exist, especially on the shorter end. Each of the stages, including the preparation step, may easily take an hour of coach and client meeting time and be best followed by some individual reflection or activity time by the client. Bear in mind that not all Stage Four modules (modules focused on developing specific areas of client conflict communication) may be relevant to each client. Also bear in mind that a given stage or stage module may require more than one session, especially when the coach and client are working under the assumptions that a moderately extensive coach-client relationship is in place and the conflict is quite challenging for the client. Also, a one-hour coaching session is certainly possible. Such a time-limited session could not be expected to offer the richness of a longer coach-client relationship but might be appropriate given various constraints and needs. For instance, a one-hour session incorporating an abbreviated version of the various stages might be routinely used as the favored model for a volunteer peer conflict coaching model, a mediation intake mechanism, or as triage for the ombudsperson process. Finally, a brief intervention based on the CCC is arguably also beneficial in constrained circumstances of less than one hour, although this would represent the fringe of what is commonly understood as conflict coaching.

Breadth and Depth of Coach Knowledge and Skill in Relation to Commitments to the Client. Different model adaptation combinations can result in quite different requirements as far as a coach's requisite knowledge and skills are concerned. A professional conflict coach advertising the capacity to work with clients across multiple sessions has a responsibility to have a considerably richer knowledge and skill base than a volunteer peer conflict coach who offers basic conflict coaching in a one-session short duration format and operates in a system in which referrals to others who are professionals are easily made. The key point is that coach knowledge and skill are in some way verified by a third party (e.g., conflict coach training development specialist), limits in knowledge and skill are represented in the boundaries of the kind of client cases that the coach seeks and accepts, and the extent of coach knowledge and skill are reasonably stated to the client at the beginning of the coach-client relationship and again throughout the coaching session as needed.

Conclusion

The purpose of this chapter was to introduce the CCC model that is detailed in the remainder of the book. We began with a consideration of the models that have been most common in executive coaching as well as the two early models of conflict coaching from ADR practitioners. We then presented the CCC model in terms of its theoretical underpinnings and specific stages. Finally, we pointed out some areas of adaptability for the model. We now go on to explore the various individual stages of the model in a chapter-by-chapter format.

Chapter Summary

This chapter introduces the Comprehensive Conflict Coaching (CCC) model that is explained in extensive detail in the remainder of the book. The chapter begins by noting the promise and perils of models and then touching on the use of models in executive coaching and conflict coaching. The majority of this chapter explains the CCC model, which is theoretically grounded in a communication perspective, assumes a constructionist orientation to conflict, and also assumes a systems orientation for purposes of conflict analysis. The model begins with a preparation component to ensure that conflict coaching is appropriate. It then proposes four stages that can generally be seen as operating in sequence and learning assessment as a parallel process throughout. Stage One involves discovering the story. Stage Two involves exploring the three perspectives of identity, emotion, and power. Stage Three involves crafting the best story. Stage Four involves enacting the best story, especially by focusing on communication skills, conflict styles, negotiation, and awareness of other ADR processes.

The chapter ends with some important areas of adaptability for the model, including different coach-practitioner business/organizational approaches, different client audiences, the length of coaching sessions and the overall coaching relationship, and the breadth and depth of coach knowledge and skill in relation to commitments to the client.

SECTION 2

Conducting Conflict Coaching

3

Stage One

Discovering the Story

Stories are the creative conversion of life itself into a more powerful, clearer, more meaningful experience. They are the currency of human contact.

—Robert McKee

Alex has been working for a very successful, elite consulting firm for the last three years. In the last year his professional relationships with the CEO and the director of research at the firm have become strained. While there are several things that Alex can point to as poor performance incidents, he cannot explain the extreme decline in collegiality and good will that he has experienced this year. He knows that his future with the firm is in serious jeopardy, which means his career future is in doubt. Two years ago Alex thought his future was fast-track and unstoppable. Now he is simply hoping to salvage something.

Alex's relationship with the company CEO, Taylor, goes back more than a decade; Taylor was a faculty member in Alex's graduate program in organizational development. Alex and Taylor first met when Alex was a young graduate student straight out of an Ivy League undergraduate institution in the same region. Alex was bright, ambitious, and creative. He was clear about his goals of obtaining his master's degree and doctorate and working for a high-powered think tank or consulting firm specializing in large-scale organizational change initiatives. Taylor was an associate professor who was rapidly becoming disenchanted with the academy. He openly discussed his dissatisfaction with colleagues, students, and administrators. As Taylor planned his consulting firm, he made it known that he was recruiting the best and brightest graduate students as potential future employees.

Alex quickly identified Taylor as a promising potential mentor and worked very hard to gain his respect. After Alex completed his master's degree, he enrolled in the doctoral program with Taylor as his doctoral adviser. The two became very close and worked together on academic and consulting initiatives.

Taylor left the department two years before Alex completed his PhD. Within two years Taylor's firm had quadrupled revenues and staff and had landed several plum contracts. Alex worked as an independent contractor during the two years in which he finished his dissertation. Alex's dissertation topic on organizational dispute system design (ODSD) for geographically dispersed organizations using project team structures was a topic that he decided on with Taylor's advice, largely because of Taylor's vision that it would be quite lucrative for several of the firm's clients.

As soon as Alex graduated, Taylor hired him as a senior consultant in the firm. Taylor put Alex in charge of soliciting clients for the organizational dispute system design models he had developed in his dissertation. Taylor told Alex to do whatever research he felt was necessary to perfect the model and prove the organizational impact of the dispute system designs.

For the first two years Alex and his team worked independently of the rest of the firm. Alex knew what others were doing in terms of major consulting contracts, but no one other than Taylor and the director of research knew of Alex's progress. Even in staff meetings Alex was not asked to report on his clients or contracts but was often asked to comment on projects overseen by other consultants. The impression that most of the firm had was that Alex had already been selected as a future partner, and as such, he was treated with almost as much respect as Taylor.

Alex thought his work was going well, although there had been some setbacks recently. His largest clients were four pharmaceutical firms that had all been involved in major mergers and acquisitions in the last three years. These firms were most interested in the application of Alex's work to manage conflict among international, dispersed teams of research scientists planning research agendas for their R&D divisions. Given the rapid changes in the pharmaceutical industry, the client organizations were particularly interested in systems that identified low-level conflict before escalations that resulted in interteam struggles and attrition of top-level scientists. The setbacks in the last year were mostly about the difficulty of developing stochastic modeling processes that had high predictive power. The setup and implementation of the systems were good, but the data were just not showing the kinds of outcomes the clients wanted.

Even with these setbacks, Alex assumed that he would prevail. He thought it was only a matter of time, and once he produced the results the clients wanted, the firm would be over this hurdle and on to applications in other industry areas. But, about a year ago, he sensed a chilling between him and Taylor. He couldn't quite put his finger on it, but he started feeling that Taylor was avoiding him. Three months ago Taylor asked Alex, for the first time, to justify the expenses on his research budget.

Alex has tried to find times to talk privately with Taylor but in the last two months has not seen him except at staff meetings. When he's pushed for an appointment, he gets rescheduled with the director of research, who seems reluctant and uninterested. Last month Alex received a call from one of his clients indicating that they wanted to make sure the new guy coming on to help Alex would be brought up to speed by Alex before starting his work. Alex was caught completely unaware.

Alex's entire life has been his work and his dedication to Taylor's firm. Most of his friends work at the firm and are past students of Taylor's; they depend on Taylor for consulting contracts. Alex feels he has no sounding board for the current situation.

Given his work in organizational dispute system design, he has a number of professional contacts in the ADR field. One person whom he greatly respects, Don, is an ombudsperson at a government agency who sometimes works with private clients as a conflict coach. Alex makes the call and is scheduled to start coaching with Don as soon as possible.

E very conflict is a story waiting to be told. In the story and in the telling, there is a wealth of information about the conflict experience, the conflict context, and the conflict management potential. The first important task of the conflict coach is to help the client discover and clarify the client's story. As we present in this chapter, the conflict management and dispute resolution field has a rich history of attending to narratives or stories as a means of understanding and intervening in conflict. How that process works is slightly different in conflict coaching than in mediation. But, as you will see, there are strong similarities.

We begin this chapter by summarizing some of the humanistic and social science theory that focuses on narrative as an important communication and cognitive process. We follow that with an explanation of insights from two areas of narrative theory applied to conflict management. Then we discuss the specific steps of discovering the story and some of the techniques that can be used. And as we do in all of our stage chapters, we finish the chapter with a statement of principles and approaches for this stage.

Narrative Theory

A cogent overview of narrative theory and its application would easily take this entire volume and more. Why is narrative accorded such power both analytically and socially?

Stories have "persuasive functions, and more generally, they may contribute to the reproduction of knowledge, beliefs, attitudes, ideologies, norms, or values of a group or of society as a whole" (Van Dijk, 1993, p. 125).

There is something about a story that is inherently sensible, memorable, and persuasive as well as entertaining. Stories allow us to challenge the taken for granted "ordinariness or normality of a given state of things in the world" (Brunner, 2002, p. 6). Telling a story a certain way can create heroes and villains, can produce alternate realities, and can elevate the mundane. As Witten (1993, p. 106) summarized,

> In addition to their cognitive impact, narratives can have strong per- suasive effects. Narratives are more effective than facts or statistics in generating belief among listeners who agree with the argument. . . . The narrative form contributes further to a narrative's credibility by imposing a sense of coherence on the disparate elements the narrative contains. This effect occurs through structuring devices of plot, which unifies episodes; narrative sequence, which unifies time; and character- ization, which unifies action.

FISHER'S NARRATIVE THEORY

As communication scholars, we naturally gravitate to narrative theories developed in the communication discipline. In a series of several works, Fisher (1984, 1985, 1987, 1989) argued that all human experience con- sists of narrative texts. People naturally tell stories, think in terms of sto- ries, and organize information into narrative forms without consciously intending to do so.

People gravitate to narrative. Since the time of the Greeks, orators have understood that telling a good story is the most effective way of presenting a key argument. Historians and folklorists appreciate that people become emotionally attached to narrative and that stories are the most lasting, powerful and effective means of cultural transmission. Campbell's (1972) work on myth is an excellent example of scholarship that illustrates the universal power of a good story.

But, there are distinctions between a good narrative and a bad nar- rative. One of Fisher's main contributions was elucidating the character- istics of narrative that can be used in critique and construction. Fisher argues there are two key tests of the validity of a narrative—the extent to which the story hangs together, or has narrative coherence; and the extent to which the story rings true, or has narrative fidelity (Fisher, 1987). Fisher later added the concept of narrative comparison, or the extent to which a story is consistent with other stories about the same basic thing. Let's review each of these in slightly more detail, because the ideas of coherence, fidelity, and comparison are other ways of talking about the refining and testing tasks in the CCC model.

Narrative Coherence. A coherent narrative exhibits three characteristics: (1) internal or argumentative consistency; (2) external consistency, which is a measure of the extent to which the focal story matches other stories considered accurate; and (3) believable characters (Brown, 1990). Another way of thinking about narrative coherence is to ask the question, "Does this story make sense?" If it doesn't make sense, the story-teller must add information or clarification that will bring its elements into line.

One of the aspects of narrative that contributes greatly to coherence is the plot. "A plot can be seen as a theory of events" (Ochs, 1997, p. 193). The plot of a story is the statement of assumed cause and effects in a sequence of events. If events seem to happen out of order, or if characters cannot be seen performing certain acts in the plot, the audience will reject the narrative.

Narrative Fidelity. A narrative's fidelity, its truthfulness, rests in its ability to present values that are aligned with the values of its audience. Fisher (1987) believed a narrative's fidelity is bolstered when the values presented are seen to be appropriate, positive, and indicative of a better life for those involved. Stories encapsulate the narrator's values and reduce uncertainty about that which is being described (Brown, 1990). Brown also asserted that the strength of narrative fidelity may be assessed by focusing on the "extent to which the story fits with the history, knowledge, background, and experiences of the audience members" (1990, p. 171).

Narrative fidelity plays a fundamental role in evaluating the quality of persuasive appeal. The degree to which the message resonates with the audience will play a part in whether the audience accepts the persuasive message. Conversely, audience members who do not find the story faithful to their lives may simply ignore it.

Narrative Comparison. In addition to coherence and fidelity, Fisher also talked about how a narrative compares with other narratives. While he did not introduce this as a test of narrative, we see powerful application of the idea in conflict coaching. For, as Fisher argued, "The meaning and value of a story are always a matter of how it stands with or against other stories" (1985, p. 358). Stories do not exist in a vacuum; they reside in a cultural context in which other stories compete with their message. If a client has a story that makes less sense than a competing story, the client will have a difficult time persuading others to adopt his story and act on his behalf.

Narrative Theory Applied to Conflict Management

Narrative theory has found a strong application in the field of conflict management. There are two areas where narrative has been highlighted—narrative theory of mediation and narrative theory of dialogue and change. We will very briefly review both and concentrate on insights from Winslade and Monk's (2000, 2005) narrative mediation model and Kellett and Dalton's (2001) narrative approach to achieving dialogue and change.

Before introducing narrative theory in other areas of conflict, we want to briefly address why we believe it is essential in conflict coaching. We see narrative as an inherently powerful way people understand their experience. The coach best understands the client's experience and perspective through the client's story. Without that story the coach's ability to engage the client in analyzing and altering the conflict is limited. As important is the power of narrative to help the coach and client consider how to transform the conflict. And part of that transformation of the conflict will be the ability of the client to craft and present a narrative that has coherence and fidelity to other listeners. Given our basic belief in the importance of narrative for all conflict management, including conflict coaching, we now turn to previous applications of narrative theory in mediation and dialogue to discern how we may appropriate these concepts for coaching.

COBB'S VIEWS OF NARRATIVE IN MEDIATION

Sara Cobb (1992, 1993) and her colleagues (Cobb & Rifkin, 1991) are usually credited with introducing narrative theory to the field of mediation. They suggested that mediators should focus on the stories that are being told by disputants in the mediation and that the mediator's response to those stories—the extensions of the narratives—had great impact on the unfolding and outcome of mediation. Cobb's views of mediation were one of the first social constructionist orientations to mediation and one of the first theories that challenged the notion of mediator neutrality.

Within this genre of research, Cobb (1994, p. 50) suggested two approaches to a narrative framework: structural and poststructural. The structural approach makes a distinction between the story and the telling of the story and "emphasizes the representation of real events as a whole, as a unit, as a structure" rather than focusing on the interactive unfolding of the story. A structural approach to narrative in mediation focuses attention on the content of the story regardless of how it is told or how someone responds to it. Cobb said that a poststructural approach to narrative "not only begins to focus attention on the role of discourse in mediation . . . but it permanently *includes* the mediator as a co-participant in both the construction and the transformation of conflict narratives" (pp. 61–62). The poststructuralist approach is more concerned with how the narrative is extended and encouraged in interaction. For example, Cobb suggested that the poststructuralist perspective "*requires* attention to narrative politics; as they unfold, some stories become dominant, others can be marginalized" (p. 52)

Both structuralist and poststructuralist insights about narrative are helpful in conflict coaching. In our orientation, there are two levels of narrative analysis that can be pursued. On the structural level we are interested in the story content and what that content says about the conflict experience and the conflict potential. The story helps the client make sense of the conflict and the context. Ultimately, the story will help the client consider how to respond and how to enlist the support of others in the response. There is great value in examining the story as well as the telling, and we devote the majority of our attention in this chapter to that focus.

At the same time, we acknowledge that there is merit in understanding how the telling of the story is a co-construction that can influence insight and action. These poststructuralist analyses can be focused on interaction between the client and the coach and on interaction between the clients and others outside the coaching relationship. There is definitely a mutual influence process occurring between the coach and the client. In fact, this entire stage of the conflict coaching model is an exercise in the interaction of influence between coach and client in presenting, refining, and testing the narrative. Similarly, when the client and coach, in Stage Three, concentrate on crafting the best story, we clearly see the mutual influence process at work.

WINSLADE AND MONK'S NARRATIVE MEDIATION

Winslade and Monk (2000, 2005) have developed and elaborated their narrative approach to mediation. Drawing heavily on narrative therapy, their approach shares some assumptions with Cobb but branches out into new orientations to practice. Obviously, both Winslade and Monk and Cobb see narrative as a primary discourse structure that mediators influence intentionally and unintentionally. While Cobb's work focused more on explaining how a mediator might privilege one narrative over the other and, by so doing, empower one party more than another, Winslade and Monk advocate a certain approach to a mediator's intervention in the narratives of the disputants. Cobb adopts a more critical theory perspective, and Winslade and Monk are more prescriptive.

With their theory based in narrative therapy, Winslade and Monk see people as stuck in conflict-saturated narratives. They suggest that people get caught up in the conflict cycle because they see themselves bound to it. As mediators, they invite the stakeholders to label the conflict-saturated story. Then, through a series of careful questions, they invite each stakeholder to slowly distance himself or herself from the conflicted part of the story.

Increasing perspective taking is a goal in narrative mediation. Each party gets the opportunity to hear the story from the perspective of the other individual and finds out whether the other person wants to be in the conflict. People who are deeply involved in a conflict often believe the other person somehow enjoys the conflict. Finding out that the conflict is unpleasant and negative for the other party helps the person let go of the conflict-saturated story.

Winslade and Monk have provided examples of questions and discourse mediators might use to move the mediation in a more constructive direction. For example, they suggest that a common block in mediation is a party who feels entitled to treat the other badly, even if such individuals don't realize that is what they are doing. Narrative mediation provides mediators a way to listen for entitlement in a narrative and challenge it through questions.

The goals of narrative mediation are to help people separate themselves and their relationships from a conflict-saturated story and to reconnect with a story of cooperation, understanding, peace, or mutual respect. Following White and Epston (1990), Winslade and Monk suggest that securing constructive conflict action (e.g., making agreements or accommodations) does not precede but follows the construction of a new narrative that allows for the recognition and embrace of the effectiveness of these actions. They emphasize the use of externalizing language— language that presents to the parties the assumption that the conflict is not inherent to them as people or to their relationship or situation. Thus, the parties are free to stand apart from the conflict and approach it as such.

Among the critical procedures of narrative mediation are

- Mapping the effects of the conflict story on the participants and on the relationship between them
- Asking questions that attempt to deconstruct the dominant story by raising taken-for-granted assumptions
- Asking the disputants to evaluate the conflict story and the future trajectory
- Inviting the participants to articulate their preferences for a future that is not limited by the conflict story
- Listening for the implicit story of cooperation or understanding that is always in the midst of a conflict story and inquiring into its possibilities (Winslade & Monk, 2005, p. 224)

KELLETT AND DALTON'S NARRATIVE APPROACH TO ACHIEVING DIALOGUE AND CHANGE

Kellett and Dalton (2001), in their book *Managing Conflict in a Negotiated World*, introduce the idea that any conflict may be better understood through a narrative lens. They encourage people to tell conflict stories as a way of deepening interpretive understanding of their own and others' conflict processes and experiences. They suggest that the more clearly we see our conflict narratives, the more we empower ourselves to create change in ourselves and our relationships.

The majority of their work is focused on helping average individuals understand their conflict narratives. What is implied in the stories we tell ourselves and others about the conflicts that we live? They reference Langellier (1989) who says that narratives give us information about the social context, information about what the teller expects as reaction to the story, insight into the teller's culture, and insight into the power dynamics and political situation of the story. Later, we will revisit these perspectives as we suggest some questions that can be asked by conflict coaches when they hear clients' initial stories.

While Kellett and Dalton strongly encourage a narrative approach to understanding conflict, they are quick to remind us that there are limitations to narratives. Narratives can convince the teller of their "rightness." If Alex convinces himself that his story of the conflict with Taylor is the only possible correct explanation of the conflict, he is shutting down the possibility of dialogue and new interpretations leading to new actions and insights. We should always be mindful that narratives are inherently political, so there is always some degree of self-serving bias in them. Our tendency is to see ourselves as innocent and the other as blameworthy.

Discovering the Story

In Chapter 2 we presented the CCC model of conflict coaching, and we explained that the first stage helps clients construct a coherent narrative of their experience of the conflict and engage in perspective taking about the possible narratives of other parties in the conflict. In this stage, the coach concentrates on discovering as much of the story as possible to have a full understanding of the conflict, the parties, and the context. The discovery process is systematic and is aimed at increasing comprehension. Most coaching will involve at least the following three levels of clarification: the initial story, refining the story (increasing coherence), and testing the story (assessing fidelity).

INITIAL STORY

This refers to the client's story that comes with little urging from the coach. The conversation begins with the coach asking very general questions about the conflict and listening as the client tells his or her story for the first time to the coach. The initial story provides information about how the client sees important issues, persons, and opportunities in the conflict. The initial story often presents characterizations of other parties and assumptions about information and actions.

The initial story may unfold much as Alex's initial story presented at the beginning of this chapter. The main task of the coach in this stage is to listen and assess the extent to which the client has presented a narrative that has basic coherence and fidelity. The coach is trying to understand the conflict from the client's point of view but is also listening for how well the client understands the conflict. In some cases the coach may suspect that the client is not competent for coaching based on the quality of the initial story. Obvious confusion, paranoia, or delusions that are presented in the initial story are certainly warning signs that an alternate referral is necessary.

However, in most cases, the coach will hear a client who has a basic story in need of considerable elaboration. Incomplete initial stories will usually take one of several forms:

What's happening? The client, like Alex, has a sense of unease and indicates that there is a problem, but the story consists of a great deal of suspicion and innuendo rather than a detailed description of events and actions that can be verified and examined. The "What's happening?" story suggests a need for significant information acquisition and investigation before strategies for action can be considered.

Why me? The client has a detailed list of events and actions and characters but has trouble understanding the reasons why she or he is involved in this conflict or is being treated this poorly. The most important missing element in the story is the motivation of the others and the contributions or responsibility of the client.

Where's the connection? The client has a voluminous set of facts and events but they are relatively or completely unconnected and do not seem to be presented in order of chronology or cause and effect. It is as if the client is throwing out segments that have no link, and the client does not or cannot see the need for a coherent framework that ties things together.

There's no hope. The client has painted a pessimistic story about a very negative future; the story is presented as conclusion rather than expostulation, and there is little detailed information to justify the conclusion.

Self-righteous rant. The client is presented as a complete innocent who has been treated badly by those with evil motivations. The story is told, often as a repetitious recounting of specific attacks (real or perceived) that demonize the other and eliminate the apparent possibility of a cooperative resolution. This form of narrative usually identifies clients who are using the narrative as a protective devise, one in which they can feel better about themselves while making very hostile attributions about the other. As we discuss later, this type of initial story should signal a coach that more testing of the narrative and its assumptions is needed.

The conflict coach should assume that the initial story, even if it appears complete, is not. While listening to the story, the coach should make notes of areas that need elaboration and testing. As Clegg (1993, p. 31) says,

> The first step in orienting to the narratives of everyday life in this way is to listen to what people say. Not necessarily to retell it in exactly those terms but to inquire into how it would be possible for them to say that. What kinds of assumptions in what types of possible worlds could produce those accounts?

Sometimes the coach can ask clients to reflect on their story and consider questions of elaboration. Returning to Kellett and Dalton's (2001) reference to Langellier's perspectives, the following questions can be posed to clients to have them reflect on the story they have just told:

1. From the context of social and political discourse
   - What are the storyteller's goals in creating this narrative?
   - What does the story tell about the social and political context of the conflict experience?
   - What is the essential moral of the story?
   - How does the story represent the power dynamics of the parties in conflict? What are the points of resistance, empowerment, and oppression?
   - What social constraints and boundaries are confirmed in this story?

2. From the standpoint of a culture
   - How does the story reflect the social and cultural values of the conflict context?
   - How does the story define who is in the in-group and who is in the out-group?*

REFINING THE STORY

After the client presents the initial story, the coach helps the client refine that story. The story is expanded through some basic questions that ask the client to add information or detail. Part of the refinement is encouraging the client to provide information about how other parties in the conflict may be experiencing the conflict and talking more about how

SOURCE: *Kellett, P. M., & Dalton, D. G. (2001). *Managing conflict in a negotiated world: A narrative approach to achieving dialogue and change.* Thousand Oaks, CA: Sage

the conflict is affecting others in the system. A key aspect of refinement is that coaches do not challenge the narrative of clients but encourage them to provide the most comprehensive and coherent version of their narratives. The story refining comes to closure when there doesn't seem to be more important information for the client to add.

In Alex's story there is obviously a need for refinement. The conflict coach can begin with a standard list of questions that can be applied to refine most conflict narratives. We can discuss the process of refining in three general ways. First, the coach can refine by identifying "missing pieces" in the story and asking for information concerning those pieces. These questions address the issue of coherence. In the following list, we present a short set of exemplar questions that could be asked by most coaches and a specific question that may be asked by Don in his work with Alex. (The general question is in italics and the question specific to Alex's story follows it.) We do not intend this list to be exhaustive or even comprehensive. We present these examples to suggest the kinds of questions a coach should consider.

Are there characters presented in the story who are not well explained in terms of roles, actions or motivations? Tell me more about the director of research. She seems to be a critical part of the organization, but I don't have a good sense of her role in the organization, her relationship with Taylor, or her relationship with you.

Are there characters not presented in the story who should be? Is there someone else in the situation who has something important to add to our understanding of the situation? Who are the liaisons you work with at the pharmaceutical companies and what is their relationship with Taylor?

Is there additional information about the context (for example, the nature of your organization) that would help us understand what is happening? Can you give us more detail about the consulting firm in terms of size, operations, and patterns of practice? How atypical would you say this firm is compared with other firms you know?

Are there important events that have not been included in the story? Why? Why not? Did anything happen in your interactions with Taylor or the director of research that may have been misunderstood or have led to the current situation?

Are there patterns of events that could help explain this situation that haven't been discussed? In the past, have you noticed that Taylor has a tendency to act out against junior associates or people he perceives as a threat? Have you seen Taylor behave this way (the way you believe he is behaving toward you) toward someone else in the firm?

Second, since we are dealing with workplace conflicts, it is helpful to encourage clients to refine their story by giving more attention to the impact of the organizational culture and climate on the conflict. Often a client will "telescope" his understanding of a conflict, giving attention to the immediate issues and actions rather than the context within which this is happening. Clients may not have a strong "systems sense" and may be unaware of questions they could or should ask about the workplace. Kellett and Dalton (2001) suggest specific questions from the organizational point of view. The following is an incomplete and restated list (pp. 134–135):

- How might the organization and relationship of management and employees have contributed to the conflict?
- In what ways was the storyteller resisting or supporting organizational power and domination through his actions in the conflict ?
- How might leadership style of management be contributing to this conflict?
- How might the organization's approach to motivation, reward, and assessment be contributing to this conflict?
- How might the story reveal or capture broader tensions or conflicts in the organization?
- How does the organizational culture create and maintain conflicts such as this?
- How does this conflict demonstrate the need for organizational change?
- How might this conflict serve as a lever to increase or decrease the chances for organizational change?
- What kinds of resistance could be expected if the organization started to change in the ways suggested by this conflict story?
- What communication skills would the organization and key personnel need to develop to implement change effectively?*

A third way to refine the story is to ask the client to reflect on the meaning of the story and to add information or make changes based on this reflection. This third level is the most sophisticated and should be used after the missing pieces and additional context questions have been considered. The more refined and complete the narrative is before attending to this level the better.

Once again, Kellett and Dalton present an excellent list of potential questions in this area (2001, p. 95–96). The following list is an elaboration of some of the questions originally posed by Kellett and Dalton.

- How does the story create the sense that the conflict is both inevitable and necessary in this relationship?
- In what way does the conflict seem to be both beneficial and damaging to the client and the other?
- How are the actions and reactions in the story different from an ideal form of collaboration or peacemaking in this relationship?

SOURCE: *Kellett, P. M., & Dalton, D. G. (2001). *Managing conflict in a negotiated world: A narrative approach to achieving dialogue and change.* Thousand Oaks, CA: Sage

※ What clues do you have that communication skills are lacking or absent in this conflict?

※ What clues do you have that conflict style choice skills are lacking or absent in this conflict?

※ What clues do you have that negotiation skills are lacking or absent in this conflict?

※ What clues do you have that emotional competence is lacking or absent in this conflict?

※ What clues do you have that political competence is lacking or absent in this conflict?

※ What clues do you have that identity management skills are lacking or absent in this conflict?

※ How might hearing this story be beneficial or damaging to the other party?

※ What are the motives of the participants in the conflict? What do they want to achieve?

※ In what ways could this story limit or open up dialogue with the other?

※ How might this story help the client recognize her or his negative patterns in the conflict?

※ How might this story help the client recognize her or his positive patterns in the conflict?*

TESTING THE STORY

At this point the coach becomes more assertive by "testing" the refined narrative. Testing addresses the fidelity aspects of the narrative. The coach is trying to make the client see the situation in a different way. As we mentioned earlier, especially when a narrative seems very self-serving or paints the client as innocent victim to another's evil actor, the coach can focus on testing this story to see whether denial or bias is preventing the client from entertaining a different and more helpful reality for moving through the conflict. There are a variety of tests that can be applied by the coach.

One common test is whether the story is created to persuade and is intentionally or inherently biased. This test often asks the client to consider the narrative from another person's point of view.

How would the story change if it were being told by the other? If Taylor were explaining this situation to me, what would the story be?

How would the story change if it were being told by bystanders or witnesses to the conflict? If you were telling this story in a staff meeting of the firm, or to one of the pharmaceutical representatives, what parts of the story would change? What would you say differently? Why? What wouldn't you say at all? Why?

SOURCE: *Kellett, P. M., & Dalton, D. G. (2001). *Managing conflict in a negotiated world: A narrative approach to achieving dialogue and change*. Thousand Oaks, CA: Sage

The coach can ask questions to challenge the client's understanding of facts or information. Or, the coach can test assumptions that the client is making about the situation or the people involved. In this way, testing can lead to challenges of hostile attributions the client is making about the other party and can increase the client's ability to consider alternative explanations for a person's actions.

Is it possible that you are misunderstanding the behavior? Are there alternative explanations? Are there other reasons that Taylor has not been meeting with you? If you assume the best, what might explain the behaviors you've seen in the last year? Can you put a positive spin on these behaviors in a way that makes sense?

What does the other party gain from this conflict? What is Taylor getting from this conflict, if your interpretation of the situation is correct? What benefits are there to his antagonizing you in the way you perceive?

Why would the other party risk the damages that you describe? Taylor must realize that this conflict is making the firm look bad to the organizational clients. He must see that other members of the firm are negatively affected by this conflict. Why would he incur those damages? If he wanted to hurt you, isn't there a way he could do it without causing himself harm?

Through the testing process the coach can help identify information that the client does not have and needs to have to make strategic decisions.

What don't you know that would change your perception of this conflict? Do you know what the implications are of ownership of the ODSD model? Do you own this model? Does the firm? Does Taylor stand to gain the model if he loses you? Vice versa?

How are others impacting the conflict in an unforeseen way? What do you know about the reaction of the pharmaceutical clients to your work?

The testing process can be repeated with each new iteration of information until the client finds a rough edge that simply won't be denied or becomes comfortable given the coherence and fidelity of the narrative.

> *Of course that is not the whole story, but that is the way with stories; we make them what we will. It's a way of explaining the universe while leaving the universe unexplained, it's a way of keeping it all alive, not boxing it into time.*
>
> —Jeannette Winterson

As a parting note, it is important that a conflict coach appreciate the balance between refining and testing the story and "finalizing" the story.

The former processes, as we have described, bring the narrative more clearly into focus in terms of content and utility. But the latter suggests that the perfect and final story can be told, and that is a view that we do not support. There is always a tension between discovery and clarification and the reality that a story is a constant possibility for elaboration and construction. Stories are truly never ending in that sense. And a conflict coach is well served by remembering that no story is ever completely told, nor should it be.

General Principles for Discovering the Story

Principle #1: Never treat the narrative as factual; help the client see the narrative as a construction of reality. While a narrative presents actions, events, and characters, it is rarely something that can be thought of as factual and should not be thought of as factual. The client should be reminded that stories are what we make of them, and we construct our realities through our stories. This orientation prevents clients from getting bogged down in "proof" and encourages them to think about how they are creating a situation and whether they want to live through that situation.

Principle #2: Appreciate that most clients will be strongly attached to their stories and that change of the story may be met with resistance until they see that the change serves them. Our stories are an extension of our identity, a discourse about our power, and a rendition of how we feel about the situation. Don't be surprised when a client owns a story and actively resists having it refined or tested. Before you test a story, talk with clients about why this step is important and how the step can be helpful to them.

Principle #3: Assume that most clients will not have a completely coherent narrative or be ready to tell you a narrative that is complete or coherent. Helping them tell the story is a significant part of the coaching experience. A good conflict coach endorses the idea of the never ending story— the idea that a narrative is never complete and that there is always room for expansion. Most coaches realize that clients are often not practiced storytellers and are likely to have problems putting their conflict experience in the form of a well-articulated narrative.

Principle #4: Emphasize that there are always alternative stories that could be told. This principle is most important in terms of encouraging perspective taking. A good conflict coach will encourage a client to try to tell the story from as many points of view as possible. Even when the retelling stretches the clients' abilities to conceive an alternative story, the exercise is valuable because it encourages them to explicitly surface assumptions they are making that may be problematic.

Principle #5: Understand that narrative tries to simplify (motives, identities, actions, time lines, etc.) but that simple is not always empowering. Sometimes clients want a neat and simple story that makes sense to them, and they actively resist refinements and testing that make the story messy. A conflict coach should be able to explain that a richly detailed and comprehensive story will ultimately give the client more potential power by helping him or her consider alternatives for interpretation and action, even if the details result in a few loose ends.

Specific Approaches for Discovering the Story

Throughout this chapter we have presented a number of specific ideas about how a conflict coach can help a client discover his or her story. In this section, we present some additional ideas about techniques that may aid in the development of narratives.

Approach # 1: Script the story.

What is it? Have the client talk out or write out the narrative as though it were a screen play or script.

Why is it important? The act of writing or carefully detailing a narrative (rather than simply presenting it as stream of consciousness) helps clients to reflect more specifically on behaviors, events, and chronology. The act of recording the "script" in writing or on audiotape also makes them slow down and more carefully consider the content of the narrative.

How do you do it? Give the client a script worksheet or a set of prompting questions, and ask the client to present the narrative accordingly.

Approach #2: Retell the story.

What is it? It is asking the client to repeat the same basic story more than once in order to see which elements of the story are told the same way and which elements change, are omitted, or are embellished.

Why is it important? This is one way of identifying which aspects of the story seem to be most critical to the client. Items in the story that are told in basically the same way over and over again are likely to be components that are very meaningful and often are emotionally triggering the client.

How do you do it? The easiest way is to ask clients to give you an initial story and, after a break or in a subsequent session, ask them to repeat the story. Ask them to identify the factors that were consistent and the factors that changed.

Approach #3: Re-place the story.

What is it? Ask the client to tell the story of the conflict but change the context. Tell the story as though the conflict were happening in a different workplace or in a different context all together.

Why is it important? This exercise helps the client consider what parts of the narrative are most context dependent. For example, if the client cannot tell the story of a character in a different context, it may help the client see that the character's behavior may be much less volitional and much more contextually scripted than the client had previously assumed.

How do you do it? You can give clients an alternate context and ask them to tell the story assuming that was the context. Or you can give them the ability to generate their own alternative context.

Approach #4: Tell the next chapter.

What is it? This application asks the client to project what the next chapter in the story will be. If none of the critical aspects of the story are changed by anyone or anything, what does the client think will happen next? Where will this story go next and why?

Why is it important? Forecasting into the future helps give a sense of the trajectory of the conflict from the client's point of view. It suggests how the client sees escalation or deescalation tendencies. It also indicates what the client has assumed may be potential courses of action for him or her to take, or potential courses of action the other may take.

How do you do it? Simply ask clients to fantasize about what they think the next natural steps in the story will be if the situation does not change.

Approach #5: Tell the story from another's point of view.

What is it? Select another character in the client's story or another party to the conflict, and ask the client to tell the story of the conflict from that character's point of view.

Why is it important? This pushes the client to take the perspective of another party and to create a coherent narrative from that person's point of view. It increases the client's perspective taking, and it makes clear assumptions the client is making that may need to be tested.

How do you do it? One technique that has already been mentioned is to simply ask the client to tell the story as the other would tell it. This can be done orally or in writing, the latter may be more helpful if the client is having a lot of trouble taking the other's perspective. Another technique is to have the coach take the part of the client and repeat the client's story while the client takes the role of the other and interjects comments and alternative facts or interpretations. In this way, clients actually challenge their own stories but from the point of view of another.

Chapter Summary

The first stage in the conflict coaching model is helping the client to tell a coherent story about the conflict that makes sense. Drawing from narrative theory as applied to mediation and dialogue processes, this chapter suggests why narrative is a powerful tool for conflict analysis and includes techniques useful in uncovering, clarifying, and testing the story. We suggest that during this stage the coach help the client to present an initial story that the coach and client then refine and test.

GENERAL PRINCIPLES FOR DISCOVERING THE STORY

Principle #1: Never treat the narrative as factual; help the client see the narrative as a construction of reality.

Principle #2: Appreciate that most clients will be strongly attached to their stories and that change of the story may be met with resistance until they see that the change serves them.

Principle #3: Assume that most clients will not have a completely coherent narrative or be ready to tell you a narrative that is complete or coherent. Helping them tell the story is a significant part of the coaching experience.

Principle #4: Emphasize that there are always alternative stories that could be told.

Principle #5: Understand that narrative tries to simplify (motives, identities, actions, time lines, etc.), but that simple is not always empowering.

SPECIFIC APPROACHES FOR DISCOVERING THE STORY

Approach #1: Script the story.

Approach #2: Retell the story.

Approach #3: Re-place the story.

Approach #4: Tell the next chapter.

Approach #5: Tell the story from another's point of view.

4

Stage Two
The Identity Perspective

Know thyself.

—Thales

Charlotte leads the office of housing and community development, a stand-alone department within the government of a major city. The organization is responsible for building and maintaining housing within the city as well as generally trying to improve the economic prospects for residents in low- and middle-income areas of the city. She moved up through the organizational ranks over a 25-year period.

Outside of her organization, Charlotte is seen as a consummate professional and courageous individual. She has the respect of her peers (the heads of other city departments) as well as her superiors (the managing director of the city and the mayor). Respect for Charlotte has a number of sources. She worked her way from entry-level secretary to the top of the organization. She has continuously developed her talents, most notably earning a bachelor's degree and later an MBA while continuing to work full-time. In recent years, she led two small- to medium-scale neighborhood redevelopment projects that won recognition at the regional and national levels. Throughout her tenure at the organization, she has also moved from being an insecure single parent struggling to make ends meet to the proud mother of two accomplished adult children.

Unfortunately, Charlotte does not feel respected inside her organization and faces a number of obstacles related to her identity. There have traditionally been two power blocks within her office—the social work set and the architecture and planning set. Charlotte has always preferred to not reinforce these camps, but others seemed to place her in the social work set for much of her life in the organization. She ended up in this category because her personal situation had required the assistance of social workers from a sister organization, and because she undertook her bachelor's degree in social work. This categorization changed, though, when she began taking MBA courses in the late 1990s.

Entry into the MBA program signaled that Charlotte was aspiring to a new professional level. Administrators and staff within the office began to talk informally about Charlotte getting restless and looking at prospects beyond the organization. Although Charlotte never said as much, there was a period when she entertained such thoughts. As she neared completion of her MBA, the reaction of others became more pointed and negative. Administrators who had for years been very friendly and supportive of her began to pull away from her. Staff members, a couple of whom had been close friends to Charlotte outside of work, also seemed to distance themselves. People in the office frequently joked about the workplace teams: social work versus architecture and planning. Charlotte did not seem to fit into this mix, as there was no precedent for someone holding an MBA within the office.

When the position for head of department suddenly came up, it was widely assumed that the director in charge of architecture and planning would get the job given that he had the most seniority and was well known both inside and outside the organization and given that the director in charge of social work was not throwing her hat in the ring. Charlotte did not immediately consider applying but did so in part because she was encouraged to do so by a respected mentor in another organization. To practically everyone's surprise, including her own, she got the position.

Charlotte now faces a very challenging situation. Using a budget with negative year-to-year growth, she has been charged with greatly expanding neighborhood redevelopment within the city. While this is theoretically possible by winning one or more major grants, the granting agencies insist on projects that strongly integrate social, economic, and aesthetic concerns. Further, grant awards are only decided after onsite consultation with applying team members.

Charlotte does not have a high degree of confidence in her core team of the director of architecture and planning and the director of social work, because they only grudgingly tolerate her as the leader, and because they do not show the level of collaboration needed to secure a major grant. Doug, the director of architecture and planning, has reportedly questioned whether she is simply holding on until she can use her MBA as a ticket to a position outside of government. Michelle, the director of social work, has informally jabbed at Charlotte in terms of "possibly forgetting where you come from." Both of these directors tend to sit on information, providing it to Charlotte on a need-to-know-type basis. Charlotte is not in touch with how the staff in the organization views her, but she suspects that they look to their directors for indicators.

Charlotte recognizes that each director has valuable knowledge to contribute to a grant application. Also, she remembers a time when each of these individuals was supportive of her role in the organization. Charlotte knows that she needs to demonstrate leadership and deal with the immediate conflict concerning Doug and Michelle, yet she does not want to needlessly threaten anyone. An important grant deadline is only three months away—a fairly tight timeline given the scope of the proposal.

Identity answers the question, "Who?" A given individual usually has a number of identities even within a single situation. Identities are important for orienting to the environment, including making sense of information, knowing how to act, and knowing how to relate to others. Identity is central to conflict interaction, because conflicts often announce themselves as identity threats, because a high degree of identity threat usually signals that a conflict is intractable, and because carrying out action that is respectful of all parties' identity needs can be an important yet challenging feat.

In the 25 years that Charlotte has been with this organization, some of her identities have stayed the same, and some have changed. Tensions between old and new identities have made it difficult for her to communicate effectively. Many of those around her have also been challenged by her changing identities, although in a different way. Charlotte's identities as an MBA and organizational leader have threatened the identities of others. In this respect, Charlotte has been living with an ongoing workplace conflict since the late 1990s. In another respect, she faces a more circumscribed conflict in the form of how to handle a troubled team given a looming grant proposal deadline. While Charlotte's situation may not necessarily be intractable, it is certainly challenging.

While the first stage of the coaching model emphasizes the client's baseline view of the conflict, the second stage involves the introduction of perspectives by the coach. This chapter and the two that follow outline content for the second stage by explaining critical dimensions of the disputant's personal experience of the conflict—identity needs, emotional needs, and power relations. The current chapter begins with consideration of some of the ways that identity intersects with emotion and power in conflict interaction. It details a number of key assumptions for understanding the importance of identity. The identity framework is then presented as a way of assisting clients in making sense of identity issues within the specific conflict that they must navigate. Tools from the areas of preventive and corrective facework are described, so that clients have clear intervention options. The chapter ends with various specific principles and approaches for coaches working with clients on this stage of the conflict coaching model.

Identity in Relation to Emotion and Power

It is notable that in introducing his pioneering writing on *facework*, or the management of individual identity, Goffman (1955) addressed the connection between emotion and face from the outset. For Goffman, face and emotion are clearly related. Essentially, people tend to experience no remarkable feelings if treated in the identity-related manner to which they are long accustomed. If they are accorded more respect than expected for their valued identities, they feel good. If, however, people are treated with less respect than they expect, they can feel bad or hurt. Goffman pointed out that people's emotions are tied not only to their own face issues, but also to the face issues of others. In both instances, social rules and situational features are closely connected to face-related feelings. Emotions are not only an outcome of identity-related interaction, they are also an important consideration for assuming and maintaining face. Again as Goffman (1955) pointed out, selecting an appropriate and effective face usually provides a person with feelings of confidence and assurance. These feelings, in turn, are likely to facilitate the continued successful enactment of face. An implication of Goffman's thinking is that the bad or hurt feeling associated with a face threat basically announces conflict to one or both parties. While Charlotte probably feels very good regarding perceptions about her identities by those outside her organization, perceptions within her organization and especially with her senior team are no doubt making her very uncomfortable.

An important distinction concerning face loss and emotion is face threat or actual loss that is initiated by self versus face threat or actual loss that is initiated by the other toward self. These usually result in two different emotional and behavioral responses. When the client self-injures, shame and guilt often result. When the other injures the client, hurt and anger frequently arise. While shame and guilt may lead to a damaged sense of personal competence and some level of social withdrawal, hurt and, particularly, anger may lead to a hostile attribution about the other that is combined with some sort of counterattack on the other. Charlotte's situation is unique in the respect that she does not seem to exhibit strong feelings of hurt and anger given the face threats initiated by Doug and Michelle. Perhaps this is because she has difficulty reconciling feelings of shame and guilt with these other emotions. It may be useful for her to clarify these self and other identity threat issues so that she can gain more emotional clarity, not to mention determine the most effective actions moving forward.

Goffman's writing is, in many respects, foundational to contemporary scholars addressing the intersection of emotion, identity, communication, and conflict. Jones and Bodtker (2001) noted that the existence of an identity is necessary for an emotion to take form. Shapiro (2002) incorporated the work of Lazarus (1991) and Parkinson (1995) to show how individuals scanning for identity-related matters use emotion to clarify what is at stake. Emotions are therefore used in a reactive manner, but they may also be used to determine future identity goals and threats. While Charlotte has been operating with identity conflict for many years, the fact that it is tied to an important new work initiative and her relatively new role of department head is almost certainly generating heightened anxiety and therefore highlighting a very specific conflict that needs to be addressed.

Another way that emotion is intimately linked with identity is in relation to self-esteem. As Hewitt (2003) noted, it is in the social world that our identities occur and develop. Likewise self-esteem, or how we feel about our identities, arises in social interaction but is also something we bring to each new social situation. Lower levels of self-esteem are connected with higher levels of anxiety. Heightened levels of anxiety can detract from self-esteem in terms of the intrapersonal experience and in terms of one's ability to successfully communicate as well as maintain and build face with others. While Charlotte has been successful in maintaining a positive identity outside of her organization at the same time as she handles considerable face threats inside her organization, the emotional burden of handling this situation is probably unsustainable and certainly unwelcome in the near future.

Power is closely connected to identity, in that an identity affirmed by others includes opportunities to exert power as well as expectations about the limits of using power. Power is also closely linked to identity in the way each identity requires different kinds of resources in order for the identity to be sustained. Finally, identity shapes not only the potential for power but also the kinds of power we are more or less comfortable enacting from a specific position. Some good news for Charlotte is that her new identity as department head provides her with new resources for asserting the identities of her choice. However, it may be necessary to get more comfortable with her new identity as department head in order to exert power to claim these various identities.

Overview of Research and Theory on Identity

Identity is one of the most powerful, all-encompassing and elastic concepts in the humanities and social sciences. It has a long intellectual history in the area of conflict theory and practice. We begin by offering an introduction to the concept of identity as a foundation for our suggestions on working on identity reflection with conflict coaching clients.

INTRODUCTION TO THE CONCEPT OF IDENTITY

Borrowing from the contributions of Goffman (1955, 1967) and of Harré and van Langenhove (1999), identity involves an individual establishing, maintaining, and/or developing social space and/or being positioned in social space by others and/or by contextual factors. Other related terms include *face* (defined virtually the same as *identity* here), *self-image* (i.e., an individual's view of him- or herself), *status* (i.e., a person's relative position of social importance), and *role* (i.e., a social category with identity implications that is assigned to and/or assumed by an individual). To keep matters simple, *identity* and *face* will be relied upon here. Accordingly, it will be understood that it can take on different meanings. For instance, Charlotte may view her professional identity differently from the directors who report to her or the managing director and mayor of the city to whom she reports. The following assumptions will enlarge the consideration of identity.

KEY ASSUMPTIONS ABOUT IDENTITY

The following assumptions are not an attempt to compose an exhaustive list. They are, however, put forward as some strong considerations for assisting clients in getting clearer about their conflict situation and the opportunities available to them vis-à-vis identity issues.

The concept of face is one of the best ways to make identity accessible to clients. While other metaphors of identity are certainly common and perhaps even unavoidable (e.g., identity as space), the face metaphor is especially appealing because of the role it has played in research and theory and the way it can be easily understood and extended in everyday contexts.

- A face is an identity.
- A particular face can be shaped by the individual, another person, and/or a situation.
- A face can be directly or indirectly supported or attacked.
- Conflict involves face threat or at least potential threat to one or more parties.

The modern concept of face was initially advanced by Goffman (1955, 1967) and has since been expanded upon by a number of others. Face is a social claim of self-identity or social attribution of another's self-identity. Individuals regularly engage in facework through behaviors that represent self-respect and consideration of others (Goffman, 1955). Individuals largely do so unconsciously by employing basic rules of politeness when stating preferences, making requests, and communicating in other routine ways. From a distance, Charlotte's most obvious face claim is arguably department head or leader of her organization. Within her organization, this claim is contested, as she is not given basic respect by others and, arguably, as she fails to successfully communicate her own self-respect by asserting herself.

Goffman (1955) wrote, "To lose face seems to mean to be in the wrong face, to be out of face, or to be shamefaced" (p. 215). Losing face involves a lost or damaged claim to desired identity. It is inherently conflict-oriented. Face loss can occur as a result of the actions of one or both communicators, or it can come as a result of an altered situation. Goffman emphasized the emotional nature as well as significance of face loss when he described it as possibly leaving a communicator with feelings that include not only shame but also inferiority, threat, and confusion, among others. These strong feelings can deeply impact the trajectory of a conflict. Brown (1977) made the point that face threats can overtake a concern with tangible issues, intensify the conflict, and add to the costs of resolution. Northrup (1989) claimed that a conflict is very likely to be intractable whenever a core sense of identity is in jeopardy. The undesirable nature of face loss in most situations puts a premium on the importance of preventive and corrective facework. These are explored in greater detail later on in this chapter. Suffice to say at this point that Charlotte is in a delicate situation of dealing with her own face loss at the same time as Doug and Michelle are dealing with their own version of the same issue. For instance, Doug probably lost face when Charlotte leap-frogged him in the organizational hierarchy and secured the department head position. Although Michelle did not enter the race, she may regret that she sat on the sidelines and may still feel like she deserved the position.

Identity is contextual. Most simply, it makes sense to say that identity is situated, because nothing in the social world is isolated from its surroundings. A given identity takes on meaning with respect to adjacent and intersecting identities as well as other contextual factors. As Blumer (1969) pointed out, meaning is neither fixed nor random, but instead reflects pragmatic realities.

There are numerous contexts that may be relevant to a client's conflict situation. More important, given the topic at hand, these contexts can shape and give an increasing and decreasing weight to an individual's identities. A large number of these contexts can fall into the category of the client's relationship to people and the environment beyond the organization. These can include the overall economic climate, trends in the organization's sector, and individuals and groups with whom the client has a relationship beyond the day-to-day work setting. Another major category of client contexts encompasses intraorganizational realities. This can include the organization's history, stated goals, and lived goals as well as the client's reporting relationship and links to colleagues and subordinates.

Everyone in the situation experienced the contextual nature of identity in the way that Charlotte's success on a couple of small- to medium-scale projects (projects that reflected the new direction of the department and the city) strategically situated her to assume the department head vacancy. Basically, changes in the organization's external environment elevated the importance of Charlotte holding an MBA and not being aligned with a traditional intraorganizational camp. In this respect, the organization's context defined her as the most appropriate and effective leadership candidate. In terms of the more immediate conflict, Charlotte's identity as a capable department head is closely tied to her ability to work closely with the two directors.

Identity is multiple and ongoing. Identity exists on many overlapping levels. The Russian literary theorist Bakhtin (cited in Baxter & Montgomery, 1996) outlined a view that has come to be known as *dialogism*, wherein identities exist communicatively, and a person necessarily negotiates a world of diverse meaning. Identities flow out of the interaction of past, present, and anticipated future conversations and reflect community connections. Given this rich and complex notion of identity, it is easy to see how individual identities can proliferate, especially if someone is associated with many different communities. Individuals may have multiple identities, with each identity becoming predominant depending on the situation or event and the parties involved. The shifting nature of identity means, in part, that identities are not always clear, and some level of conflict is virtually inevitable.

It is easy to see how Charlotte has had multiple identities both across the span of her tenure with this organization and at any particular point in time, including the present moment. Most obviously, she has had different formal professional identities. Yet even these appeared differently to different audiences, for example, organizational insiders versus senior leaders with the city. Adding nuance to her current formal professional identity is the fact that it exists (positively for some and negatively for others) in relation to a work identity (e.g., entry-level secretary) that she may have left over 20 years ago.

Of course, identity can exist beyond the personal level. For instance, teams, organizations, nations, and ethnic groups can certainly have identities. In Charlotte's case, it is notable that her organization has a structural and cultural split between social work and architecture/planning. From an internal organizational perspective, she assumed an incommensurate identity when committing to her MBA program and has not fit in since that time.

A client may have identity conflicts among his or her own identities as well as with the identities of others. Charlotte may be experiencing intrapersonal conflict in terms of reconciling her identity of origin (possibly both personal and professional) with her identity as department head. Perhaps those with whom she is working through conflict are facing similar challenges. For instance, it might be that Michelle is in a very similar situation.

Identity includes issues of freedom and constraint. Goffman's (1959) term *impression management* dealt directly with the effort of the individual to shape and be responsive to identity issues and have power and encounter limits in doing so. The individual is like an actor who wants his or her role and definition of the world to be accepted as legitimate. Any specific identity opens up options for action but also necessarily limits what is achievable. As part of this process, the individual is casting others into certain roles. Others are not passive and can contribute to the process by validating or challenging identity claims as well as the very nature of the situation.

Given the many identity shifts that Charlotte has accomplished throughout her career, it may be the case that she fails to fully appreciate the way in which her identity as department head fundamentally changes her communicative freedom and constraint. In terms of freedom, she may now have the opportunity, far more so than in the past, to directly confront the traditional divide of social work versus architecture and planning. This means that she could conceivably reshape the identity of the organization, so that her own professional identity would be a better fit. Yet this could be much more than a self-centered act, as emerging work opportunities fit a more unified organizational structure. Charlotte might also be invited to see how she has the power to insist that she know what is happening throughout the organization (rather than have her directors sit on information). In terms of constraint, she may be compelled by her role as leader to not allow others to make derogatory remarks concerning her. While Charlotte has a certain level of power to take action as the formal leader of the organization, she should also be cautioned in terms of making sure that she directly or indirectly offers attractive identities to others, so that they do not get defensive and attack her. This might mean giving Doug and Michelle a certain degree of latitude in redefining their roles while insisting that they respect her leadership.

Identity is both individual and social. Identity is located in people's heads and in observable interactions among people. These two are linked in the way that individuals make internal sense of themselves in relation to their experience of self-in-the-world.

The theory of coordinated management of meaning (Griffin, 2006; Pearce & Cronen, 1980) explains the challenge of managing meaning as the quest for coherence while the challenge of interacting with others is the quest for coordination. The unavoidable overall challenge involves working to achieve both coherence and coordination. This depends on changes people make in terms of meaning, interaction, or contextual changes that take place. The dual nature of identity means, in part, that a coach can work with a client to explore the social influences that shape desirable or undesirable individual identities. In the case of an unwanted identity, the coach may support the client as he or she challenges the identity-framing of the self by another. Many conflicts involve identities that are individually assumed but that are not shared among others or are not effectively communicated to others. Charlotte could be offered the opportunity to systematically decide which identities she wants to reinforce and which identities she wants to challenge. An obvious identity message to consider challenging is the one thrust on her by Michelle, when Michelle strongly implied that Charlotte somehow did not belong in her current position and was out of touch with her roots. While some of the meaning of Michelle's words was ambiguous, Charlotte has the opportunity to partially address her current conflict by skillfully asserting her legitimacy as leader, attributing importance to connecting to all organizational members, and actually connecting with all organizational members. In this respect, Charlotte could reassert her identity as someone who knows what it is like to live without a certain kind of privilege—a kind of experience that is foundational to the mission of the organization.

Morality flows out of identity. Positioning theory (Harré & van Langenhove, 1999) explains that when an individual belongs to a specific community, he or she can be said to have an identity position. Likewise, an individual may have an identity position at the intersection of two or more communities. These positions suggest specific possibilities and limits on actions and also indicate moral responsibilities. The connection between identity and morality is important, because it can explain how different social groups and individuals can have different understandings of what is right and wrong. The fact that virtually every human being has a composite identity (an identity with many influences) helps explain why moral questions are often complex. Positioning theory also helps explain why shifts in identity are accompanied by moral questioning and why identity challenges in the midst of conflict are folded together with moral conflict.

The various identities that Charlotte has held in the past and currently holds create some tension for her. For instance, as the organizational leader, she implicitly accepts responsibility for addressing the lack of collaboration among Doug, Michelle, and herself. Yet, as a former staffer and midlevel manager in the organization, she may feel an obligation to not threaten the identity of her senior team members. Charlotte may also feel moral outrage toward Doug and Michelle, because they seem contemptuous of the way she has become increasingly empowered throughout her career. A coach can work with a client to clarify whether feelings of right and wrong are connected to former identities and should be discarded or whether these feelings remain valid because they are connected to one or more enduring identities.

Coaches should also work with clients so that clients become more aware of and possibly indirectly or directly address issues of morality with other parties. Obviously, this needs to be done with considerable care. In Charlotte's case, she might choose to view Doug and Michelle as legitimately protecting their professional identities and work communities of architecture/planning and social work, respectively. A task she might take on is directly encouraging these individuals to make sense of these identities differently and modify their loyalties in light of changing extraorganizational realities that demand cross-function collaboration. Of course, Doug and Michelle may also feel anger and jealousy given that each feels a rightful claim to the leadership position for which Charlotte was selected.

Charlotte has been through such a whirlpool of conflict and identity issues that it may make sense to take stock of not only her key identities but also her moral obligations and opportunities. What can Charlotte, Doug, and Michelle accomplish in their respective roles and as a team of senior leaders? What are these individuals morally obligated to accomplish?

The relationship between identity and culture can be complex. Arguably, no theory is more relevant for understanding culture and identity in conflict communication than Ting-Toomey's (1988, Ting-Toomey & Kurogi, 2004) face negotiation theory. This theory is based on the assumption that face is the best concept for understanding the way that individuals from different cultures work through conflict. The theory uses the concepts of collectivism and individualism that were well developed by Hofstede (1980, 1991). Collectivism refers to cultures that value group harmony over individual needs. Individualism refers to cultures that promote the individual in terms of uniqueness and importance. Ting-Toomey claimed that people in collectivist cultures (e.g., Japan) differ from people in individualist cultures (e.g., the U.S.) in the way they construe the self, the manner in which they maintain face, and in their preferences for conflict management. Clients should be cautioned about classifying others according to culture of origin, as there are ranges of behaviors within cultures, and as evidence has shown that an individual's self-construal is a better predictor of conflict behavior.

Although culture is not highlighted in the opening case, it is important to emphasize the degree to which it could greatly impact the coaching experience. For instance, if Charlotte comes from and self-identifies with a collectivist culture such as that found in China or Japan, it almost certainly would not feel right for her to directly insist that Doug and Michele show respect because she is the leader. In this situation, she would probably find it preferable to assert her status indirectly in terms of opportunities to advance the organization's welfare. She could potentially work with a coach to determine ways of doing so. If Charlotte is any kind of visible minority, she may be dealing with direct or indirect forms of racism. If Doug and/or Michelle are visible minorities, they may perceive or be understandably sensitive to potential exploitation of privilege by those above them. Of course, as a woman, Charlotte may also be experiencing sexism regarding identity expectations.

An Identity Framework for Interpersonal Conflict in the Workplace

The coordinated management of meaning or CMM (Griffin, 2006; Pearce & Cronen, 1980) is an excellent way of understanding identity in interpersonal conflict. CMM posits that communication is the way we create our social world. While not a theory of identity per se, CMM explains that who we are is simultaneously shaped by the social world. Accordingly, every communication occurs within the contexts of episode, relationship, identity, and culture (Griffin, 2006). We have modified this list of contexts in order to emphasize the identities that we see as generally relevant among those working in organizational settings.

The identity framework presented in Figure 4.1 breaks down different kinds of identity. Clients may find it helpful to get an understanding of the different kinds of identity in a conflict before considering which identities are most relevant in terms of problematic conflict communication or for pointing ways to effective conflict management. Three CMM-related assumptions that may be helpful to share with clients in order to get them acquainted with this dynamic approach to identity are these: (1) A given identity operates in tension with other identities and contextual factors in a conflict, (2) particular identities and contextual factors may be in the foreground, midground, or background of a conflict, and (3) identity issues can play a major role whether or not they are foregrounded.

When facing an interpersonal conflict in an organizational setting, six fairly standard types of identity to consider are personal, professional, situation, relationship, organizational, and cultural identity. An important

- Personal
- Professional
- Situational
- Relational
- Organizational
- Cultural

Figure 4.1   Identity Framework: Types of Identity Frequently Implicated in Organizationally Based Interpersonal Conflict

part of most conflict coaching sessions will involve the coach working with the client to clarify these different kinds of identity and the ways in which they interrelate.

Personal identity refers to the clients' and other parties' identities that exist primarily beyond the work setting yet may have considerable impact on work-related conflicts. Personal identities can have relevance, because some are enduring and others are permanent. Obviously, individuals do not put these aside (or certainly not all of them) when they enter the workplace. Enduring personal identities include attitudes, values, and character. Permanent personal identities (with few exceptions) include gender, race, ethnicity, age, and national and regional origin. In Charlotte's case, personal identity could be quite significant if Charlotte were a visible minority who had or did not have this identity in common with others in the conflict and broader organization. Likewise, it could be quite significant if Charlotte held religious or spiritual beliefs that she described as affecting the way she acted across her life, including at work. Of course, these matters would also be important to consider for Doug and Michelle. Personal identities can be particularly challenging to consider, because, in many cases, individuals do not speak of them in the work environment, and therefore they may not be entirely obvious, or we may not be able to directly refer to them with other parties. On the other hand, it can be appropriate and effective for a client to have the opportunity to consider these within the coaching session, because they can sometimes function as the proverbial elephant in the room, both in the coaching relationship and in the direct conflict environment.

Professional identity refers to clients' and other parties' work-related identities beyond the immediate situation and the conflict-related relationships. Charlotte's primary work-related identities are her formal role as department head and her professional credential as an MBA. Noticeably, her professional credential as a social worker has effectively been stripped away from her. Charlotte can also be said to have a work identity of consummate professional in terms of interorganizational peers and extraorganizational overseers. She has an ambiguous work identity with staff in her organization who are not directly involved in the conflict. Doug's primary work identities are his formal role as director of architecture and planning and his closely related professional credential as an architect. Michelle's primary work identities are her formal role as director of social work and her closely related professional credential as a social worker.

Situational identity refers to who the parties are in relation to each other in the interaction. Although Charlotte has not yet brought the directors together to meet regarding the grant proposal, she anticipates that without a coaching intervention her identity will be that of leader while Doug and Michelle will be blockers.

Relational identity refers to who the parties are with respect to one another beyond the situation. Charlotte, Doug, and Michelle have a relatively long history together. Doug and Michelle knew Charlotte when she was a lower-level professional in the organization. Doug and Michelle were supportive of Charlotte at that time. Michelle used to consider herself to be on the same team as Charlotte given their shared social work backgrounds, but this changed for Michelle once Charlotte began making headway on her MBA. The relationships between Charlotte and Doug and between Charlotte and Michelle have been seriously strained since that time. Both relationships have seemed competitive, even though only the relationship between Charlotte and Doug was plainly competitive, as Charlotte and Doug were vying for the department head position.

Organizational identity refers to the identity of the institution especially as it affects the framing of identities and the conflict. This case is unique in that the city department basically composes its own organization. The title of the organization (i.e., "Office of Housing and Community Development") can be seen as an identity. Arguably, another relevant organizational identity is hinted at in the integrated functions and financially self-sustaining trend that runs through Charlotte's projects that earned acclaim, the city's expectations for the organization, and the demands of at least one major grant provider.

Cultural identity refers to local or broad cultural categories. On the local level, there may be cultures unique to the organization, such as those among organizational members with particular functional specializations, team assignments, or worksite locations. On the broad level, there may be more widely recognizable cultural differences that are present in the organization, including differences among organizational members that are of a particular race or ethnicity, socioeconomic status, gender, or sexual orientation. In Charlotte's case, the most prominent cultural identity present is the professional divide within the organization. Other, broad cultural differences may also be factors that could emerge as a coach continued to work with Charlotte.

Coaches should be aware that a systematic application of the identity framework to the client's case will likely reveal intrapersonal conflicts that link with conflicts between the client and others. As noted earlier in the chapter, CMM explains these sorts of struggles as unavoidable features of social life. We are constantly working to reconcile the stories we tell ourselves and others (issues of coherence) with the stories contained in our actual interactions (issues of coordination) (Griffin, 2006; Pearce & Cronen, 1980). Charlotte can be seen to be encountering a unity-diversity tension both internally and with others. Her ambiguous professional identity (as it is clearly aligned neither with social work nor with architecture and planning) combined with her professional identity as an MBA fits well with the emerging organizational identities of integrated functions and financial self-sufficiency. In fact, she may have been selected to lead the organization because she was seen as a unity candidate. However, the ambiguity of her past professional allegiance conflicts with the professional identities and related expectations of Doug and Michelle. In other words, unity in the organization does not seem to meaningfully exist at the present moment, and yet it may be required for both Charlotte and the organization to truly succeed. If she decided this were the case, she might proceed by referencing the diversity of her own history as someone who was a relative outsider and who became an insider in an honorable fashion and whose story powerfully reflects the mission of the organization. Of course, such a move can be quite bold and is not without risk, at least in part because it uses an "I'm different" argument to advance a "let's work together" mission for the organization.

Obviously, other identity issues could be important. However, an elaboration of the six identities and their interrelationships may be effective, and is certainly a good start, most of the time. The six identities can be used to make identity issues visible. They can assist in determining which identities are central to conflict escalation and effective conflict management. A careful consideration of identity dynamics is important, because identity goals tend to drive conflict (Wilmot & Hocker, 2007), and intractable conflicts are fundamentally identity related (Northrup, 1989). In Charlotte's situation, this kind of inventory would arguably be helpful in making the centrality of identity clear to her. It might be helpful for a coach to work with Charlotte to note possible themes across identity types. In addition to the unity-diversity theme noted above, Charlotte's case also touches on the inevitability of identity change coming from the outside of the organization and the need to reassure traditional insiders they have talents to be a successful part of the change. These themes could provide the basis for determining what communications need to be crafted.

Facework as the Primary Means of Managing Identity

While the previous section offers a model for charting important identity issues, the current section offers ways of intervening regarding these issues. Charlotte could benefit from an introduction to this material in order to consider appropriate and effective tactics for both protecting and enhancing face not only for herself but also for Doug and Michelle.

For the purposes of conflict coaching, we organize facework tactics into four categories. The first category involves avoiding or lessening the importance of potentially threatening behavior when identity conflict is not prominent and problematic. This category functions from a proactive standpoint and puts relatively equal emphasis on managing the face needs of self and other. The remaining categories apply when identity issues are currently prominent and, very possibly, problematic. The second category involves decreasing responsibility for behavior. This category can be used for the face needs of self and other. The third category involves taking personal responsibility for behavior. Its use is mainly concerned with the management of self face needs. The fourth category involves challenging the other to take responsibility for behavior. Putting this category into action concentrates effort on managing the face needs of the other. Coaches and clients will find these four categories and the respective tactics helpful for communicating regarding identity in conflict or potential conflict situations.

The specific facework behaviors that we outline below are derived from the work of Brown and Levinson (1987); Cupach and Metts (1994); Folger, Poole, and Stutman (2005); Hewitt and Stokes (1975); and Stokes and Hewitt (1976). Of course, it is unlikely that a client would use all of the facework behaviors in a particular interaction or even over the span of a given conflict. Also, other facework behaviors are certainly possible. Finally, it is often the case that a specific facework tactic can be used across categories, variously emphasize self and other identity concerns, and be variously linked with success. We have simply attempted to propose some major facework categories and multiple tactical choices within each. The facework categories and tactical choices are summarized in Table 4.1.

Table 4.1   Facework Categories and Tactical Choices

Categories	Tactical Choices

1. Avoiding or lessening the importance of potentially threatening behaviors when identity issues are not currently prominent and problematic	▨ Not performing a face-threatening act
	▨ Requesting suspended judgment
	  ▨ Hedging
	  ▨ Credentialing
	  ▨ Sin license
	  ▨ Appeal for suspended judgment
	▨ Going off the record
	▨ Humor

2. Decreasing responsibility for behavior	▨ Accounts ▨ Excuses ▨ Counterclaim ▨ Quasi-theories
3. Taking personal responsibility for behavior	▨ Apologies ▨ Conversational repair ▨ Justifications ▨ Remedy
4. Challenging the other to take responsibility for behavior	▨ Principled confrontation

FACEWORK CATEGORY #1: AVOIDING OR LESSENING THE IMPORTANCE OF POTENTIALLY THREATENING BEHAVIORS WHEN IDENTITY ISSUES ARE NOT CURRENTLY PROMINENT AND PROBLEMATIC

It is important that clients appreciate the opportunity to manage identity proactively, thereby maintaining a positive conflict climate. The following tactics can be used in the absence of prior conflict escalation as preventive measures. (Note that each may also be used effectively in more charged circumstances. As such, examples from Charlotte's case can still apply.)

▨ *Not performing a face-threatening act.* Thinking through whether potential communications will threaten face for self or other and then refraining from carrying out such acts (or at least having the ability to moderate such acts) is vital to being a competent conflict communicator. For example, Charlotte might stop herself from boldly telling Doug and Michelle that they must either accept her leadership or leave the organization. This is first and foremost a way to respect face for others.

Holding back on launching a major face attack can also be seen to protect Charlotte's face.

⫸ *Requesting suspended judgment.* There are a number of measures for getting another party to more deliberately and favorably assess the speaker's coming words. This technique is essentially asking the listener to give the speaker the benefit of the doubt before passing judgment.

⫸ *Hedging.* The speaker indicates uncertainty and an openness to input. For example, even while more firmly acting as organizational leader, Charlotte could insist that she does not have all of the expertise needed to succeed and that she welcomes the input of Doug and Michelle. This could proactively enhance face for Charlotte as she displays the foresight of knowing that she will need the help of others. It also gives face to Doug and Michelle even while Charlotte asserts her status in relation to the others.

⫸ *Credentialing.* The speaker indicates a rationale and relevant qualifications. For example, Charlotte could make the point that the organization needs to be run more like a for-profit company in terms of generating revenue in a competitive environment and that she is fully qualified to run it given her MBA and background with the organization. This enhances Charlotte's face but could be combined with an acknowledgment of others' relevant talents as a way to protect their face.

⫸ *Sin license.* The speaker indicates this is an exceptional circumstance in which a rule can be violated without offense. The sin license can apply to the speaker and/or others. For example, Charlotte could point out that it was somewhat reasonable for individuals to take verbal shots at one another during the time in which the lead position was open and even shortly after it was filled, but now the time had come to work together. This particular sin license functions as face repair for Charlotte and others in the organization.

⫸ *Appeal for suspended judgment.* The speaker can indicate a request to give the sender a chance to elaborate before casting judgment. For example, Charlotte might share a collaborative vision for the future of the organization and ask Doug and Michelle to take basic next steps rather than immediately buy into Charlotte's vision or reject her vision. This can save and protect face for all concerned, as Doug and Michelle are not forced to make an immediate reversal of their previous stance, and there is a neutral period for everyone to carefully consider all aspects of the matter.

⫸ *Going off the record.* The speaker can suggest that the conversation be unofficial. For example, Charlotte might privately acknowledge to Doug and Michelle, possibly even one-on-one, that she recognizes it may have felt unfair to them that she ended up as lead, but that she is committed to working as a relative equal. This demonstrates face sensitivity to Doug and Michelle (in the form of a private meeting) while also protecting Charlotte's face (against a potential attack).

✄ Humor. The speaker can signal that the situation should not be taken too seriously or that a more serious breach has been overcome. Obviously, humor needs to be used with sophistication, especially when tensions are high. For example, Charlotte might judge it appropriate at some point in the future to joke with Doug and Michelle that the speed of organizational musical chairs means that she better treat them well, just in case she ends up working for one of them as lead one day. If successful, this self-deprecating humor can acknowledge Doug and Michelle's talents while making Charlotte appear as a comfortable and, therefore, competent leader.

FACEWORK CATEGORY #2: DECREASING RESPONSIBILITY FOR BEHAVIOR

This facework category is relevant in situations where a client wants to deflect responsibility from self or other. Whether done proactively or reactively, it often occurs when identity issues are prominent and at least potentially problematic.

✄ Accounts. The speaker provides reasons for a behavior—reasons that justify the actions. For example, Charlotte could explain her taking a firmer leadership role by saying she needed to respond to a more competitive financial environment for the organization. Charlotte's action in this situation could protect or enhance her face in making it more difficult for others to attribute less attractive motives to her firmer role. An individual might also give a favorable account for another's behavior in order to support that person's identity.

✄ Excuses. The speaker accepts causality but denies responsibility. The speaker admits to an action but claims there was no intent or ill will and that something happened beyond the speaker's control. For example, Charlotte could claim that she in no way plotted to overtake Doug and Michelle but that circumstances shifted and ended up suiting and rewarding her training as an MBA. This is mainly about Charlotte saving face. It may be especially risky, because it can be seen as an attack on the others.

✄ Counterclaim. The speaker denies negative intent and suggests there is evidence of positive intent. For example, Charlotte could insist that despite direct and indirect accusations, she has always acted in the best interests of those served by the organization as well as all those working in the organization, including staffers in positions representing her own roots. This is primarily a reactive move for the individual to save face. It also recognizes, at least indirectly, those making such a claim.

✎ *Quasi-theories.* The speaker uses one or more simple explanations or alternate ways of seeing the situation. For example, Charlotte could explain that the traditional professional areas of architecture/planning and social work were not being abandoned but that they were being strongly integrated in order to more fully realize peoples' strengths and best adapt to a new operating environment. If delivered well, this explanation could save face for all concerned.

FACEWORK CATEGORY #3: TAKING
PERSONAL RESPONSIBILITY FOR BEHAVIOR

This facework category is relevant in situations where a client wants to wholly or partially accept accountability. It is typically accomplished reactively and often occurs when identity issues are prominent and at least potentially problematic.

✎ *Apologies.* The speaker expresses regret while taking responsibility. For example, Charlotte could apologize for times in the past when she did not address rumors about her commitment to the organization. This action shows respect for those who were wronged or inconvenienced. It also can build Charlotte's credibility.

✎ *Conversational repair.* The speaker corrects or restates a verbal error. In some ways this technique assumes that sounding good helps the speaker look good. For example, while talking with Doug and Michelle, Charlotte might immediately rework a given sentence if it is not as face sensitive as she might want it to be. This can save face for Charlotte as she regains a sense of conversational competence, and it can also save face for Doug and Michelle as they are portrayed in a more favorable light.

✎ *Justifications.* The speaker accepts responsibility but denies consequences. Through justifications the speaker indicates that the actions were intentional, but the effects of the actions were neither anticipated nor justified given the circumstances. For example, Charlotte could point out that she worked hard to earn the lead position but that she did not deserve the innuendo that ensued. This is an act of face-saving by Charlotte that somewhat decreases potential face threat to Doug and Michelle because she does not directly attribute the innuendo to them.

✎ *Remedy.* The speaker offers behavioral correction or repair of physical damage. For example, Charlotte could be clearer in indicating her organizational intentions by instituting a weekly statement. This action could save and build face for Charlotte and also provide clear information so that others do not threaten her and simultaneously can protect their own face in the future.

FACEWORK CATEGORY #4: CHALLENGING THE OTHER TO TAKE RESPONSIBILITY FOR BEHAVIOR

This facework category applies in situations where a client wants the other to accept some level of accountability. It may be accomplished proactively or reactively and often occurs when identity issues are prominent and at least potentially problematic.

Principled confrontation. The speaker directly addresses an issue of importance with another party and either insists on a specific course of action or invites joint exploration of the issue and possible next actions. Principled confrontation may be an effective option especially if it is behavioral (rather than speculative in terms of a person's attitudes and motivations, etc.), specific (as opposed to general), and otherwise delivered in a face-sensitive manner (e.g., the message is communicated privately and in a reasonable tone of voice). This kind of confrontation is dealt with in considerable detail in the conflict communication skills chapter. For example, Charlotte might have one-on-one meetings with Doug and Michelle in order to explore how they can best support each other's success within the organization. As part of each of these conversations, Charlotte may end up insisting that she not be criticized behind her back and that any face-to-face feedback be respectful of her role as the leader of the organization.

General Principles for Identity Work With Conflict Coaching Clients

Principle #1: Encourage the client to orient to conflict and identity given his or her pre-existing knowledge, attitudes, and skills. This involves making identity central at this point in the conflict coaching process. It also involves recognizing that the client brings a complex mix of knowledge, attitudes, and skills to this conversation. The client should leave the coaching with a sharper understanding of his or her baselines in these areas and specific ways to grow. Optimally, the client is also able to move beyond understanding of self and other by developing knowledge, attitudes, and skills within the coaching session.

Principle #2: Invite a comprehensive understanding of the concept of identity through the exploration of key assumptions. Client insight into the role of identity in conflict is facilitated in part through consideration of identity-related assumptions. This kind of conversation may naturally develop or be systematically introduced by the coach. While the coach may draw from considerable expertise in explaining different assumptions, the significance of a given assumption to the client's situation should be ultimately left up to the client.

Principle #3: Assist the client in getting clear about important identities for self and other as well as the interrelationships among these. A focus on identity and conflict must provide the client with opportunities for determining his or her identities and the identities of important others. Some level of clarity about identities is vital to examining connections among identities as well as making sense of more and less productive conflict communication.

Principle #4: Foster the client's ability to recognize identity goals, specific tactics, and ongoing face dynamics as well as the larger conflict interaction. Given the pervasive yet often taken for granted nature of identity, the coach may be of considerable value to the client in simply introducing key opportunities for change. The possibility of reflection by the client should be seen as a valuable benefit of conflict coaching.

Principle #5: Support the client in acting in relation to identity goals, specific tactics, and ongoing face dynamics as well as the larger conflict interaction. Conflict coaching in regard to identity means going beyond opportunities to increase awareness by also offering opportunities to develop identity-sensitive communications. The coach may overview fairly standard types of identity-related communication tactics and then work with the client in terms of trying out and possibly tailoring those that are most applicable.

Principle #6: Remember that the client should remain in control of claiming identities and enacting identities. Identity is not only foundational to who we are in conflict, it is also fundamental to making sense of our very existence. While sometimes it is adaptable, other times it is not. Although no part of the conflict coaching model involves directing clients outside of the conflict coaching session itself, coaches should show extra sensitivity when offering opportunities to clients, particularly when opportunities may challenge long-cherished assumptions on the part of the client.

Specific Approaches for Identity
Work With Conflict Coaching Clients

Approach #1: Map the identity landscape of a particular conflict.

What is it? This approach consists of using the identity framework to generally consider the identities of the parties to a conflict, including the way that some identities function as context to a conflict. (For example, the identity of the organization can determine the range of permissible individual identities within that organization.)

Why is it important? For many clients, this process involves getting clear on the identity webs that surround each party as well as the core drivers of a conflict. For instance, there may be a confluence of identity-related concerns within and across individuals that makes the conflict of considerable complexity and importance.

How do you do it? (1) Introduce the identity framework to the client. The model includes the personal identity of each individual, the general professional identity of each individual, the identity of each individual within a given situation, the identity of the individuals within their larger relationship, the identity of the organization, and any cultural identities that may be relevant. (2) Encourage the client to specify details for each identity type. Be sure to include consideration of self and other. (3) Once the entire typology has been populated, invite consideration of appropriate and effective communication given the identities of both parties. (4) Invite overall reflections on the meaning and value of the activity.

Approach #2: Explore identity threat from a preventive point of view.

What is it? Drawing from the introduction to facework, the facework categories (especially the first), and the specific facework tactics, the client and coach can explore a basic framework for protecting the identity of self and other as well as apply that framework in the client's conflict context.

Why is it important? Clients can often spot challenging relationships in which the conflict potential is high because of face-related issues. Moving to the level of specific preventive practices can be especially empowering to clients, because it involves the execution of a proactive strategy that decreases the likelihood of conflict polarization.

How do you do it? (1) Encourage the client to describe his or her situation so that it is clear whether the need for preventive facework concerns self or other. (2) Introduce or review the use of facework behaviors as a means for addressing face concerns. (3) Ask the client to decide on the appropriate use of preventive facework in relation to the degree of face threat. (4) Support the client's effectiveness in this area by working with him or her to craft specific communications. (5) Offer the additional opportunities to role-play and debrief specific communications. (6) Encourage consideration of alternative approaches given the contingencies of interaction. Note that it may very well be useful, even essential, to develop preventive strategies and tactics beyond those listed in the chapter.

Approach #3: Determine the anatomy of a particular face loss incident.

What is it? A face loss event occurs when one or both parties experience an attack on one or more valued identities and particularly when there is a perception of injury. This activity aims to clarify whether an interaction threatened face and, if so, how.

Why is it important? Face loss incidents can be worth analyzing in some detail because they can function as negative turning points in conflicts. Also, given the stress of these situations, details may have been underconsidered at the time and yet these details may be suggestive of effective future action.

How do you do it? One approach to positively addressing a potential face loss incident is to chart the relevant conflict situation. (1) Using a piece of paper with two columns, the client can be encouraged to recount what was said verbally and/or nonverbally (column A) and what it meant in terms of identity (column B). (2) Areas of heightened face communication can be explored in more detail to consider specific communication behaviors, effects of those behaviors, and possible alternative behaviors. Although this activity focuses on interpersonal interaction as the site of face loss, face loss can also occur as a result of change in the larger context.

Approach #4: Explore corrective identity.

What is it? Remedying face loss situations can be important in the short term and the long term, particularly if negative conflict patterns are to be avoided or curtailed. This activity supports a client in identifying instances of face loss as well as in delineating repair opportunities both in the moment and beyond.

Why is it important? Even well-intentioned and interpersonally skilled individuals can make face-related mistakes, especially in rapidly unfolding conflict situations. This activity assists clients in productively learning from these mistakes in terms of both the conflict at hand and conflict communication in general.

How do you do it? (1) Introduce the client to facework behaviors as specific ways to correct identity. (2) Provide the client with a piece of paper divided into five columns, and ask the client to write in each of the columns. The first column is for a list of important identities. The second column is for an indication of which identities from the first column suffered harm. The third column provides an opportunity to note actual and possible repairs in the moment. The fourth column is for possible delayed repairs. The fifth column is for notes on a general corrective strategy given the overall exercise. (3) Get the client to talk through his or her written responses as a way of checking assumptions and further elaborating the client's responses. (4) Offer the possibility of role-playing or otherwise preparing for any of the action items generated as part of this activity.

Approach #5: Clarify identity-consistent action.

What is it? This activity connects identity and related action.

Why is it important? This activity can be useful for showing the way identity opens up and closes off different opportunities for action. It can be used to explore the suitability of possible action in view of a predetermined identity.

How do you do it? (1) Present the client with a sheet of paper that is labeled at the top with a specific identity, possibly a composite identity of the client's choosing. Divide the page into three equal rectangular sections. The first represents action that is inconsistent with the listed identity. The second represents action that is somewhat consistent with the listed identity. The third represents action that is highly consistent with the listed identity. (2) Invite the client to write down and, in doing so, consider his or her past or prospective actions in terms of degree of identity consistency. (3) The client can also attempt to do this from the perspective of the other party by using a separate activity sheet. (4) Debrief the activity by encouraging the client to consider ways to take action and influence the overall interaction so communication is consistent with both the client's identity and the other party's identity.

Chapter Summary

Identity is closely connected to emotion and power issues and therefore serves as one of the three basic lenses through which coaches can assist clients in understanding and strategically responding to conflict. Identity is a complex phenomenon that can be introduced with a selection of key assumptions. Consideration of an identity framework may be useful for determining many of the most relevant identities in an interpersonal workplace-based conflict. Facework techniques can be grouped in four major categories and can offer the client communication tools for proactively and reactively supporting the conflict-related identity needs of self and other.

(Continued)

(Continued)

GENERAL PRINCIPLES FOR IDENTITY WORK WITH CONFLICT COACHING CLIENTS

Principle #1: Encourage the client to orient to conflict and identity given his or her preexisting knowledge, attitudes, and skills.

Principle #2: Invite a comprehensive understanding of the concept of identity through the exploration of key assumptions.

Principle #3: Assist the client in getting clear about important identities for self and other as well as the interrelationships among these.

Principle #4: Foster the client's ability to recognize identity goals, specific tactics, and ongoing face dynamics as well as the larger conflict interaction.

Principle #5: Support the client in acting in relation to identity goals, specific tactics, and ongoing face dynamics as well as the larger conflict interaction.

Principle #6: Remember that the client should remain in control of claiming identities and enacting identities.

SPECIFIC APPROACHES FOR IDENTITY WORK WITH CONFLICT COACHING CLIENTS

Approach #1: Map the identity landscape of a particular conflict.

Approach #2: Explore identity threat from a preventive point of view.

Approach #3: Determine the anatomy of a particular face loss incident.

Approach #4: Explore corrective identity.

Approach #5: Clarify identity-consistent action.

5

Stage Two

The Emotion Perspective

There is no necessary clash, no dichotomy between man's reason and his emotions—provided he observes their proper relationship. A rational man knows—or makes it a point to discover—the source of his emotions, the basic premises from which they come.

—Ayn Rand

Randy and Sue have been lifelong friends. They grew up together in a small hometown and moved after college to the city where they decided to follow their dreams and develop a software design firm ten years ago. Over the past decade they have established their practice and are currently one of the leading firms in their area. As they built their company, they had a number of very lean years. Almost like spouses in a marriage, they counted on each other as more than business partners. As a result, when they became successful and established it was all the more gratifying.

During the last several years as the business stabilized, Randy and Sue started their individual families and developed a close network of clients, family, and friends. The firm operated as a nexus for their lives to the point that the boundaries sometimes seemed blurred. Yet the connections were very positive. Conflicts happened and were handled, as you would expect in a healthy family or community.

Last year the honeymoon ended as Randy and Sue realized they had very different visions for the future of the firm. A large software company offered to acquire the firm as a subsidiary due to the quality of database search software that Randy had designed. The offer was much more than Randy had ever thought possible, and it contained the incentive of his being the president of the subsidiary. It was common knowledge that this software company often acquired promising smaller companies and targeted certain leaders for the fast track within the larger company. It was clear that Randy was being targeted as fast track material. Sue's status in the new configuration was much less certain. While there was no indication that she would lose her job, there was also no indication she would be given the same consideration as Randy.

The acquisition would not involve a physical move (at least not soon) or a basic change to the everyday operation of the firm. But it would fundamentally change the autonomy and freedom they had always taken for granted, even when things were not going well. Sue was shocked that Randy was seriously thinking about this offer.

Sue was even more shocked when Randy indicated that he might consider taking the offer as an independent, basically splitting the firm and allowing his portion to be acquired. She felt this was a great betrayal and was very angry and bitter about Randy's disloyalty. She was also quite fearful, beginning to wonder whether dissolution of the firm (if it came to that) would leave her able to recoup and rebuild. And there was some jealousy involved. Why was Randy getting the attention and fanfare, and why was he so willing to let the spotlight fall only on him? Sue was certain that whether or not she went along with the acquisition, her partnership with Randy was over on the most profound level.

S ue is in the middle of one of the most life-changing conflicts we face. One of her definitive, bedrock relationships is in serious danger of termination. She needs help to manage the conflict well in order to respect her past, hopefully salvage her relationships, and move forward to a promising future. A conflict coach can help Sue understand her emotions about this conflict, manage her emotional reactions during this conflict, and use her emotions to identify what she needs to move past this conflict. The conflict coach must be able to be an emotion coach to do the job well.

In this chapter, we introduce one of the three perspectives that are essential in conflict coaching—the emotion perspective. We begin with a brief discussion about the nature of emotion and the centrality of emotion in conflict. In this discussion we link the significance of the emotion perspective to the identity and power perspectives, as explained in Chapter 2. We follow this with a quick overview of some of the emotion theories that are most helpful to conflict coaches, and we refer you to resources outside this text for more information. Then we turn our attention to how you can use this information in conflict coaching to help your client use emotion to his or her advantage.

Introduction to Emotion

Over the past several years, we have been continually struck by the frequency with which conflict practitioners raise questions about dealing with emotion. Until recently, emotion was ignored in the conflict theory and practice literature or, when addressed, discussed in a limited manner in terms of anger management with an emphasis on how that impacts conflict escalation (Adler, Rosen, & Silverstein, 1998). Fortunately, more recent literature has treated emotion more seriously, discussing the importance of emotion for conflict practitioners (Cloke, 2001; LeBaron, 2002) and examining research about emotion in conflict and conflict management processes (Jones, 2000, 2005; Jones & Bodtker, 2001).

As mentioned in our model explanation in Chapter 2, we believe that emotion is one of the three key components of all conflict. To understand the conflict between Randy and Sue, one must understand and appreciate how they are feeling about this situation and about each other. Without attention to the emotional component of this conflict, Sue's conflict coach will be unable to help Sue get to the root of the conflict. If emotion is central to the creation and nature of conflict, the influence of emotion on the management of conflict becomes central as well.

UNDERSTANDING EMOTION

For a conflict coach to be effective in helping clients manage emotions in conflict, the coach needs to have a basic understanding of emotion. Social scientists studying emotion agree that emotion involves three elements—cognitive, physiological, and behavioral (Kitayama & Markus, 1994). The cognitive component of emotion is an appraisal process. Ortony, Clore, and Collins (1988) argue that an event or change in the environment is appraised, and the appraisal leads to an emotional response. Later in this chapter we will suggest one appraisal theory of emotion that coaches can use to help clients identify what they are feeling and why. Different appraisals lead to different emotions and suggest different needs in order to move past the emotion (Dillard, Kinney, & Cruz, 1996). Thus, when a coach clarifies a client's emotions, the coach also narrows the possible resolutions that will be most effective.

Emotion also involves a physiological component—a physical sensation and a physical reaction. Denzin, in his book *On Understanding Emotions* (1984), labels emotions "embodied experiences" that radiate through the body. Lyon's (1995) description of emotions as "embodied thoughts" provides a similar description. Sometimes the physical element of emotion can make it difficult for a client to think clearly, an idea called "emotional flooding" that we'll discuss later.

The expressive component is how we communicate what we are feeling. Sometimes our expression of emotion is completely spontaneous, but often it is at least partly strategic—we let people see what we want them to see (Buck, 1984). Clients may not understand how their expression of emotion affects the other people in conflict, and they may not appreciate how they are being affected by the other's emotional communication.

All three components together constitute an emotional experience. Conflict coaches should be able to help clients understand how their appraisal has led to an emotion, how they can use the appraisal to identify options for the conflict resolution, how their physical response to conflict may be influencing their thoughts and behavior, and whether their expression of emotion is contributing to or impeding effective conflict management.

EMOTION AND CONFLICT

Jones (2000) articulates basic principles that illustrate the strong relationship between emotion and conflict. In these principles we clearly see the relationships between emotion and identity and between emotion and power as well.

1. Conflict is emotionally defined. Most definitions of conflict assume that conflict occurs when people perceive incompatible goals or interference from one another. These are the triggering events that cause conflict. They are also, by definition, events that elicit emotion. Perceived interruption of plans or perceived discrepancies between our goals and reality are the things most identified as emotion eliciting (Ortony, Clore, & Collins, 1988). Because the triggers of emotion and the triggers of perceived conflict are the same, whenever we are in conflict, it means that we have been triggered emotionally. Put simply, we don't realize we are in a conflict until we have an emotional reaction that leads us to define the situation as problematic or conflictual.

If the trigger of a conflict is inherently emotional, a conflict coach must access emotional information to help the client understand the conflict. To gain a full understanding of the nature of the conflict, coaches have to know how to uncover and discuss the emotional triggers that influenced how clients recognized and defined the conflict. For some conflict coaches, this attention to emotion will already be ingrained in their approach to working with conflict. For others it may require a profound shift in their thinking about emotion in conflict management. If you were the coach working with Sue, you would want to help Sue think about how she is feeling about this potential acquisition of the firm and where those feelings are linked to her reactions to Randy.

2. Emotion reveals what we value. Emotional experience is fundamentally moral. Our values impact how we experience emotions, and our emotions reveal what we value (Manstead, 1991). We don't have strong emotions about trivial things. Instead, we get emotional about something because it strikes us as right or wrong, good or bad, appropriate or inappropriate. When we think about what "makes sense" in solving a conflict, we are guided by our assumptions about what outcomes are "fair," "just," or "good."

Emotion can serve as a coach's lens into the ideology and morality of the client. The emotional response of the client provides insight to both the coach and client about the client's moral framing of issues and options. The client and coach can better appreciate what the client sees as "right" solutions and how the client can enact these options in the "right" way. Other scholars have noted that understanding the moral dimension of conflict is necessary for the creation of a "transcendent dialogue," in which individuals in conflict not only learn to reflect on their own ideology but also become willing to consider changing their values in order to resolve conflict (Pearce & Littlejohn, 1997). Sue, in the example above, has very strong values about friendship and loyalty. Her reaction to this conflict is strongly linked to her sense that "friends just don't treat each other this way." No amount of economic argument or convenience argument addresses the foundation of her perception of what is really important about this conflict. Helping her understand this point, how it impacts her views, and how it affects potential conflict management is key.

3. Emotion reflects identity issues that impact conflict. In the previous chapter, we explained how important identity is in conflict. Understanding who you are in a situation is critical to understanding how you perceive things and how you feel about them in conflict. If we don't have a strong sense of self, we don't have clear emotional experiences (Saarni, 1999). We can't see clearly what may be personally important that is at stake, because we aren't clear about what is "personal." Sometimes, sorting out emotions can help us clarify our identity. Sue may be very upset and have an idea of why she is upset, but during coaching she comes to understand that her identity of business partner is actually more an identity of life partner (in a nonromantic sense) with Randy, and that is why she is so affected by this conflict. In a very scary way for her, Sue's identity is linked with Randy's. If Sue and Randy split, it raises questions about who Sue really is; these are questions that Sue (like most of us) finds threatening and uncomfortable.

A client's emotional responses also reveal identity needs and face concerns to which coaches should be sensitive. We know that threats to identity often lead to conflict escalation and make conflicts harder to resolve. The more our identity or face is threatened, the more defensive we become (Rubin, Pruitt, & Kim, 1994). Threats to identity may also result in shame, which can lead to anger and withdrawal. Without reducing the feeling of shame, these cycles will almost certainly escalate destructive conflict (Retzinger, 1993).

If we were Sue's conflict coach, we would want to help Sue understand how she sees her identity threatened by the acquisition and the ways she and Randy have been communicating about the acquisition. We could help her see how increasing perceptions of identity threat have resulted in escalation of conflict intensity and behavior. And we may discover that she feels very uncomfortable and ashamed at the way she has been thinking about and feeling toward Randy. Her shame, coupled with her other feelings, has fueled her inability to handle this conflict as she would prefer.

Working through conflict can help a client decide on the identity that she wants to emphasize. Sue may come to understand that she wants to be a business mogul, and her insights may lead her to be more accepting of the acquisition. She may realize that she wants to be a true and valued partner and that serving in a secondary role in this acquisition will never sit well with her.

Emotion coaching under the umbrella of conflict coaching not only helps the client think about identity issues, it also encourages the client to engage in some perspective taking; to consider the identity needs of the other party and how those needs are affecting the other's behavior. Sue may need to have a better understanding of how Randy sees himself and of who Randy wants to be in order for her to appreciate what the acquisition means to him. As we'll discuss later in this chapter, a sign of emotional competence is the ability to engage in empathic perspective taking and to consider what actions are "caring" based on that insight.

4. *Emotion reveals the power relationship.* According to Kemper's (1978) sociological theory of emotion, emotions are influenced by and influence two key relational elements—power and social status. Emotion is important in how we make sense of our relationships, both in the moment and retrospectively. Emotion, especially in conflicts between intimate partners, reveals much about the power and status expectations in their relationship that influence opportunities for resolution. Understanding emotion provides another way of understanding how parties have currently defined their relationship and how motivated they are to retain that definition or change it.

Sue's reaction to the acquisition may be based on her perception that this will significantly alter her preferred power relationship with Randy. Up to now they have been equal partners, both getting credit for the company's success, both having a say in what happens, and both getting their share of the economic rewards. Sue may perceive, and probably rightly so, that the acquisition will give Randy a great deal more power in the relationship than she will have. Randy will be seen as the boss by the software company. He will have the power in decision making, he will get the credit, and he will reap more of the rewards. If this is the case, this emotion and power analysis suggests that Sue will be very motivated to resist this acquisition or very motivated to find other ways to maintain her power in the relationship.

As we can see with this brief overview of emotion, conflict coaches have a great deal to work with when they address emotional roots of conflicts with their clients. In the next section we give you a deeper introduction to some of the relevant theory on emotion and conflict. This theory will help us introduce some basic principles that conflict coaches can follow when addressing emotion, and it will serve as the foundation for specific approaches and techniques in the last section of the chapter.

Theories of Emotion

The social science literature on emotion is vast. We will cherry-pick our way through this wonderful resource in order to introduce you to theories that we find particularly valuable in application—theories that we believe make a real difference in the practice of conflict management. We'll begin with the cognitive component of emotion.

As we suggested earlier, our judgments that lead to our emotional experience are very dependent on our sense of identity and power. Given our model of conflict coaching, we believe it important to begin with theories that help us understand this relationship between the three critical perspectives—identity, emotion, and power. Then we will discuss theory that pertains to the physiological aspect of emotional experience, and that will be followed by discussion of the expression of emotion.

COGNITIVE APPRAISAL OF EMOTION

Appraisal theories of emotion emphasize that emotion is an inherently cognitive process and should be understood in terms of the appraisals or evaluations of the situation that give rise to the emotional experience. There are two bodies of work that we feel are particularly germane for conflict coaches: Lazarus's theory of emotional reappraisal and Gottman, Katz, and Hooven's work (1997) on meta-emotion.

Emotional Reappraisal. While there are several appraisal theories of emotion, we concentrate on Lazarus's model, because we believe it has the most demonstrated impact for therapeutic situations or other situations where people seek change to create a better experience. Lazarus's (1991) appraisal theory of emotion argues that there are two kinds of appraisals that are key: primary appraisals and secondary appraisals. The identification of the emotional experience is a function of both appraisal processes acting in tandem.

Primary appraisals focus on the question, "Is the event or situation personally relevant?" There are three elements to be considered in making the primary appraisal:

- *Goal relevance*—Does it impact on personal goals?
- *Goal congruence*—Does it make it easier or harder for me to achieve my goals?
- *Ego involvement*—Is it related to my identity in some important way?

The primary appraisals are about the link of the situation to the identity or personal interests of the perceiving party. If the primary appraisal is that the situation is not personally relevant, we will have a neutral or very low-intensity emotional experience. But, if the primary appraisal is that the situation is linked strongly to identity and personal interests, we will have a strong emotional experience. Whether that experience is positive or negative depends on whether the appraisal is favorable to or antagonistic to our identity. All negative emotions arise from appraisals that the event or situation impacts on personal goals (is goal-relevant) in a way that makes it harder for us to achieve those goals (is goal-incongruent). In conflict, negative emotions are more likely to lead to aggression that may be enacted in a variety of ways (e.g., avoidance, hostile attribution, verbal or physical aggression, blaming, building coalitions, intransigence). Izard (1977, 1993) argues that the experience of a negative emotion heightens the propensity to focus on negative information and form negative evaluations of the other party.

Secondary appraisals focus on additional issues that help determine the specific positive or negative emotion felt. While primary appraisals are the essential perceptual link between emotion and identity, secondary appraisals are the essential link between emotion and power. According to Lazarus, secondary appraisals consider three additional issues:

- *Judgments of accountability*—What or who is to blame for the event/situation?
- *Coping potential*—How well can you solve the problem and manage your feelings?
- *Future expectancy*—How likely is it that things will get better or worse?

Let's look briefly at each of these in terms of the relation to power concerns. The assumption of blame suggests that the person you can blame has lost some sort of social power or justification for his actions. If Sue can blame Randy for splitting their friendship, she can suggest that he owes her, that he should be obliged to act in some way that reimburses, protects, or redresses her for the harm he has caused her. To be able to blame is a "one-up" power position and to be blamed is a "one-down" power position. The more intentional the blameworthy behavior, the more the blameworthy person has lost power. One can be blamed for an incident and still be seen as not intentionally causing that incident (Kottler, 1994). Perhaps Sue blames herself for the conflict. Perhaps she thinks that she has not been working as hard as Randy or giving as much to the company. Her self-blame is as debilitating to her power in the relationship as the other-blame would be debilitating to Randy's power.

Coping potential encompasses a sense of empowerment. When coping potential is high, people are less likely to feel trapped or desperate and more likely to realize they have options other than "fight or flight." When people feel that they can handle whatever happens or solve whatever problem presents itself, they are much less likely to feel threatened and disempowered. If Sue feels that no matter what Randy's decision is, she will be able to start a wonderful firm on her own and succeed without Randy's help, she is likely to feel more positive about the whole situation.

Future expectancy is linked to perceptions of power in two ways. First, it's linked to power in terms of your perceptions of what you can handle and for how long. If Sue believes that this conflict is going to get worse and worse, she may feel that she doesn't have the strength to withstand this experience. Or, if she believes that this tension is going to pass quickly and she and Randy will be able to get back on track soon, she may feel that she can handle what's coming. The second way that future expectancy is linked to perceptions of power is the extent to which people feel they can affect whether the situation will get better or worse. If Sue knows that she can do something that will stop this situation from getting worse, she has a heightened sense of power—especially when compared to her feelings that she cannot do anything to affect how long this will go on.

It is the combination of primary and secondary appraisals that define the specific emotional experience. We can use the analogy of a map. The primary appraisals let us know the general negative or positive nature of the emotion—much like we might know we're in the state of Kansas. But it is the secondary appraisals that let us know the specific positive or negative emotion we are experiencing—whether we are in Lawrence or

Kansas City. If we look at the combination of primary and secondary appraisals, we can see how someone may experience certain emotions that may be germane in a conflict:

Sadness is usually felt when there is the loss of something or someone very close to or important to one's identity but where there is no one or nothing to blame for the loss, and where there is nothing that can be done to repair the loss.

Anger is usually felt when there is an interference or blockage of a desired goal, especially when that goal is linked with identity and the blockage is seen as unfair and where someone is to blame. Usually the assumption is that someone intentionally committed this offense against us.

Shame is usually felt when we fail to act in a way that we think we should and thus cause ourselves a serious loss of face; we are to blame, and we are responsible for repairing our identity by enacting the appropriate behavior.

Contempt is usually felt when we need to denigrate others in order to increase our perceived status or identity; others are to blame for their own inferiority, and we are permitted to act against them, because we are superior. Contempt is often linked with personal ideology and exclusionary politics.

Fear is usually felt when we realize a potential loss of something that is personally important, when that loss may be inflicted by someone or something beyond our control, and where we anticipate little if any ability to repair the situation or replace the loss.

Meta-emotion. Meta-emotions, quite simply, are emotions about emotions. They are the ways we feel about having certain kinds of emotions. For example, Sue may be angry at Randy but feel ashamed of that anger. The latter (feeling ashamed) is Sue's meta-emotion.

The link between meta-emotion and conflict is empirically supported in family research (Gottman, Katz, & Hooven, 1997). Differences in meta-emotions can be the basis for misunderstandings or disputes. For example, "I" feel shameful about being proud, but you feel happy about being proud. "I" might see you as arrogant because of this.

Awareness of meta-emotions can allow a person to think of the best ways to respond behaviorally in a conflict. For example, if Sue feels ashamed about being angry, she may need to work on how she can express anger in a way that is less threatening to the identity she wants to maintain with Randy.

THE PHYSIOLOGICAL ELEMENT OF EMOTION

There are two areas of theory and research on the physiological nature of emotion that are very helpful for conflict coaching practice: the impact of emotional flooding and the influence of emotional contagion.

Emotional Flooding. Emotional flooding is system overload—being swamped by emotion to the extent that one cannot function or think effectively. As research by Perry, Pollard, Blakely, Baker and Vigilante (1995) confirms, intense emotion blocks us from thinking in a cognitively complex way and inhibits our ability to engage strategic (e.g., either competitive or problem-solving) orientations in conflict.

Usually, emotional flooding occurs when we are experiencing a very strong negative emotion that has been triggered by some perceived threat. When people feel unfairly attacked, misunderstood, wronged, or righteously indignant, they are responding to a core identity issue. From a behavioral point of view, threats to identity are usually linked to behaviors of criticism or contempt. In fact, Gottman (1994) argues that these behaviors are the most corrosive to relationships, precisely because they have the potential to trigger emotional flooding and its consequences. Sue may be so upset about what she sees as Randy's betrayal that she cannot think clearly about what she wants to do. Likewise, Randy may be so frustrated that he can't make Sue see reason that he is emotionally flooded and unable to use perspective taking to better understand her reaction.

Not all causes of emotional flooding are external. Sue's flooding is not necessarily just due to Randy's statements and vice versa. In some cases, our own negative thoughts can cause flooding. Sue may have rehearsed telling Randy off—a very seductive internal dialogue that increases the negative emotions she has about Randy. Randy may be repeatedly replaying a nasty argument with Sue in his head, or dwelling on an interaction in which he felt intentionally shamed or humiliated by Sue. The more Randy and Sue persist in these negative inner scripts, the more they literally talk themselves into an emotionally flooded state.

Emotional Contagion. The issue of emotional contagion is closely related to flooding. Sometimes people can be "infected" with the emotions of others. If they are happy, we get happy. If they are angry, we get angry, etc. This phenomenon is called emotional contagion (Hatfield, Cacioppo, & Rapson, 1992). Basically, we may have relatively unconscious emotional responses to the other.

If Randy is susceptible to emotional contagion—likely to pick up the emotions of others—and he interacts with Sue when she is angry, Randy is likely to leave conversations with Sue feeling angry himself. Randy can become angry around Sue's anger without ever understanding why Sue is angry or sharing her feelings that anger is an appropriate response in this situation. Clients who are highly susceptible to emotional contagion should be cautioned against face-to-face interactions in which their emotions and reactions may be influenced by the other's.

THE EXPRESSIVE ELEMENT OF EMOTION

The physiological and cognitive elements of emotion are important in terms of how we individually experience emotion. But, the expressive element is how we communicate to others what we are feeling or what we want them to think we are feeling. The expressive component consists of the verbal and nonverbal behaviors through which we intentionally or unintentionally communicate emotional states.

Rules about when and how we should express emotion are heavily influenced by culture. Different cultures are more or less expressive, more or less comfortable displaying certain kinds of emotions (like anger), and more or less likely to use certain behaviors to express that emotion— e.g., smiling to indicate discomfort rather than happiness, or screaming to indicate sorrow rather than crying (Lutz, 1988, Markus & Kitayama, 1991; Shweder, 1993). However, we usually interpret other people's emotions as though they were members of our culture. In this sense, we can think of culture in the more generic sense—as encompassing gender, race, age, affinity groups, etc. In the case of Sue and Randy, Sue's emotional expression of sadness is something that is much more culturally appropriate for women than men in this society. When Randy fails to show sadness at the thought of the end of their company, Sue may interpret this as a lack of caring on Randy's part, when it may actually be his tendency to be "manly" and hide sadness, as boys are usually taught in American society. Still, Sue sees the lack of a sadness display as proof that Randy does not care, and this may make her even more angry and embittered toward him.

Emotional expression can create conflict as well as reflect conflict. Conflict may result from inappropriately enacting emotional display rules. For example, the emotional display may be "wrong" or inappropriate because we have displayed the "wrong" emotion (e.g., Randy feels sad but shows it by laughing instead of crying), because we have displayed the emotion with the wrong intensity (e.g., Randy looks sad but not sad enough), or because we display emotion in the wrong situation (e.g., Randy laughs at a mediation session held to deal with the conflict).

Conflict may also result from an inability to decode emotional expression. For example, you may think you are accurately reading the nonverbal cues of another, but in actuality, you are unable to see them or accurately interpret them. Senders of the message are likely to become upset, because they assume their message was received but not respected. Randy may be trying to act sad, but Sue fails to see it. Randy's likely to think that Sue saw the sadness and just disregarded or devalued it; this provides more disconfirmation that fuels the conflict.

Emotional Competence

Carolyn Saarni explains in her prologue to *The Development of Emotional Competence* (1999, p. 2) that

> emotional competence sounds straightforward and simple, but in fact is subtle, complex, and sometimes downright elusive. This is because the ideas behind each of these concepts, namely, emotion, competence, resilience, self-efficacy, character, emotion elicitation, and social transaction, represent whole sets of theories and assumptions, all of them very much anchored in cultural context.

There are many skills involved in being emotionally competent. Rather than present a laundry list of skills, we prefer to think in terms of underlying tenets of emotional competence. Within the explanation of these tenets we will discuss the key skills of emotional competence.

TENET #1: EMOTIONAL COMPETENCE REQUIRES EMOTIONAL AWARENESS

The most basic ability is to be able to identify what you are feeling and why you are feeling it. Sadly, there are many people who are not able to do this easily, because they have not been given adequate opportunity to talk about their feelings (Saarni, 1999). Emotions are often uncomfortable for people to talk about, because they feel vulnerable, too disclosive. Giving people emotional words helps them get in touch with their emotional experiences.

Being able to label your own emotions is a necessary first step in being aware of someone else's emotions. Other-awareness has two parts. The first is knowing enough about emotions to be able to recognize and label the feeling itself. If Randy doesn't have a word for jealousy, he can't think about it in terms of a feeling Sue may be having. The second part is our ability to read the physical cues others use when they are trying to express that emotion. As we mentioned, there is a wide range of decoding ability, and this ability is influenced by age, gender, culture, personality, and family history.

TENET #2: EMOTIONAL PERSPECTIVE TAKING IS THE ROOT OF EMPATHY

Emotional perspective taking is the ability to recognize and understand what others are feeling, the kind of emotional experience they are having. One way to appreciate emotional perspective taking is to understand it in relation to a series of related terms: cognitive perspective taking, empathy, and caring. Cognitive perspective taking is being able to understand how others see a situation, what their needs and interests are in that situation. Cognitive perspective taking elicits valuable information but does not include an awareness of how people feel about the situation they see. Emotional perspective taking is understanding how someone feels about what is happening. But, knowing how others are feeling is not the same thing as feeling it with them. When that happens, you are empathizing with the other person. Empathy is the ability to feel what they feel, although often to a lesser extent. The development of empathy is absolutely essential to emotional competence and to the development of a moral society, as both Saarni (1999) and Greenspan (1997) agree. Caring is an action; it is taking action to reduce the negative experience of the other.

Randy may be able to engage in cognitive perspective taking by understanding that Sue may see the impending acquisition of their firm as against her economic interests and as limiting her financial control. Randy may further be able to engage in emotional perspective taking by understanding that this makes Sue feel fearful and anxious about her future. Further, Randy may be empathic and feel Sue's fear and anxiety to some extent. And perhaps Randy is willing and able to be caring by taking the action of getting a financial counselor to sit down with both of them and consider the best ways to financially protect Sue in any number of possible approaches to the merger.

TENET #3: EMOTIONAL COMPETENCE REQUIRES CULTURAL SENSITIVITY

Cultural awareness refers to the understanding that there are different emotional cultures as well as the ability to appropriately follow display rules prescribing and proscribing emotional expression. Cultural display rules inform group members of what they should feel and how they should express it in certain situations. Therefore, cultural understanding represents an extension of perspective taking in that it requires being aware that situations may not elicit the same emotions in all people, and that people experience emotion differently. As with perspective taking, consideration of these factors influences the inferences one will make about how others are feeling and determines the attributions one will make for the other's behavior.

> *If you are patient in one moment of anger,*
> *you will escape a hundred days of sorrow.*
>
> —Chinese proverb

TENET #4: EMOTIONAL COMPETENCE
REQUIRES STRATEGIC EXPRESSION

Strategic expression is the crowning glory of emotional competence: It is the ability to regulate your emotional experience and expression in adaptive and beneficial ways. Emotional regulation means you learn to control your impulses to respond emotionally. Sue may be extremely angry with Randy, but she probably realizes that throwing a temper tantrum during their meeting with the financial consultant will only make her look immature and incompetent. Displaying her anger without restraint may flood Randy and escalate the conflict beyond a point of repair. And word of Sue's tantrum might reach the leaders of the acquiring firm, further convincing them they would rather not make a deal that includes Sue.

The more emotionally competent clients are, the more a conflict coach can help them understand how to apply these skills to their benefit in the conflict. If a client is lacking in certain areas of emotional competency, the coach can attend to those needed improvements.

General Principles for Emotion Work With Conflict Coaching Clients

Shortly we will be suggesting specific approaches a conflict coach can use to help his or her client understand how emotion is impacting and may influence the conflict at hand. As a prelude to those approaches, we offer the following general principles.

Principle #1: Help the client appreciate emotion as an analytic tool. Emotion is a huge part of conflict, whether we want to admit it or not. Many clients will not want to deal with the emotional side of their conflict or, if they are willing, they will not know how to deal with it. Helping a client appreciate how emotions are influencing the conflict is an important benefit of conflict coaching. A conflict coach can help the client examine emotions in terms of better understanding the conflict and can help consider possible approaches to conflict management.

Principle #2: Appreciate that most clients will be uncomfortable with emotion and will need to have some extra time to reflect and consider emotion as a tool before getting into activities and exercises. Clients will differ greatly in their ease with emotion, but the coach should be prepared for a client who is very resistant and uncomfortable. Giving clients the opportunity to reflect on emotions in their conflict will help. While this may necessitate more than one session with the client, the time may be well spent, especially if the coach can prepare the client with helpful questions for reflection.

Principle #3: Stress that emotion is another form of rationality, rather than an irrational response. Once clients see emotion as a reasoned response to the evaluation of a situation, it is easier for them to appreciate emotion and take it seriously in the analysis of conflict. Many clients will have the same bias against emotion that conflict practitioners have—it's irrational and should be avoided. Help the client appreciate that emotion is a valuable diagnostic tool for their orientation to conflict as well as the other party's orientation to conflict.

Principle #4: Emphasize that all three components of emotion are important in conflict, not only for the clients' analysis of themselves but also for their analysis of how to approach/respond to the other parties in conflict. As we have done in this chapter, encourage clients to understand that the cognitive, physiological, and expressive elements of emotion are all germane to their conflict analysis. Some clients will want to emphasize one element over others. But, allowing them to disregard an element limits their ability to fully consider issues and options.

Principle #5: Use the model of emotional competence to plan a response strategy for clients—what they can and should do to use emotion to their advantage. The model of emotional competence that we introduce can serve as a strategic template for conflict analysis and tactical response. To what extent are clients able to understand their own emotions and others' emotions in the conflict? To what extent are clients able to engage in perspective taking and empathic response? To what extent are they able to marshal a culturally appropriate and culturally sensitive action? To what extent are they able to strategically express emotion so that the expression enhances rather than hurts their identity and power? To what extent are clients able and willing to discuss the issue in a manner that does not manipulate the other's emotions for personal gain?

Specific Approaches for Emotion Work With Conflict Coaching Clients

There are numerous ways that a conflict coach can help a client to appreciate and manage the role of emotion in the conflict. As we did in the explanation of emotion and conflict, we begin here with issues of awareness, move to questions of perspective taking, and then focus on possibilities for expression. Some clients will need help in all of these areas, while others will benefit from focus on one or two. To determine their readiness for working with emotion and conflict, we suggest a beginning conversation as a diagnostic for the coach.

Approach #1: Determine the client's emotional orientation to the conflict.

What is it? During the initial discussions, the conflict coach can ask clients to talk about how the conflict has made them feel and what role they believe their feelings have played in the way the conflict has unfolded.

Why is it important? The coach should be able to determine how facile clients are with discussions of emotion, the sophistication of their emotional vocabulary, whether they see the strategic element in emotion, and their willingness to consider the emotional reality of the other person in the conflict.

How do you do it? The coach can use a simple schedule of questions to have clients get in touch with their feelings. The coach can provide clients with emotional vocabulary lists and have them identify all the terms that describe how they are feeling in the conflict. Using these as a guide, the coach can ask clients to elaborate on how and why they are feeling each of these emotions.

Approach #2: Explore the client's meta-emotions.

What is it? Exploring clients' meta-emotions is asking them to think about the emotions they are experiencing in the conflict and how they feel about those emotions—whether they are comfortable or uncomfortable with these feelings.

Why is it important? Clients are likely to vary in their sensitivity to their meta-emotions. If the coach feels that meta-emotions may be impacting the conflict, as in the case of Sue's feelings of shame about her anger that inhibits her willingness to explore the bases for her anger at Randy, the coach can help the client explore meta-emotions.

How do you do it? This exploration has three simple parts. First, the coach can give clients a meta-emotion interview that focuses on their comfort level with certain emotions and where that comfort or discomfort comes from. Second, the coach can talk with clients about how this discomfort or emotional blockage affects their ability to work through parts of the conflict that make them feel the uncomfortable emotion. For example, Sue may recognize she is ashamed of anger, but she may not realize that her shame has kept her from expressing her anger in a way that lets Randy know how deeply she cares about the conflict and how hurt she has been. Third, the coach can help the client consider whether this meta-emotion and its impact is part of a pattern. Perhaps Sue has always inhibited her expression of anger toward Randy, putting on a mask that convinces him Sue is fine with his taking the lead or setting the direction. Perhaps this pattern is what has influenced Randy to feel it was all right to take the lead in exploring a merger; he assumed that Sue would follow along, as she had done in previous situations. He may think, "She wasn't bothered before; why should she be bothered now?"

Approach #3: Clarify the client's emotional experience of the conflict.

What is it? Clients may not really know what they are feeling about the conflict. One of the most important interventions that a coach can do is to help clients gain a better understanding of what they are feeling and why.

Why is it important? The more that clients understand judgments they are making that are leading them to feel a certain way, the better able they will be to use that knowledge to empower themselves through reappraisal—a process we'll discuss in the next section. Clients have to know how they feel before they can figure out how to change the situation so they can feel better.

How do you do it? There are a few ways that a coach can clarify clients' emotional experience. (1) In the absence of "emotion words" coming from clients, the coach can listen for implicit appraisals that clients are making and assess what they may be feeling. Sue may talk about her sense of unfairness with the way Randy is taking the lead and her concern that she will not be able to survive professionally if she goes out on her own. A coach conversant with Lazarus's theory would hear in those statements an indication of anger and fear. (2) For clients who are comfortable talking about emotion, a coach can use questions to help them identify or clarify their emotions. A coach may ask questions such as these:

- ⁂ How are you feeling about this?
- ⁂ Do you know why you are feeling this way?
- ⁂ Do you think someone or something is to blame? If so, who or what?

Good clarification questions are ones that focus on the aspects linked to the primary and secondary appraisals discussed earlier. Questions will focus on how the conflict is impacting goals and identity; whether the situation can be blamed on someone, and whether the client feels able to deal with or better the situation.

Approach #4: Facilitate reappraisal: Help the client know how to feel better.

What is it? To change the emotion, you must change the appraisal. A coach can help guide clients through a process called "facilitating reappraisal" that helps them think differently about the situation.

Why is it important? It's not enough to help Sue understand that she is angry and ashamed and afraid. A conflict coach needs to know how to use that information to help Sue consider what she can do to change the situation for the better—to work her way through the conflict.

How do you do it? After a coach has helped the client clarify emotions, the next step is the use of questions to help the client reappraise the situation. This process focuses primarily on the coping abilities of the client, which is similar in many respects to the process of empowering in some models of mediation. According to Burleson and Goldsmith (1998), helpful questions in this effort could include these:

- How important is this event to you? Now and in the future?
- What might make it less important?
- How might this event have helped you in ways you haven't discussed?
- How important is it for you to blame the other in this situation?
- What have you done to deal with the situation?
- How well is that working for you?

We suggest that different question sets fit different emotions. One way to think of this is to think of finding the critical key that will unlock the emotion or make it possible for the client to know how to move past that emotion. For example, if fear is a primary emotion, questioning can concentrate on why clients value what they fear losing, what other things might be substituted for the potential loss, what could be better if the loss occurred, why they assume the other wants to cause this loss, what they can do to replace the loss, or what they can do to honor the loss so it has symbolic richness for them. Each emotion has its critical key; and a good conflict coach will craft the questions that best unlock that emotion.

Approach #5: Encourage emotional perspective taking.

What is it? The process for encouraging emotional perspective taking is the same as for clarifying emotion and facilitating reappraisal. The only difference is that this time the subject of the clarification is the other party rather than the client.

Why is it important? Not only is emotional perspective taking a hallmark of emotional competence, it is also strategically powerful. The more you understand the other, the better you can plan how to work with the other. In almost every situation, helping a client understand the other party will benefit the client strategically.

How do you do it? Ask your clients to engage in the same kinds of clarification questions discussed earlier, but to answer in terms of how they believe the other party may be feeling. The coach can listen for hostile attributions and challenge the client's perspective taking if it seems the client is refusing to do anything but demonize the other. The coach can also role-play the question-and-answer sessions, taking the part of the other to help clients rehearse conversations they may want to have at some point in person. In some cases, clarification of emotion will result in a client who can strongly empathize with the other party and, by so doing, is motivated to find a way to work with that person in a collaborative manner.

Sue could benefit greatly from this approach. In considering Randy's feelings, Sue may better understand that Randy is truly happy about the potential merger and is angry that Sue may get in the way of his happiness. Randy may also be confused about why Sue is so resistant, because Sue has always supported his leadership in the past. But Randy may also feel guilty about making Sue unhappy, because he does care about her. Sue can think about what critical keys are for Randy's emotions of anger and guilt and happiness. Randy may feel less guilty if he lives up to his standards of friendship by protecting Sue's interests in the merger. Randy may dissipate his anger if he believes that Sue is not to blame for the problems, and if he sees Sue as acting from her orientation of fairness (even if it is not Randy's). And Randy may cease to be as happy about the merger if he can be convinced that the merger is actually going to inhibit his professional goals and growth in the long term.

Approach #6: Uncover and defuse physiological triggers for conflict escalation.

What is it? This approach assesses the client's tendency to be emotionally flooded.

Why is it important? If Sue is becoming emotionally flooded whenever she talks with Randy, she is not able to engage in optimum critical thinking and problem-solving. Her tendency to become flooded (whether through emotional contagion or not) is a handicap that must be recognized and overcome.

How do you do it? Recognizing a client's tendency to emotionally flood or be susceptible to emotional contagion that leads to flooding can be done with simple self-assessment instruments. A self-aware client can recognize these tendencies without the use of such instruments. The coach can help the client identify triggers that encourage flooding. Identifying triggers often involves clients in thinking about issues, loaded language, or nonverbal behaviors that cause them to become incensed. Talking about self-calming provides information about the stimuli that facilitate mood repair. Reducing internal causes of flooding requires the coach to interrupt the negative inner scripts that the client is using. Coaches can help clients tame their negative inner script by identifying it and substituting a self-soothing script. For example, if Sue is using an innocent victim script, the coach can encourage her to think of things she is doing that contribute to the conflict (i.e., take responsibility for her part of the conflict). If Sue is using the righteous indignation script, the coach can offer guidance on thinking about positive qualities about Randy, positive things Sue and Randy have done, and positive aspects of their relationship.

Approach #7: Interrupt the client's tendency to flood the other.

What is it? This approach helps clients recognize verbal and nonverbal communication they use that may trigger emotional flooding in the other party.

Why is it important? In most conflicts, someone is dissatisfied with something and wants to be able to express it. The assumption is that voicing dissatisfaction will motivate the other to stop the offending behavior. But, the expression of dissatisfaction may cause emotional flooding in the other. Thus, it is important to understand how to express dissatisfaction without escalating the conflict.

How do you do it? There are three choices a person has in communicating dissatisfaction: to communicate a complaint, to communicate a criticism, or to communicate contempt (Gottman, 1994). A complaint is a specific statement of displeasure directed toward a specific action or event; for example, Sue could say, "I am very upset that you didn't check with me before accepting that invitation to discuss a possible merger." A criticism is much less specific and usually has blaming language in it; for example, "Randy, you never ask what I want to do with the future of the firm. You just don't care about my opinion." A contempt statement, which is the most incendiary, involves language that is verbally aggressive, intended to insult and psychologically abuse the other. For example: "Randy, you're an idiot to think I'd want to go into this kind of merger with you." Coaching a client to avoid using criticism and contempt messages can decrease the chances that the client is an external cause of emotional flooding for the other party.

Similarly, there are a number of nonverbal behaviors that can antagonize the other (Remland, 2004) (see CD-ROM), such as rolling your eyes, using a very slow rate of speech, invading the other's space, patting the other on the head, etc. A coach can help clients consider whether their nonverbal behaviors are insulting the other and are contributing to emotional flooding that halts the progress of collaboration.

Approach # 8: Plan effective emotional expression.

What is it? This approach coaches clients in how to express their emotions in the most appropriate and competent manner for the context.

Why is it important? When clients know how to express emotion effectively, they get the best of both worlds. They are able to communicate what they are feeling and to do so in a manner that increases the chances the emotional expression will be constructive rather than destructive in the conflict.

How do you do it? Helping clients to plan effective emotional expression involves walking them through several key questions:

- ※ What are some important rules for emotional expression in the conflict context?
- ※ Are there ways of expressing emotion that are more appropriate, more respected, or more accepted in the context of the conflict? If so, does the client know what these are?
- ※ Can the client think of examples when such expressions were used effectively?
- ※ Can the client think of examples where the rules for expression were broken?

While coaches can't engage in an anthropological study of the relational or organizational culture that the client is involved with, they can help the client to identify what seem to be consistent boundaries on behavior that need to be respected. A coach can help clients to craft language that assertively complains and expresses dissatisfaction in a way that others can hear. Similarly, a coach can help the client tackle the all-important question of timing. When should negative emotion be expressed? In what circumstances is it likely to have the most positive effect?

Approach #9: Consider and prepare an apology.

What is it? A coach helps the client decide whether an apology is in order and, if it is, how to do it well.

Why is it important? A sincere expression of regret is more powerful than any single behavior in conflict, and that regret is best manifested through apology. Given the importance of an apology, there is a right way to apologize.

How do you do it? A coach can help a client to craft an apology that meets the following criteria. The apology should acknowledge that some moral norm, or rule in a relationship was violated, and the person apologizing has to accept responsibility for that. To be successful, an apology has to be specific, articulating the behavior that was the transgression. Although this is not always easy, the person apologizing must give some reason for why he or she committed the offense in the first place. And, finally, a good apology has to express genuine regret if the apology is to be taken as sincere. On the CD-ROM, we provide more information about how to give a good apology.

Approach #10: Decide to forgive.

What is it? A conflict coach can help a client decide whether forgiveness is a possibility and a benefit in a particular conflict.

Why is it important? When you forgive others, you make it clear that you will no longer be upset with them because of what they did. You don't forget what they did, but you no longer try to punish them for doing it. Forgiveness releases the client from the emotional control of the other party's transgressions. Forgiveness may free a client from focusing on, reliving, or even obsessing about a conflict and, by so doing, failing to move on.

How do you do it? The coach can talk with the client about what it is costing the client to hold on to negative feelings about the other, and the client and coach can discuss how to understand forgiveness as empowering for the client.

Chapter Summary

Conflict coaches need to understand emotion in conflict so they can help clients to use emotion strategically. Understanding emotion involves recognizing the physical, cognitive, and expressive parts of emotion. Since emotion is linked with identity and power issues, emotion serves as one of the three important lenses through which coaches can help clients understand and strategically respond to client conflicts.

GENERAL PRINCIPLES FOR EMOTION WORK WITH CONFLICT COACHING CLIENTS

Principle #1: Help the client appreciate emotion as an analytic tool.

Principle #2: Appreciate that most clients will be uncomfortable with emotion and will need to have some extra time to reflect and consider emotion as a tool before getting into activities and exercises.

Principle #3: Stress that emotion is another form of rationality, rather than an irrational response.

(Continued)

(Continued)

Principle #4: Emphasize that all three components of emotion are important in conflict, not only for the client's own analysis but for the client's analysis of how to approach/respond to the other party in conflict.

Principle #5: Use the model of emotional competence to plan a response strategy for the client—what he or she can and should do to use emotion to his or her advantage.

SPECIFIC APPROACHES FOR EMOTION WORK WITH CONFLICT COACHING CLIENTS

Approach #1: Determine the client's emotional orientation to the conflict.

Approach #2: Explore the client's meta-emotions.

Approach #3: Clarify the client's emotional experience of the conflict.

Approach #4: Facilitate reappraisal: Help the client know how to feel better.

Approach #5: Encourage emotional perspective taking.

Approach #6: Uncover and defuse physiological triggers for conflict escalation.

Approach #7: Interrupt the client's tendency to flood the other.

Approach #8: Plan effective emotional expression.

Approach #9: Consider and prepare an apology.

Approach #10: Decide to forgive.

6

Stage Two

The Power Perspective

The sole advantage of power is that you can do more good.

—Baltasar Gracian

Jane is the vice president of advertising and marketing of a large home improvement chain. Her main job is to serve the various regional operators of stores that are spread across the country. In this respect, the overall organization is both centralized and decentralized. Regional operators must maintain companywide quality standards and manage costs but are also given room to advertise and market in ways that reflect local tastes. All of the individual stores' communications must be developed in conjunction with or purchased through Jane's office.

While Jane has been with the company for many years and was part of the team that facilitated its explosive growth, Jane has recently experienced unprecedented tension with a number of regional operators. This is partly due to the fact that the housing market and related demand for home improvement products has cooled. Nonetheless, her job depends on her ability to effectively work with regional operators.

Regional operators tend to be very money-oriented and competitive. This makes sense, because they largely live and die within the company based on quarterly profitability as demonstrated in national performance rankings, which give some consideration to regional economic differences. Regional operators generally want quick turn around time from Jane's office. They also want to get their voices heard in terms of marketing and advertising designs. Of course, their overarching goal is to increase sales and profitability within their respective regions.

Jane and her departmental colleagues tend to have a friendly service-first philosophy. This is understandable given that they are largely meeting the needs of others in the organization. It also fits with the fact that much of their work is team oriented and time constrained, from developing a design to technically executing the design to making a media buy to ensuring the proper final placement of the design.

Each regional operator submits an extensive report and meets face-to-face with the chief operating officer on a yearly basis. The COO has commented to Jane that there is a pattern of blame directed at her by the regional operators with whom he has been meeting lately. In particular, the COO has asked Jane to respond to Bob, a regional operator who in the past seemed to work well with her. However, Bob has recently led the charge in calling Jane "slow to take action in implementing new advertising and marketing initiatives" and therefore "bearing a large measure of responsibility for dampened results," at least in his particular region. While Jane does not feel like her job is threatened, she wants to do everything she can to maintain a workable relationship with Bob, best support regional operators, and protect herself from unfair allegations, especially those voiced toward the COO.

S triving for outcomes is an essential feature of organizational life (Kipnis, Schmidt, & Wilkinson, 1980). Accordingly, individuals are using power whether working to cooperate, compete, or be left alone. Not only is the presence and use of power unavoidable in work life, it is inevitably intertwined with conflict. Longstanding definitions of power (e.g., Dahl, 1957) emphasize that power involves getting others to do what they might not do in the absence of influence. However, power involves much more than the motivation and resources of one individual.

In the opening case, the entire home improvement store chain is experiencing a challenging time as the business is in a sluggish period, individuals remain responsible for performance, and accountability is not always clear. Jane's conflict centers on her interactions with Bob and the COO, but it can be seen to extend across all regional operators as well as Jane's own department. The issue of power is clearly implicated in terms of what each party has the ability to do with respect to work performance and also in how communication about this workplace performance conflict is carried out.

This chapter introduces power by touching on connections with identity and emotion. The section on research and theory clarifies a number of important assumptions about power, offers goals and power sources as a primary step to selecting conflict strategies and tactics, touches on conflict patterns as a caution against adopting short-sighted emphasis on individual tactics, presents three strategies as a way of navigating the many different tactics, and touches on some of the ways cultural considerations can play an important role in power communication.

The general principles and specific approaches at the end of the chapter assist the coach in moving from the introduction of power concepts to their application in a conflict relevant to the client.

Power in Relation to Identity and Emotion

There are very close links between power and identity. Identity involves power in terms of a person's ability to lay claim to one or more positive identities and have those identities respected and engaged by others. A given identity opens up and closes off access to specific conflict tactics. This link between identity and power can be especially relevant, as identity is selected not only by self but very often is cast by another (Goffman, 1955). In terms of the case, Jane is in a position to exert power to remain in control of her professional identity. The service-first aspect of her identity will probably make it inappropriate and ineffective to adopt tactics that are plainly aggressive or run the risk of being framed by others as aggressive, as this would undermine a basic role that she has in the organization.

In terms of emotion, individuals can feel comfortable or uncomfortable with the very notion of power. Because emotions are connected to goal congruence and incongruence, they are triggers for the impulse to use power (Lazarus, 1991). This can mean that emotions have power over us, although not necessarily in a negative respect. For instance, emotion can announce the need for the use of power and focus our efforts in terms of effectiveness and efficiency. Emotions exist within relationships, and so it can be valuable to consider the ways in which specific feelings reflect the power that others hold over us, the power we hold over others, and the power that we share. Emotional responses in the sender can vary on the basis of relative power of the sender. For instance, emotional responses to persuasive messages have been shown to be shaped by perceived dominance and explicitness (Dillard, Kinney, & Cruz, 1996). At the same time that Jane recognizes the limits of her power vis-à-vis her identity, it may be useful for her to receive a reminder that it can nevertheless be appropriate and effective for her to exert power in this conflict despite the fact that her typical approach is more friendly and, possibly, not emotionally consonant with assertion.

Overview of Research and Theory on Power

Power has been defined in many different ways. Synonymous or allied terms include *compliance, control, dominance, empowerment,* and *influence.*

One study of people in positions of influence in corporate law, sales, and government found six orientations toward power: power as good, power as resource dependency, power as instinctive drive, power as political, power as charisma, and power as control and autonomy (Cavanaugh, Larson, Goldberg, & Bellows, 1981). A basic definition of power is the individual's ability to achieve goals within a situation (Deutsch, 1973). Power in this respect is most contingent on the individual's personal power (e.g., the individual is more or less able to meet goals on his or her own), relationship power (e.g., the individual is more or less able to influence and fall under the influence of others), and environmental power (e.g., the individual is more or less able to benefit from and influence environmental conditions). However, given the interdisciplinary nature of the study of power and the considerable diversity in definitions, a focus on assumptions is an approach that is appealing, as it provides a more complete definition of power while maintaining accessibility for the purposes of conflict coaching.

KEY ASSUMPTIONS ABOUT POWER

Power may mean directly causing behavioral change in another. Dahl's (1957) description of power as one person's ability to get another person to do something that he or she would not otherwise do is considered to be foundational to the modern study of power. This view emphasizes intentionality on the part of the person attempting to act with power. This view also emphasizes power as a behavioral outcome in a target. Of course, sometimes it is the case that people use power unintentionally and in ways that are not observable in a target, such as by changing someone's attitudes, perceptions, or values. In the opening case, Bob can be seen to have used power in simply causing Jane to be engaged in a conflict with him.

Power can include the potential to cause behavioral change in another. Another way that power is understood is as the potential to act and effect change. The relationship between possible and actual power is worth consideration. One view is that power exists only as it is put into action. Another view is that power in action amounts to weakened power, because the need for action is taken to imply a threat to power. Jane certainly has legitimate power in her work, presuming, for example, that her department is able to enforce a timetable for executing requests for advertising and marketing services. This may translate into power in the conflict that she faces, as she can objectively document Bob's and others' use and compliance with the policies and procedures of her department.

Power may involve shaping the decision-making possibilities for another. Bachrach and Baratz (1962), in responding to Dahl's (1957) work, pointed out that power can involve limiting the decision-making opportunities of another. This can mean controlling how decisions are framed and even whether a decision gets explored, as in cases of failing to make a decision. Also, individuals may actually exert control over the perceptions that others have of their own interests. This means that a conflict coaching client should be encouraged to assess whether taken-for-granted frames are the strategic impositions of others. Shaping the decision-making possibilities for another is a sensitive ethical issue but one that most professionals are confronted with in their careers, particularly in conflict. This issue can be richly explored within a conflict coaching session. In the opening case, Bob attempted to shape the decision processes of the COO by making an allegation that Jane was responsible for his region's poor performance. A coach could work with Jane to locate ways that her own decision-making possibilities have been impacted by Bob's actions and determine how best to protect against this threat in the future.

Power exists in organizational structures and in wider social and cultural structures. Power certainly involves individuals and interpersonal relationships, but it also exists beyond them (Lukes, 1974). The tendencies to not deeply question vested power and, in most Western societies, to focus on the individual nature of power mean that there is often a lack of awareness of the way power may be structured at various cultural or social levels. Power in this respect is not only tied to conflict but may shape needs, so that conflict does not even arise. The fact that there are virtually always different ideologies of power (Mumby, 1988), or competing frameworks of values and behaviors, can make it challenging to make sense of and actively negotiate power. A client may find it instructive to consider the ways deeply entrenched social power shapes interpersonal conflict. Likewise, a client may find it helpful to explore the way different values are linked to different understandings of power as well as different acceptable behaviors. The structure of Jane's organization can be seen to protect Jane and challenge Bob in this conflict. Jane's department has the obligation to demonstrate good service to the regions, but it is the regions that must demonstrate financial results, a seemingly more challenging responsibility. Of course, Jane should be cautious in terms of how much weight she gives this observation and whether or not she refers to it in her communications. Also, as noted above, the use of power is different in Jane's and Bob's respective locations in the organization. The friendly service-first environment in which Jane works probably has expectations of assertive to integrative tactics, while Bob's competitive environment may have norms that extend from assertive to aggressive tactics.

Power is always relational. Dahl (1957) touched on the relational nature of power when he pointed out that the basic challenge is not to identify power but to make comparisons. Yet the relational quality of power involves more than the comparison of two individuals. It speaks to the fact that the exercise of power always incorporates interdependence (Grillo, 2005). Displays of power are often combined with relational work (Locher, 2004). This reflects a fundamental human tension between autonomy and connection (e.g., Tannen, 1994). In terms of the case, Jane is probably sensible in recognizing that she needs not only to take action to protect or even extend her position in the organization but to do so in a way that takes into account her need to have an ongoing working relationship with the regional operators.

Power is always, to some extent, negotiable. There is always some opportunity to affect the exercise of power (Clegg, 1989; Fairclough, 1989). This depends greatly on the circumstances. For instance, when parties are balancing power and working in a collaborative manner, power becomes more negotiable. A client without formal power and clients who are in conflict with those who may not have formal power should be reminded that power is never fixed.

Skilled use of language is arguably the number one way that power can be reconfigured. Language is so closely connected to power that it cannot be considered separate from it (Grillo, 2005). Language is frequently the way power gets exercised (Locher, 2004; Ng & Bradac, 1993). Successful individuals often have linguistic variability (King, 1987), meaning they demonstrate the ability to customize messages based on self goals, sender factors, and situational characteristics. Careful consideration of language can reveal power even in relatively hidden forms. In a review of the research literature on power and language, Ng and Bradac (1993) concluded that language: reveals power (i.e., a listener may infer power in another because of the way that person communicates), creates power (i.e., the way a person communicates may achieve power within a conversation and beyond), reflects power (i.e., those with established power may display power through special forms of speech), and obscures or depoliticizes power (i.e., language can be used to exert or seize power yet do so in a subtle way).

It would be prudent for Jane to see that despite possibly having certain structural advantages in her conflict with Bob, his efforts along with the efforts of others in the organization could act as a counterbalance. However, coaches should not only work with clients to determine potential power renegotiation threats. They should also help clients identify and even create opportunities to expand or grow power. Possibilities for integrative power, especially in the form of mutual empowerment, are probably underappreciated and underutilized. What might it mean for Jane to meet with Bob or the COO to transform the working relationship between her department and the regional operators in order to make arrangements better for everyone concerned? Coaches should generally work with clients to determine multiple opportunities for all parties to a conflict to (re)negotiate power.

Power is also negotiable in the sense that the value an individual places on power resources can change through active (re)negotiation within a relational context. Here Jane might want to consider how she can persuade Bob to engage her rather than the COO in order to boost his workplace performance. Another issue concerns the degree to which we are willing to or have to depend on another for needed resources. In this respect, Jane might reflect on developing positive opportunities for Bob to achieve better results without feeling like he is relying on her.

The following questions may be used to prompt client exploration of power assumptions:

※ How do the power assumptions help to make sense of past interaction between self and other?

※ How do the power assumptions inform likely or possible future interaction between self and other?

Using Goals to Determine the Relevancy of Power

The Merits of a Goal Approach. In all but the most pressing situations, clients have the opportunity to consider conflict goals prior to taking action. A systematic consideration of goals, reflection on power sources, awareness of conflict interaction patterns, and the thoughtful selection and execution of conflict tactics can lead to a better conflict communication process as well as better outcomes.

Coaches recognize that clients may propose or even enact behaviors that are dangerously shortsighted. Fortunately, Jane's view of her situation is not so limited, as she acknowledged at the outset that she seeks to maintain a workable relationship with Bob, best support regional operators, and protect herself from unfair allegations. While it would no doubt be wise to consider Jane's goals in more detail, it is important to point out that she should also be encouraged to give equally thorough consideration to Bob's goals as well as the goals of the COO.

It needs to be acknowledged that a goal approach has its limitations. For instance, it can overemphasize the individual and underemphasize the other party. It can also underemphasize the challenge of translating goals into relevant behaviors as well as the interactional nature of conflict, including the impact of contextual factors. Nonetheless, goals can be very helpful. They help parties to manage information. They clarify action. They create meaning. Even in instances when goals are flawed, they may still play an important and positive role (Weick, 1979).

One of the ways to increase the likelihood of success with a goals approach is to distinguish among prospective, transactive, and retrospective goals (Wilmot & Hocker, 2007). These subtypes allow us to define the term *goals* as desired future states (Hobbs & Evans, 1980), the maintenance of present states (Dillard, Segrin, & Harden, 1989), or the strategic reconsideration of past behaviors or conditions in order to better make sense of the present reality (Weick, 1979).

Jane might choose to set up a one-on-one meeting with Bob, given the prospective goal of trying to establish a more collegial and productive working relationship. If Bob launched an unfair verbal attack within the meeting, she might set the transactive goal of making one attempt to point out the offensiveness of his behavior and give him the opportunity to apologize, otherwise she would end the meeting. If the meeting ended badly, Jane might make sense of it retrospectively as an opportunity to learn about how best to present the overall conflict with Bob to the COO.

Returning to the CCC Goal Model. In Chapter 2 we introduced four types of client goals that receive considerable attention in the CCC model: content goals, identity goals, emotion goals, and power goals. *Content goals* reflect the primary influence objective. *Identity goals* refer to the positive identities that the client and other parties want to hold both individually and in relation to one another. *Emotion goals* concern the positive emotions that the client and other parties most likely want to feel in regard to the conflict issues and process. As with the identity perspective, the Stage Two emotion perspective may be the place that the emotion goal first becomes clear for the client and coach. Finally, *power goals* focus on conflict process or the optimal way to achieve the other goals given overall constraints and possibilities. Power goals are the primary focus of this chapter.

It is useful to consider two or three exemplar questions that a coach may ask a client for each goal. These are offered below along with possible answers in the case of Jane and Bob.

Content goals	*Client Focus:* From your point of view, what would it look like to have successfully resolved this conflict or at least be managing it as successfully as possible?

In part, Jane might want to work collaboratively with Bob and other regional operators to enhance profitability and have objective accountability criteria for both herself and the regional operators.

Other Party Focus: From the other party's point of view, what would it look like to have successfully resolved this conflict or at least be managing it as successfully as possible?

In part, Jane might speculate that Bob wants better support from Jane and, most important, a return to strong profitability in his region.

Identity goals	*Client Focus:* In effectively managing or resolving this conflict, who do you want to be recognized as, internally or by others?

In part, Jane might want to be seen as a credible leader in tough times. It might be particularly important to have this identity in the eyes of the COO, other senior leaders, and the regional operators.

Other Party Focus: In effectively managing or resolving this conflict, who might the other party want to be recognized as, internally or by others?

Jane might speculate that Bob ultimately wants to be seen as one of the organization's best regional operators.

Emotion goals	*Client Focus:* In effectively managing or resolving this conflict, how do you most want to feel?

Jane might want to feel happy, highly competent, and confident throughout her work world.

Other Party Focus: In effectively managing or resolving this conflict, how might the other party most want to feel?

Jane might speculate that Bob wants to feel satisfied and strong.

(Continued)

(Continued)

Power goals	*Client Focus:* How can you best take action to reach your content, identity, and emotion goals?
	Jane might initially react to this question with a strong sense that she wants to be proactive and assertive versus reactive and defensive. This might include trying to work effectively with Bob but also working independent of Bob to become the company's expert on the changing advertising and marketing landscape.
	Other Party Focus: How can you best take action to not only reach your own goals but also support the other party in reaching his?
	Jane might recognize an opportunity to determine a plan of action that offers Bob a chance to collaborate but that also protects her interests should he continue to compete with her.
	Joint Focus: How might you and Bob best work together to achieve your individual and common goals?
	Jane might see how she and Bob could team up to design a marketing strategy that not only addresses the challenges within his region but could also be used in other regions hurting from an economic downturn.

Wilmot and Hocker (2007) noted that goals may be differently foregrounded and backgrounded given the overall type of conflict or the pattern of interaction within a given conflict. In Jane and Bob's situation, the alleged advertising and marketing mishap may be in the foreground, but the issue of influencing the COO is probably of premier importance, as neither party wants to be alienated from him. From Jane's perspective, an important strategy seems to be keeping the COO in the loop without needlessly inflaming Bob and other regional operators.

Sources of Client Power in Conflict

Just as power without goals is irrelevant, so too are goals without power. One of the most resonant power concepts from the last 50 years concerns individual sources of power. These are also known as power bases or power currencies. French and Raven (1959) identified five sources of social power: reward (the person seeking change offers an incentive), coercive (the person attempting to influence has the ability to punish), referent (the person exercising power is admired), expert (the person seeking influence has specialized knowledge), and legitimate (the person using power has formal authority). There have been many other typologies that derive from this initial framework. For instance, Wilmot and Hocker (2007) use a classification system that includes resource control, interpersonal linkages, communication skills, and expertise. Lewicki, Saunders, and Minton (1999) focus on information and expertise, control over resources, and location in an organizational structure. Northouse (2007) emphasizes position power and personal power in present-day organizations. Four sources of power that we believe are particularly important in interpersonal workplace conflict include information and expert, resource, organizational structure, and informal human networks. The typology used here is therefore closely related to that of Lewicki, Saunders, and Minton (1999).

Information and Expert Power. There is power in having direct access to conflict-related knowledge and having specialized information-related abilities. Jane has access to considerably more information than Bob, because her office has data on the advertising and marketing activities of all regional operators. Jane and the COO both have access to considerable information, but each is likely to have exclusive access in some respects. It may be relevant that Jane has the ability to effectively present advertising and marketing information up the chain of command. It may be relevant that Bob has competitive abilities in an organization that seems to reward this orientation.

Resource Power. There is power in controlling conflict-related resources other than information, including time and money. Both Jane and Bob control sizable budgets. The COO obviously has more budgetary control and is most empowered in terms of using time and setting time limits for the other parties.

Organizational Structure. Conflict-related power can exist in an individual's formal position within the organization due to authority to demand or command action and compliance. Neither Jane nor Bob seems to have a clear advantage in relation to the organizational hierarchy. Both have access to other regional operators. Bob is a peer and competitor to these individuals. Jane is a service partner. The COO has a high degree of structural power over both Jane and Bob.

Informal Human Networks. Relationships create their own source of power through connections, affiliation, affection, intimacy, and trust. It could be significant if Jane has strong informal connections to senior leaders and others throughout the organization based on the fact that she has been involved with the organization since early on. The nature of informal human networks sometimes makes it difficult to assess power for other parties. The strength of Bob's informal networks is not clear. This fact alone makes it difficult to determine the balance of power between Jane and Bob.

As context changes, so may an individual's power resource profile. Nonetheless, consideration of power sources can be helpful as clients assess the viability of various goals and the best ways to enact the goals of self or other. Coaches may use the following questions in order to have clients apply the power resource concept to their conflict situations:

- How do power resource profiles help to make sense of past interaction between self and other?
- What are the current power resource profiles of self and other?
- How do power resource profiles inform likely or possible future interaction between self and other?

Power Patterns in Conflict Interaction

A focus on patterns of conflict and power reminds us that individual actions are situated and take on meaning within larger systems of behavior and interaction. Sometimes individuals take legitimate action that makes logical sense but that can produce extremely disappointing outcomes. Conflict coaching is an opportunity to highlight the nature and importance of conflict interaction patterns for the client.

Messages can be attempts to assert power (one-up), give up power (one-down), or transition away from the issue of power (neutral). But patterns of interaction are defined not only by the behavior but by the immediate response that follows the behavior. This is known as the *interact.*

When a response mirrors the same type of control as the message, the interact is symmetrical. When a response is opposite to the type of control attempted in the message, the pattern is complementary

(Watzlawick, Beavin, & Jackson, 1967). Sometimes, people are caught in repetitive cycles of using symmetrical or complementary patterns of interaction, thereby establishing power patterns in their relationship.

Symmetrical communication can be problematic, because both individuals are asserting power, which can result in more and more extreme assertions of power, or classic conflict escalation. It could be that the parties are behaving rationally in this situation, because the act of giving in to the other or failing to continue sending strong messages can signal weakness and undercut one's prior actions. This situation might get played out if Jane reacted in a directly competitive way to Bob's attack, and both parties continued to act aggressively.

There may also be a symmetrical communication in which two individuals who are reluctant to use power keep trying to give power to the other. This may take the form of an escalating avoidance spiral. The parties may be behaving rationally if each assumes that using power amounts to taking responsibility for the pressing challenge, and yet personally taking on the responsibility represents an unfair burden. This situation might take hold if the COO had individually instructed both Jane and Bob to take responsibility and reach out to the other party, but each resisted doing so, because it would feel like accepting primary blame.

One example of a complementary pattern difficulty is the case of a dominant person who keeps confronting and a submissive person who, in turn, keeps avoiding. This conflict could escalate as the confronting party takes more extreme action to engage the avoiding party, and the avoiding party acts with increasing passivity to remain disengaged. This situation might occur if Jane resists talking to Bob (possibly because she thinks he is an inappropriate communicator) and Bob (possibly sensing that going on the attack and not being deterred signals victory for his point of view) keeps attacking.

Patterns of communication can be very difficult to change. We may not be willing to give up certain goals. We may be adept or comfortable at carrying out certain tactics. Our identity may feel at stake. Alternative action feels risky. And yet the situation may be largely counterproductive. The conflict is a drain on resources. Involvement in the conflict affects overall effectiveness. And, ironically, the person on the other side of the conflict may feel the same way. The basic lesson to be taken away from a consideration of patterns is that individuals should not select tactics without considering the likely reactions of other parties and the way in which past communication interaction may impact the form and meaning of future interaction.

The following general questions may be helpful for coaches to ask clients regarding potential conflict communication patterns:

- 〆 What, if any, positive or negative communication patterns existed in the past or currently exist involving self and other?
- 〆 How might knowledge of conflict communication patterns be used to positively affect future interaction?

Power Strategies and Tactics

A strategy is an overall plan to achieve goals, while tactics are specific communications that advance a strategy. Tactics amount to power in action (Folger, Poole, & Stutman, 2005). This section provides a basic framework of strategies. While a given tactic can have different functions and meanings, the perspective outlined here is that tactics tend to be used in clusters that amount to the strategies of aggression, assertion, and integration.

Throughout this section, the meaning and success of tactics is context dependent. Context matters in terms of different orientations to power in different professional domains (Cavanaugh, Larson, Goldberg, & Bellows, 1981). Context matters at the level of a specific interaction episode (Folger, Poole, & Stutman, 2005). Context also matters in the way that a particular tactic is understood as advancing a larger strategy.

Many power tactics have been identified, and there have been numerous efforts to categorize these (e.g., Folger, Poole, & Stutman, 2005; Kipnis, Schmidt, & Wilkinson, 1980; Schenck-Hamlin, Wiseman, & Georgacarakos, 1982). Three power strategies can be used to categorize tactics in discussions with the client: aggression, assertion, and integration.

While the strategies will be presented as separate categories for the purpose of explanatory clarity, they may be better understood as points along a continuum. For instance, assertion can be seen to shift toward integration as it moves from use of competitive tactics to the use of instrumental collaboration (collaboration to further self-interest) to the use of collaboration aimed at the advancement of both parties' interests.

THE STRATEGY OF AGGRESSION

This strategy involves seeking power over the other by means that are questionable or fall outside of broad norms of social acceptability. Aggression involves a reliance on negative sanctions, basically the threat or delivery of punishment. Aggression may take the form of physical intimidation or outright attacks. Other tactics used can include creating a difficult environment for the other person, using guilt, and issuing warnings (Schenck-Hamlin, Wiseman, & Georgacarakos, 1982). Aggression is distinct from assertion, because it is largely or wholly negative from the recipient's point of view and amounts to a person-centered attack. It is self-obsessed in the sense that it is typically a shortsighted attempt to advance self-interest. It tends to be associated with conflicts in which the parties' communication and power relations are stuck, possibly in an escalation pattern of one type or another. In general, it is the least desirable strategy, because it is often seen as unethical and tends not to be effective in the long term due to the relational damage and retaliation it creates. It usually requires considerable resources to be sustained, even to protect short-term objectives.

Making attributions or interpreting the behaviors of self and others is important throughout day-to-day life but often has increased importance in instances of serious conflict—situations in which an aggressive strategy is perceived in others and/or is contemplated by self. Folger, Poole, and Stutman (2005) summarized the work of Sillars (1980a, 1980b, 1980c) and Sillars and Parry (1982) in noting three ways attributions play a major role in conflict interactions. First, a self-serving bias is in effect meaning that the negative aspects of the conflict are seen as caused by the other rather than self. Second, the self-serving bias also is in effect as each party believes it is doing more than the other to resolve the conflict. Third, each party tends to see his or her behavior as situationally determined and the other party's behavior as personally controlled. If a client makes self-serving attributions about the other, the client may be more likely to feel aggressive action against the other is warranted.

Those using or considering using an aggressive strategy would do well to note research on the use of coercion (Kipnis, 1974) in particular. Coercion tends to be used in situations where the sender believes the receiver is willfully and voluntarily resistant; however, a number of social factors affect the accuracy of such judgments. The sender's own stress can cause him or her to inaccurately evaluate the receiver's behavior.

The following tactics are generally understood as reflecting an aggressive strategy. We do not advocate their use by conflict coaching clients, although we believe it is important for coaches to acknowledge them, so that clients may better understand the assertive and integrative strategies as well as strengthen their proactive and reactive abilities when encountering (potentially) aggressive others. Coaches working with clients who are encountering or at risk of encountering the following tactics should make a point of consulting specialized resources or accessing appropriate professional services. This is certainly the case if personal safety is a real or potential issue.

- Threats or delivery of punishment (especially a heavy reliance on threats and punishments or the use of threats and punishments that are severe)
- Physical intimidation or attacks
- Name calling and other mental-emotional intimidation or attacks
- Lying, cheating, or manipulation
- Relentless use of power, especially with those who are less powerful

THE STRATEGY OF ASSERTION

This strategy involves seeking power to advance self goals by means that fall within broad norms of social acceptability. Assertion involves the use of tactics that are usually neutral or positive from the point of view of the receiver. Although assertion may occasionally incorporate the use of some negative sanctions, it differs greatly from aggression in the type and frequency as well as the weight that it places on these. Assertion tends to be distributive in the sense that it is focused on getting the sender's needs met as the primary consideration.

Assertive tactics are seen as less aggressive or more acceptable to other parties. For example, those issuing threats are viewed less favorably than those issuing promises (Heilman, 1974). Power can often be made more effective with the use of politeness (Locher, 2004). More broadly, the sophisticated use of social skills in terms of persuading, asserting leadership, taking conversational initiative, regulating conversation, being expressive, and communicating charm can reflect positive acts of power (Burgoon, Johnson, & Koch, 1998).

There is much research that informs the use of assertion from a high-power position. For instance, exercising control over floor time and topical focus often but not always indicates conversational dominance and can be reasonably linked to issues of influence over identity and relationships (Palmer, 1989). When in a low-power position, individuals generally do well mixing assertion with politeness. Levine and Boster (2001) found that being nice was strongly connected with success in the low-power position. Likewise, Locher (2004) pointed out that individuals in positions of low power can sometimes achieve power by combining politeness with assertion. Another low-power approach is to form a coalition; however, coalitions can also be effectively used by those in a high-power position. Such third party conflict communication in workplace settings is common and can strengthen or weaken a party's likelihood of acting assertively (Volkema, Bergmann, & Farquhar, 1997).

Assertive tactics are particularly difficult to definitively identify, because the assertion strategy falls in between aggression and integration. Therefore, tactics associated with it can often shift in terms of strategy alignment based on changes in context, etc. Nonetheless, the following represent some major assertive tactics. Each is also illustrated with a case-related example.

Initiating conversation	The communicator starts communication with the other.
	Jane could immediately reach out to Bob.
Regulating conversation	The communicator controls the flow of communication.
	Jane could take charge of the conversational process with Bob.
Persuading	The communicator uses arguments and otherwise designs information so that the other party adopts the communicator's point of view.
	Jane could convince Bob to partner with her to improve the results of his stores.
Asserting leadership	The communicator impacts the actions of all concerned.
	Jane could put forward a particular plan for changing Bob's situation.
Using expressiveness	The communicator displays emotion.
	Jane could be comfortable and upfront in sharing her emotions, especially as these enhance her credibility.
Displaying politeness	The communicator is socially appropriate.
	Jane could be good natured in working with Bob.
Forming a coalition	The communicator works with others to become more powerful.
	Jane could partner with other influential individuals or departments to reinforce her stance. Whether or not she does so, she should scan for Bob using this same tactic.

THE STRATEGY OF INTEGRATION

While aggression and assertion involve power over the other party, integration aims for power in partnership with the other party. Integration involves the use of tactics that are almost always positive from the point of view of the receiver. Unlike assertion, its focus on the goals of the other party as well as one's own is not to simply maximize one's own gains but to acknowledge the connection between the two parties and to value gains for both self and other.

Sillars's (1980c) integration strategies from his verbal conflict tactics coding system represent some specific behavioral opportunities for conflict coaching clients. Each of these is presented below along with one possible application in Jane's case.

Description	The communicator makes a factual statement.
	Jane might acknowledge, "Our company's operating environment, in terms of customer demand for our products, has never been more challenging than it is now."
Disclosure	The communicator shares private thoughts or feelings.
	Jane might reveal, "I am concerned that a sustained decline might result in the loss of jobs throughout our company, most notably in each of our respective areas."
Soliciting disclosure	The communicator asks the other to disclose.
	Jane might ask, "What is foremost in your mind given the current business climate?"
Understanding	The communicator indicates understanding and concern.
	Jane might respond to Bob by saying, "You are worried about your own job and those of individuals on your immediate team, because your positions in the company are directly tied to profitability."
Supportive remark	The communicator backs up another person's point of view.
	Jane might add, "Your heightened concern about our company's economic outlook makes sense given where you are placed in the organization."

Concession	The communicator indicates a willingness to give a little.
	Jane might offer, "I would like to give you the opportunity to meet with my team to explore improved ways to boost sales in your region. I am open to committing increased staff resources to implement a marketing strategy for your region in the coming quarter."
Accepting responsibility	The communicator accepts responsibility for part of the conflict.
	Jane might admit, "It is my job to work with you to face this unprecedented economic climate by initiating unprecedented efforts to craft effective messages for your customers and potential customers."
Common ground	Both communicators try to find a mutually satisfying solution.
	Jane might emphasize, "If you and I can maintain cool heads and work efficiently, my department can roll out enhanced initiatives to draw in customers, which will hopefully strengthen your bottom line and reaffirm the value of both our roles."

Based on the case and Jane's cumulative coaching experience, she might assume that she is comfortable using a blend of the assertive and integrative strategies, while Bob might fall within the assertive to aggressive range. Given her overall goals for the conflict, she might consider how to communicate effectively with both Bob and the COO in order to behave in a principled fashion and emphasize practicality as they work through the conflict. She can also use it to try to understand Bob's strategy.

Questions that coaches can ask clients to get clearer about the relevancy of strategies and tactics within their situations include the following:

- What power strategy(ies) and tactics have you been using in the conflict and to what effect?
- What power strategy(ies) and tactics has the other party been using in the conflict and to what effect?
- What power strategy(ies) does it make the most sense for you to use going forward, especially considering the likely or possible communication choices made by the other party?

Power and Culture

Perhaps the most basic point to make about power, conflict communication, and culture is that a given behavior can have very different power implications depending on the cultural point of view. One reason for the failure to effectively communicate issues of power across cultures is that individuals may be enmeshed within their own cultural context to the extent that they do not appreciate the nature of power within their own system or within the systems of others (Lukes, 1974; Mumby, 1988). Blindness to power may also occur in instances of deeply entrenched patterns of privilege. Those belonging to privileged groups and holding power may downplay or completely overlook the barriers to those who have traditionally not had equal access to power.

Another reason for the different understandings of a given tactic or set of tactics is that cultures may have different power distances (Hofstede, 1980, 1983), meaning different degrees to which hierarchical relationships are reinforced. High power distance cultures such as those in the Philippines, Mexico, and Venezuela tend to be more formal, to be more restrictive in terms of the emotions communicated from subordinates to superiors, and to place more emphasis on the individual's status rather than his or her competence. Low power distance cultures such as those in Austria, Panama, and Denmark tend to be less formal, more relaxed in terms of what constitutes acceptable behavior, and less oriented toward status differences.

While acknowledgment of national culture is important when examining power and conflict, so too is culture at the other end of the spectrum, in terms of organizational and professional microcultures. Different organizational sectors, different organizations within a sector, and even different departments within an organization can have distinct cultures and power expectations. These differences may be so stark that they rise to the significance of some general international differences. Likewise, specific professions may be unique in features such as power distance and the appropriate use of power sources; for example, the difference in power accorded to physicians versus nurses within a health care setting is unique in this way.

Coaches and clients are encouraged to take macrocultural and microcultural considerations into account when exploring implications of power strategies and tactics. For example, an assertive strategy may be seen as selfish, even aggressive, in a setting in which there is little power distance and a strong norm of collaboration. Conversely, integrative and assertive strategies may be considered weak and be seen as evidence of incompetence in settings in which aggressive displays are the accepted way of conducting business. The latter example may raise sensitive ethical issues for conflict coaches and clients.

Working With Clients Who Feel or Act Disempowered

In an era when power tends to be tied to less tangible sources such as information, expertise, and informal relationships, strong determinations of client empowerment and disempowerment are difficult to make. Nonetheless, some clients will have histories of taking action that puts them into weak positions, some will self-identify as generally disempowered, and some will atypically find themselves in constrained situations. In these circumstances, the coach may need to make a special point of working with the client to examine past conflict patterns and sketch possible new conflict interaction that emphasizes positive power in terms of self-goals, sources, strategies, and tactics. Before considering enacting power in respect to the aggressive-assertive-integrative continuum, some clients will first need extra support in conceiving of themselves as powerful. This extra support could consist of exploration of the legitimate use of power in light of the client's goals and power sources, the fact that some degree of power exists even for those in a relatively low-power position, and the different ways that power can be successfully communicated.

General Principles for Power Work With Conflict Coaching Clients

Principle #1: Integrate the client's beliefs about power with an exploration of the assumptions offered in the chapter. Beginning with a client's existing assumptions about power assists both the coach and client in determining the relevancy and need for review of the premises detailed in this chapter.

Principle #2: Invite client consideration of the goals of self and other as a necessary precursor to selecting strategy and tactics. Goals define the arena in which power is meaningful. If there are no implicit or explicit goals, then an assessment of power is not really possible. A client's deliberate selection of goals will virtually always lead to better results within a conflict coaching relationship.

Principle #3: Encourage the client to determine the power source profiles for self and other. Power sources point to the possibilities for reaching goals. Therefore, they are useful to consider as a check on goals and as a precursor to selecting particular strategies and goals. The power source profiles should be explored for self and other, because the relationship between the two functions as a basic indicator of what is possible or likely.

Principle #4: Foster an awareness of power patterns in conflict, especially as these patterns may be relevant to the conflict at hand and as they may inform the effective selection of tactics. A focus on patterns provides clients with some assessment of whether their ideal next move will continue to be attractive over the longer term. Patterns allow the client to survey the landscape of conflict and power in order to spot potential pitfalls and possibilities.

Principle #5: Support the client in determining desirable strategies and tactics. Offer the opportunity for selecting specific tactics based on prior consideration of goals of self and other, power sources of self and other, and a determination of relevant conflict patterns. Conflict coaching concerning power is arguably most helpful as it fosters clarity regarding communication behaviors.

Principle #6: Ensure that culture has been taken into proper account throughout the process. Whether at a broad national level or at a narrow organizational or professional level, culture can have a tremendous impact on the meaning of specific strategies and tactics.

Specific Approaches for Power Work With Conflict Coaching Clients

Approach #1: Explore the client's power assumptions.

What is it? This activity surfaces the client's baseline assumptions regarding power and offers an opportunity for the coach to present the client with various research- and theory-based assumptions to consider.

Why is it important? The activity can be beneficial in increasing awareness regarding existing assumptions, providing an opportunity to add to or otherwise modify existing assumptions, offering an exploration of the ways in which assumptions relate to communication behavior, and assisting in understanding the thinking and behaviors of other as well as self.

How do you do it? There are a number of different ways that an exploration of assumptions can occur. (1) The coach can provide clients with a piece of paper with the sentence starter, "Power is . . ." in the middle of the page. Clients are then instructed to complete the sentence as many times as necessary in order to capture all of their important beliefs, feelings, values, etc., regarding power. The coach can then invite clients to explain the meaning of each of the assumptions, especially in light of the current conflict. Then the coach can share the research- and theory–based assumptions and ask clients to consider how these assumptions are present in the current conflict. (2) The coach can provide clients with a blank sheet of paper and invite them to draw a picture of power in action. The coach can then request that clients consider the assumptions about conflict that are contained in the picture before inviting them to consider the applicability of the research- and theory-based assumptions. (3) After exploring clients' baseline assumptions in writing or orally, the coach can provide clients with a sheet of paper with a table on it. The table should list each of the research- and theory-based assumptions, briefly describe each, and then leave a blank space for clients to jot down notes relating the respective assumptions to their current conflict situation. (4) The assumption exploration process can also occur conversationally but still remain tied to one of the methods described immediately above. Any subtype of this activity works well, as the conversation includes a turn to the implications for the conflict in question.

Approach #2: Explore and elaborate the goals of self and other.

What is it? This activity uses the CCC goal model as a way of clarifying clients' goals as well as attempting to clarify the goals of other parties.

Why is it important? The CCC goal model usually offers insights into conflict goals, even for sophisticated communicators. It can be particularly helpful for developing a conflict strategy that then leads to the selection of specific tactics. Whatever its self-related purpose, the content, identity, emotion, and power goals work best when they are accompanied by a consideration of goals for the other.

How do you do it? The coach can ask clients to share their conflict goals as well as the goals of the other party. The coach can then present the CCC goal model as a way of integrating the baseline goal analysis with additional goals that may have not been previously considered. As well as possible, include the goals of both the client and the other party, and invite consideration of the interrelationships among the various goals.

Approach #3: Systematically assess the power sources of self and other.

What is it? Sources of power are the means by which goals can be pursued in a conflict situation. Four sources of power that we recommend clients consider are information and expert, resource, organizational structure, and informal human networks.

Why is it important? Most clients will have a bias toward focusing on their own power sources as opposed to the other's. Many will not have taken the time to consider the variety and depth of power sources, even for themselves.

How do you do it? The coach can provide clients with a simple table to populate. The vertical side can provide the different types of power sources and an additional row for overall considerations. The horizontal side can provide columns for self, for other, and for the comparisons of individual sources. After clients fill in the table, the coach can invite them to talk through their insights and make connections to related concerns such as conflict goals, patterns, strategies, and tactics.

Approach #4: Draw and discuss a conflict "power line."

What is it? This is an exercise for getting the client to consider the larger pattern of the conflict in question and how power shapes this pattern.

Why is it important? It is often the case that people in conflict take a short view. This activity can assist clients in gaining a wider perspective, which can lead to a more effective assessment of goals and tactics.

How do you do it? The coach should provide clients with a blank sheet of paper and instruct them to draw a line that captures the shape or movement of the conflict in question. The line can take any form (e.g., straight, circular, spiral, or jagged). After clients have drawn the line, they can be encouraged to plot significant behaviors or events on the line. Clients can draw a line that represents the past or future. They may also find it helpful to consider the line that might be drawn by the other party. The debrief of this activity should focus on the use of power to explain the general direction or directional shifts of the conflict line. The coach can also invite clients to consider various power enactment possibilities in relation to different conflict trajectories.

Approach #5: Apply the strategies to the conflict at hand.

What is it? This activity allows clients to look forward and back in terms of the aggressive-assertive-integrative continuum and its application to the conflict that they face.

Why is it important? The continuum can be a helpful model for making sense of the broad tactical patterns and potentials in the conflict.

How do you do it? It can work well to start by focusing on the past and separately considering where the skills of the respective individuals, the relationship, and the larger conflict situation fit along the continuum. (In each instance, it may be that a band is charted rather than a point.) Interactions among these can be explored. The client can then be invited to chart the point on the continuum to which the conflict might ideally and realistically shift (or be maintained). Finally, the client can be encouraged to determine any necessary or desirable changes in skills, the relationship, or the larger conflict situation that are necessary or desirable to arrive or remain at the charted destination.

Approach #6: Explore opportunities for balancing power and shifting toward an integrative strategy.

What is it? This activity is a chance for the client to consider whether and how an integrative strategy makes sense.

Why is it important? Sometimes individuals take part in coaching because they have a negative history of coming across as aggressive or as assertive but too self-interested.

How do you do it? The coach should not assume that an integrative strategy is best for the client's situation. However, many people fail to appreciate the potential applicability and value of this approach. One option is to move through the specific goals and consider what it would mean to advance each within the aggressive, assertive, and integrative strategies, respectively. After the client has done this with two or three goals, certain patterns may emerge. For instance, an integrative overture related to one goal may directly advance another goal and be very appealing to the client. Another possibility is that the client may not perceive that it is desirable or possible to use integrative tactics and may choose to concentrate on effectively applying assertive tactics. Whether or not an integrative strategy is selected, the client should see how this approach is, to a large extent, based on balancing power and creating power.

Approach #7: Consider the implications of culture and power in the conflict.

What is it? This is an opportunity for the client to scan for the significance of culture and power in the conflict and, if it is significant, to plan and take effective action.

Why is it important? Culture may be a blind spot, especially for someone in the dominant position. Directly considering this issue may turn out to be valuable for both parties.

How do you do it? One option is to use the following questions: (1) To what extent do you and the other party come to this conflict with similar and different cultural frames? (2) How do these cultural frames relate to power? (3) How may cultural issues have created challenges or opportunities for you and the other party? (4) How might it be effective to directly or indirectly address cultural issues in this conflict, especially as they relate to power?

Chapter Summary

Power is closely connected to identity and emotion issues and therefore serves as one of the three basic lenses through which coaches can assist clients in understanding and strategically responding to conflict. Power is a complex concept that can be introduced with a selection of key assumptions. Exploration of conflict-related goals, power sources, and power patterns can help make sense of the strategies and tactics used in the past as well as point the way forward for the client and other conflict parties. Sensitivity to cultural concerns and the phenomenon of disempowerment can also be of client value.

GENERAL PRINCIPLES FOR POWER WORK WITH CONFLICT COACHING CLIENTS

Principle #1: Integrate the client's beliefs about power with an exploration of the assumptions offered in the chapter.

Principle #2: Invite client consideration of the goals of self and other as a necessary precursor to selecting strategy and tactics.

Principle #3: Encourage the client to determine the power source profiles for self and other.

Principle #4: Foster an awareness of power patterns in conflict, especially as these patterns may be relevant to the conflict at hand and as they may inform the effective selection of tactics.

Principle #5: Support the client in determining desirable strategies and tactics.

Principle #6: Ensure that culture has been taken into proper account throughout the process.

SPECIFIC APPROACHES FOR POWER WORK WITH CONFLICT COACHING CLIENTS

Approach #1: Explore the client's power assumptions.

Approach #2: Explore and elaborate the goals of self and other.

Approach #3: Systematically assess the power sources of self and other.

Approach #4: Draw and discuss a conflict "power line."

Approach #5: Apply the strategies to the conflict at hand.

Approach #6: Explore opportunities for balancing power and shifting toward an integrative strategy.

Approach #7: Consider the implications of culture and power in the conflict.

7

Stage Three

Crafting the "Best" Story

True originality consists not in a new manner but in a new vision.

—Edith Wharton

Alex and Don, the conflict coach, have been working together to help Alex deal with his conflict with Taylor, the CEO of the consulting firm that Alex works for (see opening case in Chapter 3). After the preparation conversations, Don began by helping Alex to discover the story of his conflict. Using techniques described in Chapter 3—refining and testing the story—Don and Alex have produced a more elaborate narrative of the conflict, and Alex has a much better understanding of the situation and his initial biases:

※※ Alex realizes that Taylor has been asking Alex informally for more information on the progress of the ODSD (Organizational Dispute System Design) model for the past year. In most cases these requests have been made in passing at some other meeting or work session or as a part of a general sign-off at the end of a phone call, something like, "Keep me posted on the project." Alex has been sending short e-mails when things of note have happened, but he has not sent in any formal memos or reports. In fact, he hasn't sent in any formal report on the project since the end of the project's first year—almost two years ago. Alex realizes now that Taylor's requests were much more "formal" and anticipatory than he has assumed, and he realizes that his responses were probably inadequate.

※※ As part of the initial coaching and feedback sessions, Alex discussed the reactions of the pharmaceutical company representatives and gathered more

information from them about their satisfaction with the project. As he anticipated, the representatives were generally pleased with the progress of the model but were anxiously awaiting more hard data reflecting success. What Alex had not appreciated was that the representatives of two of the companies had become concerned about their sense that Alex was "operating in a bubble." These companies are also using Taylor's firm on other projects, and the representatives and Taylor often communicate. One of the representatives mentioned that he'd been trying to get in touch with Alex and had not had much luck, so he called the firm's offices and found that no one could give him information about the ODSD project. He assumed there would be an obvious project team with someone he could be referred to, and he was concerned that the firm was not devoting enough attention to the project He mentioned this as an aside to Taylor at a meeting some time ago. The second representative indicated that about a year ago Taylor had made a point of asking him about his sense of support on the project (meaning whether he felt the firm and Alex were giving him enough information and attention). At the time he'd answered that he was satisfied, that sometimes it was a little tough to reach Alex, but overall it was fine. The conversation seemed so minimal it hadn't really registered as important, but Alex's interpretation is that Taylor was pretty concerned if he'd initiated this request for feedback.

🕮 Although Alex is not sure about this, he believes that the director of research may be pressuring Taylor to allow her to have more influence and control over Alex's project, because it is strongly research based. He has learned that the "new guy" recently hired is a stochastic modeling expert and has been assigned to a number of other projects under the director's control. He believes that the intent is to have the new hire work with Alex or take over the research part of the ODSD project. Alex had missed a staff meeting in which the new hire was announced and introduced and had not attended to the circulation of the new hire's resume and introduction via e-mail. When he went back to the e-mail and reviewed the information, it was clear that the director intended the consultants to view the new hire as a high-level statistician who would be troubleshooting as needed on all research projects for the firm.

After discovering the fuller story of the conflict situation, Alex and Don considered the conflict from the three perspectives of identity, emotion, and power. While these discussions yielded a number of insights, some of the most critical are the following:

🕮 Alex realizes that he has been taking his identity as heir apparent for granted in the firm and that he has not behaved in a manner that is consistent with that identity. In order to do a better job of creating and maintaining that identity, he should have been more involved with other projects and consultants in the firm. He also realizes that he has not been acting professionally enough with clients. He should not create situations where they cannot reach him or where they feel he has not given them adequate support for their projects in the firm. Alex sees that his lack of interaction with the director of research has potentially been insulting to her and may have motivated her to act against Alex instead of with him. And most important, Alex sees that his nonresponsiveness to Taylor has been very disconfirming and has probably caused Taylor to wonder about his commitment and loyalty.

※ Alex's fear of rejection by Taylor has caused him to avoid dealing more directly with the conflict at a much earlier stage. Alex didn't want to be seen as insecure or immature or as someone who couldn't handle everything, and he thought that addressing his concerns with Taylor might communicate that insecurity. Now, he has become more paralyzed by his anxiety than he would have assumed. He feels that the situation has careened out of control, and he's very concerned about the possibility that things have gone too far to be salvageable. He has also reflected on previous patterns of behavior that Taylor has exhibited when angry. Alex realizes that he's seen this pattern of withdrawal before. In graduate school and in his years with the firm, Taylor hasn't displayed conventional anger in the sense of yelling, cursing, belittling, etc. Taylor's way of expressing anger is to "go cold" and distance himself from the target of his anger. Alex hadn't recognized this pattern, or that Taylor's recent behavior toward Alex was an enactment of this pattern, because Alex hadn't really accepted the idea that Taylor could get that angry with him. Now Alex feels his relationship with Taylor is more threatened than he'd thought, and he realizes it may be an uphill struggle to repair it.

※ And in terms of power, Alex sees that he has squandered a great deal of influence by simply not being careful enough about communication. Alex has sacrificed considerable power in the firm by alienating Taylor and the director of research, by acting "better" than the other consultants, and by failing to keep the pharmaceutical directors on his side by providing better service. Alex had assumed he was not expendable, and he's regretting that error. Moreover, Alex realizes that he has cut himself off from important power resources in terms of connections with and information from other members of the firm. His isolationist stance has cost him a great deal of good will and influence. But, he still has some relational connection with Taylor and has intellect and ambition. Moreover, he owns the ODSD model and knows that Taylor would rather not part with that.

A lex has come to a critical point in the conflict coaching process. Almost like a fulcrum, there is a point in conflict analysis when you deemphasize explanation, discontinue asking what happened, and start focusing on vision and what needs to happen to make the situation better. In our model we refer to this point as "crafting the 'best' story." While this stage of the model is not as lengthy or elaborate as others, it is nonetheless critical. If the coach cannot help clients know where they want to go, the coach can't be certain of providing them the resources to get there.

In explaining this stage, we begin by drawing briefly on appreciative inquiry and visioning approaches to change management. Then we revisit narrative mediation theory and the advice about narrative coherence and fidelity that we presented in Chapter 3. We illustrate how a conflict coach can work with the client through this stage, and we use Alex's case as an exemplar. We end the chapter with a discussion of principles and approaches for the coach in Stage Three.

Relevant Change Theories

The question of how you help someone move forward or change from a current state is at the heart of all change management processes in organizational and institutional development as well as at the root of therapeutic approaches to human relationships. Suffice it to say, it is not a small question easily answered. But change theories have provided some consistent insights, and we introduce those here as foundation for helping clients initiate change in their own conflict.

APPRECIATIVE INQUIRY

Developed at Case Western Reserve University in the late 1980s by David Cooperrider and Suresh Srivastva (1987), appreciative inquiry (AI) has been used by organizations and individuals to implement a strengths-based rather than a deficits-based change process (Ryan, Soven, Smither, Sullivan, & Vanbuskirk, 1999). Cooperrider and Srivastva (1987) contended that an organization frequently spends a disproportionate amount of time and resources addressing discrete problems and not enough time identifying and enhancing what the organization does best. They concluded that when stakeholders assess their organization by first appreciating what the organization does best, they are better prepared to address any negative dimensions or problems that may appear later in the process. Appreciative inquiry has been used in a number of large-scale, long-term organizational change efforts (Van Oosten, 2006).

The process of AI, whether applied to an organization or an individual, begins by asking people to identify what is good or right in the present situation. What are the aspects of the present that they want to continue into the future? Traditional change management theory asks the question, "What's wrong around here?" And AI asks the question, "What is working around here?" (Hammond, 1996). The result of an AI process is a set of statements about what an organization wants to be that are then translated into an action plan for how to get there or make that happen.

The basic philosophy of AI is that if you dwell only on the mistakes and problems, you may decide on a course of action that destroys the good as well as the bad. And by focusing on the deficits, you may completely miss creative solutions that would have enhanced the strengths. In our CCC model, the first two stages are based on explaining a reality and analyzing need. When done well, those two stages prepare a client with a thorough understanding of the present in terms of both strengths and weaknesses. But, to move forward, we need to help the client concentrate on protection and enhancement of strengths (which will usually also address weaknesses or make them much less relevant).

Hammond (1996, p. 20–21) summarizes basic assumptions of AI:

In every society, organization or group, something works.

What we focus on becomes our reality.

Reality is created in the moment and there are multiple realities.

The act of asking questions of an organization or group influences the group in some way.

People have more confidence and comfort to journey to the future (the unknown) when they carry forward parts of the past (the known).

If we carry part of the past forward, it should be what is best about the past.

An AI process is different from a traditional problem-solving process, as Cooperrider and Srivastva (1987) explained. Problem-solving starts with (1) an identification of a problem, which leads to (2) an analysis of causes, which is followed by (3) an analysis of solutions, and finally, (4) action planning. Conversely, AI begins with (1) appreciating and valuing the best of "what is," which helps us (2) envision "what might be," which leads to an opportunity to (3) dialogue about "what should be" and to (4) innovate "what will be."

The initial stage of AI presents the person or group with some questions and asks them to reflect. The questions, like those presented below, are intended to help the person identify strengths. Below, we present general questions provided by Hammond (1996).

Describe a time when you feel the person/group/organization performed really well. What were the circumstances during that time?

Describe a time when you were proud to be a member of the team/group. Why were you proud?

What do you value most about being a member of this team/group? Why?

Think back through your career in this organization. Locate a moment that was a high point, when you felt most effective and engaged. Describe how you felt and what made the situation possible.

Describe your three concrete wishes for the future of this organization (or your future with this organization).

Let's assume that Don directs these questions to Alex. He's asked about a time when Alex performed very well or when Alex felt that his relationship with Taylor was very positive. Don may ask Alex to describe what the behaviors were like during those positive times. Similarly, Don may ask Alex to reflect on a time when he was most proud of his role in the firm—to choose a high point in his professional career and describe what made it a high point. Don can add questions to this list, questions that are more tailored to Alex's experience. But all of the questions should lead Alex to reflect, describe, and consider the times, conditions, and behaviors associated with moments of strength and success in his relationships and his work performance.

We go where our vision is.

—Joseph Murphy

VISIONING AND APPRECIATIVE INQUIRY

A second step in most AI processes concerns visioning, or the creation and presentation of an idealized future state. When done from an AI perspective, visioning consists of *provocative propositions,* or statements of a future state in a particular area. For example, Alex may have identified his ability to persuade the pharmaceutical companies to use his model as a significant high point in his career and as a time when his relationship with Taylor was most positive. In most AI work, Alex would be asked to create a provocative proposition like the following: "Taylor will consider me an indispensable part of the firm due to my ability to consistently attract major clients to the use of the ODSD system." Provocative propositions are intended to state an ideal and, as such, sometimes seem grandiose or unrealistic.

Visioning has existed as a change management technique outside of AI as well. In general, visioning has been used as a facilitated dialogue exercise with groups to describe a more holistic future reality that is desired. Barge (2001) describes visioning in this more general sense as asset development. In this approach to visioning, the emphasis is still on building on strengths or assets. However, the intent is to create visions that are broader and inclusive of more assets instead of focusing as narrowly on one or two strengths as provocative propositions do.

The visions created should be as detailed as possible. For example, when visioning is used in large-scale public policy conflicts, like those described by Uyesug and Shipley (2005) in the planning of multicultural communities in Vancouver, or by Cuthill (2004) in visioning in local area planning of the Gold Coast, the emphasis is on elaborate dialogues in which the participants literally describe a future world. The more detailed the description, the easier it is for the participants to create the vision through careful action planning.

Often, the impetus for the broader visioning process is a prompt statement like, "Describe the world if. . . ." In Alex's case, Don might ask Alex to "imagine what it would be like if you and Taylor were having the best possible working relationship. Describe what it would look like, what you'd both be thinking, how you would interact with each other, how you would interact with others, and how you would feel about things." Don could break out various elements of this visioning and ask Alex to start focusing on feelings or start focusing on interactions. But, the important factor is that Don is trying to encourage Alex to describe the richest, most detailed story and a desired future.

As powerful as visioning can be, it is important that visioning not be allowed to be delusional, to ignore realities that must be faced in order for the view of the future to have a strong chance of becoming reality. The conflict coach serves an important function during the visioning process; the coach both encourages the client to be creative and reminds the client of the limits of imagination, much as a mediator reminds disputants of the "reality tests" for certain solutions.

The Link to Narrative Theory

Narrative is very much at the center of the change management process. Our commitment to the importance of narrative was presented in Chapter 3. In that chapter we described in some detail how important it was to help a client understand the current conflict by listening to the initial story, helping the client refine that story, and helping him or her test the story. A narrative approach for a story about the future is as essential as it is for a story about the present or the past—perhaps more so.

Winslade and Monk (2000, 2005) have already acknowledged this in their discussion of the importance of helping disputants distance themselves from the conflict saturated story (the narrative of the present) and move to a co-creation of a narrative of peace and understanding (the narrative of the future). Other scholars have commented on how important narrative structure (rather than propositional structure) is for articulating a vision (Ludema, 1997, 2002). If individuals are to "see" the future, they need to be able to tell the story of the future—a story or narrative that has coherence and fidelity.

In Stage Three of the CCC model, the coach is asked to support the client in elaborating the story of the future. And because the coach is again dealing with the narrative, the coach can apply the same three steps.

INITIAL NARRATIVE OF THE FUTURE

The conflict coach will need to preface this solicitation of the initial narrative with an explanation of the process. Many clients will not understand or be comfortable with AI or visioning processes for change. It may strike some clients as a little strange; perhaps a client will assume this is a waste of time because it isn't facing facts and fixing what's broken. But, once encouraged to begin, clients will probably experience a freedom in imagining something they had not expected. As many visioning novices will agree, they often see what they want much more clearly and completely in this process than if they are directed to consider only what needs to be fixed.

The most important contribution from the coach at this stage is to fashion prompt statements or questions that cover a broad range of factors, as we suggested in the example with Alex above. In fact, the coach may ask the client to identify parts of a vision that he or she would find important (e.g., relationships with co-workers, types of projects assigned, reward and incentive components, personal satisfaction and wellness, advancement in the organization, etc.) before the client is asked to begin telling the story of the desired future. The coach can then refer to these dimensions to make sure the client's narrative includes them all.

Probably the second most important contribution from the coach is to remind the client to "cut loose," "describe what you'd really like to have as a reality," and "don't feel constrained by the limitations you see in the current situation." The coach can push the client to describe a truly emotionally satisfying reality without worry about the chances that it can be achieved.

Some clients will be helped by writing out the story. Some will find it easier to freely create if they draw it, record it into a tape recorder in private, etc. Some clients are best stimulated by storyboarding the ideas or creating metaphors for this future reality and then elaborating from there. There is no one right way to accomplish this.

Alex and Don have spent the last week focusing on Alex's vision of the ideal working relationship with Taylor and the firm. The following is a much-truncated version of Alex's description of his ideal vision:

"Taylor would announce that I am going to become a partner in the firm and that the firm will be developing a second branch under my leadership. The second branch will be in a nearby urban center, so that we can build a regional presence but be in close enough proximity to allow us to communicate regularly. While both branches would deal with the full range of consulting projects like those currently undertaken by the firm, my regional branch would take the lead in ODSD design and research. We would secure intellectual property rights to the ODSD design model and become the sole distributor and training organization for application of ODSD in large organizations. Taylor and I would communicate on a regular basis—at least three or four times a week, and it would be with the same kind of informality and mutual respect that we had in the beginning of my tenure at the firm. But it would also be different, because Taylor would treat me more as an equal than as a subordinate. We would be comfortable sharing tensions and conflicts with each other and would be able to negotiate well together. Most of our time would be spent discussing new projects and innovations, because we would have a support staff that was highly competent and able to manage the implementation of current contracts with little direction. Our firm would be experiencing extremely strong revenue generation, but we would follow a reasonable growth model so we could maintain mutual oversight on the entire firm's activities."

REFINING THE FUTURE STORY

Once again, the initial narrative is only a starting point. There is more of a blend between the initial story and the refining of the story in Stage Three than in Stage One. This is because the coach takes a more active role in eliciting the future story. The coach has more influence in selection of prompts and in pushing the client to make sure to examine all factors or dimensions in the story of the future.

Yet, even after the construction of the narrative, the coach can still refine further in two important ways. First, the coach can refine in terms of the same elaboration and refinement tools we discussed in Stage One.

- Are there characters presented in the story that are not well explained in terms of roles, actions, or motivations?
- Are there characters not presented in the story who should be—who have something important to add to our understanding of the situation?

⁄⁄⁄ Is there additional information about the context that would help us understand what is happening?

⁄⁄⁄ Are there important events that have not been included in the story? Why? Why not?

⁄⁄⁄ Are there patterns of events that could help explain this situation that haven't been discussed?

The second way a coach refines is by far the more important for this stage. It is at this point that a coach leads the client into the discussion of the conflict management skills most critical to make this a reality. The appropriate timing of this refining is hard to predict; it will vary with each client. But a good rule of thumb is that the coach should wait until the narrative seems almost complete before moving to the stage of asking, "What conflict management skills are necessary to make this happen?"

Note that in this stage the coach is not asking the client to consider all possible courses of action that would need to happen in order to make the future story a reality. That conversation can happen later if desired. But at this point the coach needs to help the client target certain skills or behaviors that need to be used in order for the desired future to be more probable. The coach wants the client to begin to think about skill development and strategy so that, in Stage Four, the focus can be on which approach to conflict management makes the most sense. This approach not only moves the client forward but also links the narrative of the desired future with the deficits or problems presented in the narrative of the disliked present. Here the appreciative inquiry and the problem-solving orientations merge but within the larger framework of vision rather than limitation.

TESTING THE FUTURE STORY

Testing is less emphasized in this stage than in Stage One. The emphasis is on constructing a coherent future narrative rather than testing the fidelity of the future narrative. As such, the kinds of tests in this stage are different not only by degree but also by kind. In this stage there is not as much interest in whether the future narrative is shared by others, is biased, or is based on accurate information. And the tests of the future should not be probability based; that is, they should not address the question, "How likely is it that this can really happen?" As mentioned earlier, if the future vision is completely fanciful and impossible, the coach should raise questions about how much the client feels this future is achievable. Tests are certainly appropriate in terms of internal consistency and detail. The coach can help the client review the narrative in terms of how well it avoids internal inconsistency and whether the level of detail is sufficient to help in action planning and skill development.

Tests can also present alternative stories and ask why the client did not include this or that. For example, Don may ask Alex, "Why aren't you envisioning being the owner of your own consulting firm?"

The Transition to Stage Four—Skills Development

Once the client and coach have created and tested the "best" story, that narrative serves as the guide for identifying needed skill development (which we mean to include knowledge, skills, and attitudes on a particular topic). In the next four chapters we will present suggestions for skill development in communication, conflict styles, negotiation, and coordinating conflict coaching with other conflict management processes. To appreciate the information in those chapters, the link between Stage Three and Stage Four must be clear.

In reviewing the best story, the coach discusses with the client the kinds of knowledge, skills, and attitudes that the client will need in order to make the future vision happen. In this discussion, the coach is likely to take the lead, because the coach has a deeper understanding of relevant skills and conflict competencies. Still, the final articulation of areas for skill improvement is one that is negotiated by both coach and client.

General Principles for Crafting the Best Story

The principles for Stage Three are very similar to the principles for Stage One, because both deal with privileging the narrative. Because these have been introduced in more detail earlier, we reintroduce them only briefly here.

Principle #1: Never treat the narrative as factual; help the client see the narrative as a construction of reality. Especially when the narrative is of a future desired state, the questions of truthfulness, probability, and fidelity are not important and can be damaging to the intention to forecast desired states.

Principle #2: Appreciate that most clients will initially have difficulty visioning and will prefer to remain grounded in the narrative of the present. As mentioned earlier, it's difficult for people to imagine a future, especially when they are consumed with difficulties in their present. Asking a client to create a vision is liberating, but frightening, especially in terms of casting a new or different identity.

Principle #3: Assume that most clients will not produce a completely coherent narrative. Helping them tell the story is a significant part of the coaching experience. Clients are not usually asked to envision a different state of affairs. They lack practice and, in many professions, have learned that fantasy is not rewarded. The conflict coach should assume that the client will need help to produce a robust vision.

Principle #4: Emphasize that there may be alternative stories that could be told. Adhering to this principle takes tact and delicacy. Suggesting that the person has envisioned a future that is less than an alternative future can be face-threatening, and it is particularly so for the client who has had to stretch to engage the visioning process. Nonetheless, raising the possibility of alternative futures is an excellent means by which to test clients' assumptions that may be holding them back from exploring certain courses of action.

Principle #5: Encourage clients to reflect on what they can learn about themselves through their future narrative. In Stage One we presented some reflection questions from Kellett and Dalton (2001). These questions ask clients to consider underlying assumptions embedded in their narratives—assumptions about self, the other, the context, and the future. Encouraging the same kind of reflection on the future narrative is equally important.

Specific Approaches for Crafting the Best Story

Throughout this chapter we have presented a number of specific ideas about how a conflict coach can help clients discover their future story. In this section, we present some additional ideas about techniques that may aid in the development of future narratives.

Approach # 1: Retell the story within the coaching environment.

What is it? It is asking the client to repeat the same story more than once in order to see which elements of the story are told the same way and which elements change, are omitted, or are embellished.

Why is it important? This is one way of identifying which aspects of the story seem to be most critical to the client. Items in the story that are told in basically the same way over and over again are likely to be components that are very meaningful and often are emotionally triggering the client.

How do you do it? The easiest way is to ask clients to give you an initial future story and, after a break or in a subsequent session, ask them to repeat the story. Ask them to identify the factors that were consistent and the factors that changed.

Approach #2: Use expressive arts to elaborate the story.

What is it? Help the client to use expressive arts like visual art, creative writing, etc., to produce the narrative of the future.

Why is it important? Visioning is a very creative activity. It asks clients to step out of the tried and true, the known and comfortable, and project a different reality. And then it asks them to make that reality robust enough that they can present it in full form to another. Because this narrative production is about creativity rather than veracity or reporting, using expressive arts can unlock their creativity.

How do you do it? Ask them if they prefer or are more comfortable with an expressive art form, and encourage them to consider depicting their future story through that art form.

Approach #3: Identify a symbol of the new story.

What is it? Invite the client to select a tangible existing item that can serve as a symbol of the desired story.

Why is it important? A tangible symbol can serve as an important reminder of the new story and of the client's commitment to the new story. If it is small enough, clients may find it helpful to keep it on their person. If this does not feel appropriate or effective or if the item is larger, clients may want to keep the item in their work space (e.g., office) or personal space (e.g., car or home).

How do you do it? The coach can introduce the idea to clients and ask them if anything comes to mind. Even if an item does immediately come to mind, the coach may want to encourage the client to take some time to think about the best choice. Some clients will want to select items whose symbolic value is known only to them. Others may select items whose importance is obvious to or is explained to trusted others beyond the coaching session. This approach can be combined with the previous approach in that the art created by the client can function as a symbol. However, there may be clients who find it more fitting to use an acquired object as an ongoing symbolic reminder of the new story.

Approach # 4: Positively reframe negative self-talk associated with the old story.

What is it? Unproductive conflict interaction with others may be reinforced by unproductive internal scripts or simply by negative internally held assumptions. This activity aims to surface and change these scripts or assumptions so that positive interaction with others is more likely to succeed.

Why is it important? Shifting self-talk or implicit internal assumptions may enhance the development of the best story especially when done prior to the client initiating changed communication with others.

How do you do it? The coach can introduce the concept of self-talk and then invite the client to brainstorm negative scripts or assumptions that may be in place and, most important, to craft specific positive scripts and assumptions that help develop the new story. For example, "I failed to give my boss feedback at a key time, and I seriously damaged our relationship," may become, "Experience of past communication behaviors and patterns with my boss has given me clarity about what is desirable, important, and essential. I am using this information to build success right now and into the future."

Approach #5: Root and grow the best story beyond the conflict relationship.

What is it? The new story might not only offer the possibility for positively transforming a particular interpersonal conflict, it might offer the possibility for the client to transform roles, relationships, and actions more broadly.

Why is it important? Attention toward this broadening not only offers the promise of reinforcing the client's effort toward changing a particular conflict dynamic, it also serves to create greater change opportunities for the client.

How do you do it? The coach can introduce the concept and invite the client to identify key changes represented in the conflict narrative. Some examples include the following: "I see myself as an experienced organizational member and co-leader/co-contributor," or, "I realize I can pursue my own goals and support the goals of the other person," or "Being in this conflict doesn't mean I have to be angry." The coach can then prompt the client to explore the implications of these changes beyond the immediate conflict. For example, the coach might say, "You've made it clear how the new story can transform your relationship with the other party to the conflict. What are the key elements of the story that you changed? How might these elements expand possibilities for you and others beyond the particular conflict that we are exploring in our coaching conversations?" Clients may see opportunities to enact lessons learned from the particular conflict in other areas of their work or even personal life. The initiation of change in these other settings may reinforce the initiation of change with the conflict area that is the primary subject of the conflict coaching sessions.

Approach # 6: Assemble the story squad.

What is it? The *story squad* is one or more highly trusted individuals identified by the client who can offer practical or moral support to the client as he or she works to define and live a new story.

Why is it important? The story squad can build the client's confidence and commitment to the story as well as provide ideas for story elaboration and general support.

How do you do it? Invite the client to identify one or two trusted colleagues or friends not involved in the conflict. These should be close friends or professional confidants or mentors who will respect and support the client's efforts at positive change.

Chapter Summary

In this stage the client, informed by the initial story and the analysis of identity, emotion, and power needs, crafts a narrative of a future that is based on taking forward the best of the present and elaborating on that. Using appreciative inquiry and visioning approaches, the coach and client create and test the vision. The best story then becomes the guide for identifying areas of knowledge, skill, and attitude development that will take place in Stage Four.

GENERAL PRINCIPLES FOR CRAFTING THE BEST STORY

Principle #1: Never treat the narrative as factual; help the client see the narrative as a construction of reality.

Principle #2: Appreciate that most clients will have difficulty visioning and will prefer to remain grounded in the narrative of the present.

Principle #3: Assume that most clients will not produce a completely coherent narrative. Helping them tell the story is a significant part of the coaching experience.

Principle #4: Emphasize that there may be alternative stories that could be told.

SPECIFIC APPROACHES FOR CRAFTING THE BEST STORY

Approach #1: Retell the story within the coaching environment.

Approach #2: Use expressive arts to elaborate the story.

Approach #3: Identify a symbol of the new story.

Approach #4: Positively reframe negative self-talk associated with the old story.

Approach #5: Root and grow the best story beyond the conflict relationship.

Approach #6: Assemble the story squad.

8

Stage Four

Communication Skills

Confrontation, Confirmation, and Comprehension

Courage is what it takes to stand up and speak; courage is also what it takes to sit down and listen.

—Winston Churchill

Alan is the site manager of a regional parcel sorting facility; he has been identified as a prospect for higher-level management positions within the organization. Alan is very talented at maintaining an efficient process—quickly identifying and solving concrete problems by generating and assigning specific tasks. This is highly regarded, because it is essential to the organization's purpose of delivering packages in an accurate and timely manner. However, his strong task focus can sometimes come across as abrupt and run counter to the organization's relatively flat and friendly organizational structure. Alan has some sense that he is not as effective at people skills. His typical way of communicating consists of getting the essential facts, fixing the problem, and moving on. If someone else has the problem, he rarely sounds supportive.

Lately, a number of minor communication misunderstandings have started to negatively impact on Alan's job. One situation involves Dave, a floor supervisor, and Max, a line employee who reports to Dave.

Three months ago, Dave was in a meeting with Alan and mentioned a great idea for identifying new employees for the facility. Dave shared that the company should establish a program with the career service offices of area colleges to identify and prescreen candidates. Dave made the point that the basic idea came from one of his line workers.

Alan said he thought the idea had merit and passed it on to the head of human resources. Although the idea has not been fully implemented, the concept looks very promising. The human resources department is continuing to develop the idea while maintaining communication with Alan.

Last Wednesday, Alan dropped in on Dave's morning "round-up"—the team meeting strictly limited to three minutes at the start of each new shift. Dave spoke for two and a half minutes. In the last 30 seconds of the round-up, Alan very quickly shared the new hiring idea, thanked Dave for making a very important contribution, and held up an advance copy of the facility newsletter with the headline, "Dave Takes Us to Hire Efficiency!" Dave laughed lightly as many of his team members cheered. Alan immediately ended the meeting to keep things on schedule. Max marched off incensed that Dave had apparently stolen his idea and was willing to take credit for it.

As the rest of the line workers moved to their stations, Dave approached Alan and reminded him that it was not actually his idea. Alan simply instructed him, "Have the backbone to stand tall as a team leader. You brought the idea forward. The human resources people threw this newsletter together. Actually, as far as I am concerned, it is not about the credit, it is about all of us at this facility taking pride in doing our job better."

What seemed like an inconsequential matter got worse in the hours and days that followed. Dave tried to talk to Max about the issue but was blown off. Some of Max's co-workers, who had known that it was his idea, made the point of quietly sharing the truth with each of the other line workers on the team. After getting dirty looks from several line workers, Dave insisted that Max speak with him privately. Dave emphasized that he did not pretend that the idea was his own, but Max remained unconvinced. Dave then went to Alan and insisted that he step in to clarify the issue. Alan commented that the matter was getting more attention than it was worth but that he would come to the next team meeting in which Max was in attendance.

At the next team meeting, Alan used all three minutes to make the point that the "me, me, me, I get the credit" mentality had to stop. Not surprisingly, Alan's intervention did not seem to help. Dave remained angry with Alan and Max, and the other line workers continued to view Dave with disgust.

C onflict professionals are very aware of the importance of communication in conflict. We can have the best intentions and the most exciting and promising ideas, but we are unable to move the conflict management forward if we are unable to communicate effectively. In too many instances, like Alan's case, communication behaviors create unnecessary conflicts that can dominate our personal or professional relationships.

In this chapter, we address three functions of communication in conflict: confrontation, confirmation, and comprehension. Coaches can help their clients communicate to announce the need for conflict management (confrontation), to show respect and protect identity (confirmation), and to understand and be understood about information relevant to the conflict (comprehension).

We have chosen to discuss these communication skills in this order because they tend to be the order in which the skills are used in a conflict encounter. First, someone must confront the other in order to acknowledge that they are in conflict. During that initial and subsequent interaction, the client needs to know how to communicate in a way that respects the other person's identity (as we discussed in Chapter 4) to help maintain a cooperative and nondefensive climate and increase the chances for collaboration. And once that cooperative climate has been established, the client has to be able to communicate ideas and understand the other's thoughts and suggestions in order to decide what should be done.

Further, these skills work in concert. Confronting someone without being able to communicate respectfully or engage ideas is ineffective and potentially damaging. Creating a cooperative climate for resolution through appropriate confrontation and confirmation may actually frustrate the other party if you can't take it to the next level and work through the problem.

We have made certain assumptions that color the presentation of information in this chapter:

1. Confrontation is often, but not always, a constructive move. We focus on how someone should confront the other about the conflict issue, but we will briefly note later that there are times when confrontation is not a good idea.

2. In coaching, the emphasis is on helping clients send or encode communication. We give less emphasis in this book to clients' ability to decode the communication of others and respond to their behavior.

3. There are important communication skills that are not covered in the discussion of confrontation, confirmation, and comprehension. We see these skills as foundational—anyone in any conflict needs to know how to confront, confirm, and comprehend. We have discussed more specific skills, like persuasion or emotional expression, in other chapters where those skills are clearly germane to the conflict coaching topic of that chapter.

For coaches who are interested in a more thorough coverage of communication and conflict, especially as it applies to interpersonal conflict, there are good resources available (Folger, Poole, & Stutman, 2005; Jones, Remland, & Sanford, 2007; Remland, 2004).

Hargie (2006, p. 13) defines a communication skill as "a process in which the individual implements a set of goal-directed, interrelated, situationally appropriate social behaviours, which are learned and controlled." Communication skills stress appropriateness and effectiveness of enacted verbal and nonverbal behaviors (Cupach & Canary, 1997; Segrin & Givertz, 2003; Spitzberg & Cupach, 1984, 1989). Appropriateness means that social norms are respected. Effectiveness means that the individual's goals are achieved. And appropriateness and effectiveness cannot be discussed without attention to the issue of culture.

Culture and Communication Skills

Most modern definitions of the term *culture* refer to shared beliefs, values, customs, and symbols (Lustig & Koester, 2003; Neuliep, 2003). Culture is a product of learning. Each generation passes on to the next lessons about what to value, what to believe, and how to behave. Cultures can be racial, ethnic, generational, gender-based, family, organizational, professional, regional, etc. Throughout this book we have referred to culture as operating on a variety of levels ranging from subcultures in an organizational culture to national cultures. As coaches reflect on culture and communication for their clients, it is helpful to concentrate on the complexity and embeddedness of cultures.

Part of the complexity of culture and communication is the reality that all of us are unique combinations of several cultures, and it is this unique combination that accounts for our assumptions about appropriate and effective behavior. Think about Alan in the case example. The appropriateness of Alan's behaviors toward Dave and Max is judged in terms of expectations for an American man in a managerial position in a manufacturing organization. Those expectations would be very different if Alan were, instead, "Akiko," a woman in Japan working in a high-powered financial firm. It is simply not possible to think of "skilled" behavior apart from the cultural context in which it occurs.

CULTURAL FRAMES OF REFERENCE

Scholars over the years have discovered that some of the values we take for granted in our own culture are not shared by persons in many other cultures. One well known researcher, Dutch social scientist Geert Hofstede, investigated cultural differences among IBM employees in 64 countries. Drawing from the results of this important early study and several subsequent studies, he identified four basic dimensions that differ across cultures (Hofstede, 1980, 1991):

- *Individualism.* This dimension represents the degree to which individuals are integrated into groups. In an *individualistic culture,* ties between people are loose; for the most part, people learn to look out for themselves and their immediate family. In contrast, *collectivistic cultures* encourage interdependence among members, teaching them the importance of allegiance to in-groups (e.g., work groups, extended family) that provide continued protection in exchange for unquestioned loyalty.
- *Inequality.* Hofstede uses the term *power distance* to mean a society's willingness to accept unequal distributions of power. The key factor in assessing power distance in a culture, according to Hofstede, is the degree to which the *less powerful* people in that culture expect and accept inequality. In low power distance cultures, there is a much greater preference for equality among people.
- *Masculinity.* This is a culture's preference for male versus female values. In a highly *masculine culture,* people—men and women alike—are more likely to endorse assertive and competitive behavior than they are in *feminine cultures,* where people are more likely to endorse caring and cooperative behavior.
- *Uncertainty.* This dimension deals with a culture's lack of tolerance for ambiguity, what Hofstede calls *uncertainty avoidance.* In cultures high in uncertainty avoidance, people are uncomfortable in unstructured situations—situations that are novel and surprising. People in such cultures are more likely to want laws, rules, instructions, rituals, and the like than are people in cultures that are more tolerant of ambiguity.

CULTURE AND NONVERBAL COMMUNICATION

An unsuspecting visitor to a foreign country who takes the meaning of a gesture for granted runs the risk of offending his or her host by inadvertently using a gesture that sends the wrong message. Cultural differences in nonverbal communication occur in many areas, including personal space, gaze, touch, gestures, and voice (Remland, 2004).

Edward Hall's (1959, 1966) research on cultural differences in the use of space found members of contact cultures (e.g., Arab, Latin American, and southern European nations) use more touch and less personal space than do members of noncontact cultures, who prefer the visual mode of communication (e.g., North American, Asian, and northern European nations).

The meaning of touch often depends on one's culture. In some Middle and Near Eastern countries, shaking hands is an act of bargaining rather than a form of greeting. Same-sex touching in public is more acceptable in many Asian and Middle Eastern countries than is opposite-sex touching (Jones, 1994).

Sometimes we assume that the gestures we use to communicate are universal, but that is rarely the case. The meanings of many gestures vary from one culture to another. These differences can sometimes cause serious misunderstandings and subsequent embarrassment (Axtell, 1998; Morris, 1977, 1994).

Vocal volume varies with culture. Some researchers claim that Arabs prefer loud speech, because they regard it as stronger and more sincere than a softer tone of voice (Hall & Whyte, 1966; Watson & Graves, 1966). In contrast, Britons generally prefer a quieter, less intrusive volume than persons from many other cultures, including both Arabs and Americans (Hall, 1966).

CULTURE AND VERBAL COMMUNICATION

Cultures have different styles of verbal communication. Much of what we know about this comes from the work of anthropologist Edward T. Hall, who wrote extensively about the many differences between what he called *high-context* and *low-context* forms of communication. In low-context cultures, the speaker is responsible for getting the message across to the listener by using language that is clear, complete, and direct. In high-context cultures, the speaker assumes the listener understands hints and indirectness, because the listener comes from the same culture and knows the intent and expectations in that culture. In high-context cultures, the burden is on the *listener* to figure out what the speaker is trying to say, taking into account everything that affects the meaning of the message.

Using Hall's distinction between high- and low-context cultures and Hofstede's dimensions of culture (individualism, power distance, etc.) as a theoretical framework, communication researchers William Gudykunst and Stella Ting-Toomey (1988) identified several basic styles of communication that differ across cultures.

- *Direct or indirect styles.* A *direct style* is blunt and straightforward; speakers say exactly what is on their minds. With an *indirect style*, speakers hint at important points instead of saying exactly what they think.
- *Instrumental or affective styles.* With an *instrumental style*, speakers focus primarily on the task at hand, using language to accomplish a personal goal, such as persuading or making a good impression. In contrast, when speakers use an *affective style*, they focus as much on the listener as they do on themselves and are more concerned with the process of interacting than with accomplishing a goal.

※ Person-centered or role-centered styles. A *person-centered style* is informal, emphasizing first-person pronouns and downplaying status differences. A *role-centered style* is a more formal style, using titles and other means to focus on status and formality.

COMMUNICATION SKILL AND INTERCULTURAL COMMUNICATION

In the preceding paragraphs we've emphasized how culture influences the kinds of verbal and nonverbal communication behaviors that are seen as appropriate and effective. So, if Alan is interacting with Dave and Max, and all three are from the same culture(s), all three will have the same general understanding of whether Alan's behavior is culturally and communicatively competent.

But what if Alan is from a culture that is very different from that of Dave and Max? This would be an instance of intercultural or cross-cultural communication. It's hard enough to be culturally competent in your own culture, but being competent at intercultural communication is extremely difficult. Cross-cultural conflict interaction relies on individuals from different cultures creating a shared sense of effectiveness and appropriateness (Ting-Toomey, 1997). A good intercultural communicator is flexible with respect to the goals of self and other as well as other situational features. The more intercultural the encounter, the more important it is for the client to consider how to identify and honor communication norms of the other's culture. Likewise, the more intercultural the encounter, the more important it is for the client to explain his behavior to the other.

Key Conflict Communication Skills

There are three important kinds of communication skills in conflict encounters: confrontation, confirmation, and comprehension. In this section we briefly introduce each of these skill areas.

CONFRONTATION

Conflict management practitioners know all too well that clients often do not confront the other party before turning outside the relationship and escalating the conflict. Many people are conflict avoidant and can't face a conversation with the other party about what is wrong. Even if people are willing to confront, they may not be skilled at confrontation, and without effective confrontation, you cannot attempt to engage the other party directly in the management of the conflict issue.

Confrontation occurs when you directly address someone about an issue of actual or potential disagreement. It involves an explicit statement regarding social rules or expected behavior. Confrontation may clarify past or future behavior. When you confront another, there is no question that the problem has been put on the table—or announced—and that you are expecting a response from the other person about what to do about this issue.

Confrontation is a series of decisions. Should Dave confront Alan? When should Dave confront Alan? How should Dave confront Alan? What are the consequences if Dave doesn't confront Alan? How can Dave deal with this conflict if he decides not to confront Alan? All three aspects of confrontation—whether to confront, how to confront, and when to confront—will determine the effectiveness of the communication. Dave might choose to confront Alan but do it clumsily or at a very bad time. Dave may realize that confronting Alan won't help and might hurt (although Dave should be very careful that he's not concluding this out of his desire to not confront). But if Dave doesn't confront Alan, he can never be completely sure that Alan realizes how Dave sees the problem and why Dave believes it needs to be addressed.

Appropriateness of Confrontation. Let's look at the first question. Should Dave confront Alan? In conflict, people have three choices: to confront the conflict, to have someone else confront the conflict, and to avoid the conflict. Before we discuss the how of confrontation, let's take a quick look at when confrontation makes sense.

The decision to confront or not confront has to do with the importance of the conflict, the power dynamics in the relationship, and the potential consequences for self and other from the conflict and the confrontation. We summarize these factors and their indication for action in Table 8.1 below.

Too often, people choose not to confront another because they are uncomfortable with how to confront. Deciding to confront is one thing; knowing how to confront is another. Max's decision to not confront Dave contributed to the escalation of this conflict to other line workers and to the growing resentment of the work group against Dave and Alan. Even when Dave approached Max, Max chose to blow off the conversation rather than honestly confront the issue, further deepening the divide. But when Alan decided to confront the issue, he did it all wrong. He confronted the issue to the entire work group instead of talking with Dave and Max directly; he confronted them by blaming them for focusing on the issue of credit, which further angered them; and he confronted them by announcing the conflict and then closing it from

Table 8.1   Factors that Determine Appropriateness of Confrontation

	Importance of the Conflict	Power Dynamics in the Relationship	Consequences for Self and Other
Confront directly	⅏ Moderate to very high	⅏ Relatively equal or balanced power ⅏ Strong support from external parties or constituencies ⅏ Organizational norms or policies require direct confrontation ⅏ Protection from retaliation is offered by the system ⅏ Confronter has key skills of confrontation	⅏ Conflict will get worse (or consequences will get worse) if not confronted ⅏ Lack of confrontation will inhibit pursuing redress or protection of rights later if desired ⅏ There is no outlet for indirect confrontation ⅏ Lack of confrontation may protect self but cause serious harm to other
Confront indirectly	⅏ Moderate to very high	⅏ Significant power imbalance in a relationship where the client has low power and the other has high power ⅏ Organizational norms or policies require indirect confrontation (e.g., through ombuds) ⅏ Protection from retaliation is only guaranteed when confrontation is indirect (e.g., through ombuds) ⅏ Confronter does not have key skills of confrontation	⅏ Conflict will get worse (or consequences will get worse) if not confronted ⅏ Lack of confrontation will inhibit pursuing redress or protection of rights later if desired ⅏ There is no outlet for direct confrontation ⅏ Direct confrontation will expose self or other to serious retaliation or harm ⅏ Lack of confrontation may protect self but cause serious harm to other

(Continued)

Table 8.1 (Continued)

	Importance of the Conflict	Power Dynamics in the Relationship	Consequences for Self and Other
Avoid confrontation	🕮 Low importance	Significant power imbalance in a relationship where the client has low power and the other has high power 🕮 Organizational norms or policies prohibit or punish confrontation either direct or indirect 🕮 No protection from retaliation 🕮 Confronter does not have key skills of confrontation	🕮 Conflict will get better or be resolved (or consequences will get better) if not confronted 🕮 Lack of confrontation does not affect pursuing redress or protection of rights later if desired 🕮 There is no outlet for confrontation 🕮 Lack of confrontation will not expose self or other to serious retaliation or harm

discussion, which strengthened the workers' perceptions that Alan did not respect them. Alan's behavior was aggressive and argumentative.

Unfortunately, confrontation is often associated with aggressive communication and argumentativeness. While there may be circumstances in which both types of communication are advantageous or even culturally sanctioned, we are not advocating that coaches encourage clients to use either. In fact, we suggest coaches support clients in their reflection of whether they already use aggressive or argumentative communication and in their consideration of whether and how to change these communication styles.

Aggressive communication is an indication of hostility (Infante, 1987) and includes verbally attacking a person's character, name calling, and cursing (Rancer & Avtgis, 2006). Verbal aggressiveness has specifically been defined as attacking a person's identity or character instead of attacking the issue. Argumentation includes making logical and persuasive arguments and being able to refute others' arguments. Argumentativeness is when a person argues too much and becomes overbearing and attacking.

Basic Types of Confrontation. Productive confrontation takes one of three forms: clarify an assumption, correct a behavior, or invite joint problem solving. Each of these advances the interests of the confronter with at least modest acknowledgment of the other person's interests. In the case of joint problem solving, confrontation offers the opportunity not only to acknowledge but to fully incorporate the interests of both parties.

Confronting to Proactively Clarify an Assumption. This type of confrontation checks whether the two parties are seeing things the same way. It asks the question, "Do we agree that . . . ?" about something that is seen by at least one party as a potentially important source of conflict. When someone confronts to clarify an assumption, it may look like one of the following:

- A statement of an assumption (e.g., "Regarding X, I assume you/I/we will do Y.").
- A check to see if an assumption is shared (e.g., "Is that your assumption?").
- A request for clarification about whether the assumption is negotiable (e.g., "It's not up to us to change the company's decision that we will do Y," or "Let's see whether we're right about this; we might be able to change this.").

If Dave confronted Alan after his address to the work group, it might look something like this:

> Hi Alan. About what just happened in the meeting, it seems to me that we still need to talk with Max to make sure he's OK with what'd happened. I don't think this thing is going away until we take care of that. What do you think?

Confronting in Order to Correct a Behavior and Advance a Specific Solution. This type of confrontation labels a behavior as negative, problematic, or unacceptable and suggests a different way of behaving. It tries to correct undesirable behavior without engaging in personal attack. To make this kind of confrontation effective, the person doing the confronting has to be very specific about the behavior that needs to be corrected and why. The confronter uses some version of an "I-statement" (When you do _____ , I feel _____ and would like it if _____) that announces the negative behavior but also suggests alternatives. Here is an example:

- Identify a specific negative behavior (e.g., "When you do X . . . .")
- Point out the negative effect (e.g., "I notice that Y. . . .")
- Suggest a positive alternative behavior (e.g., "It would be better if Z. . . .")
- State one or more likely positive effects (e.g., "That way you . . . I . . . we could see benefits in. . . .")

If Dave confronts Alan in this way, his statement might look like the following:

> Alan, when you criticized the group for focusing too much on who's getting credit, you made several of them angry enough to leave the meeting. It would help if the next time you talk to the group, you also acknowledge that they have a right to expect credit for their own ideas and that we're going to look into ways of making that happen more often. I'm pretty sure that will lower their resentment and change the climate which has gotten pretty rough lately.

Confronting to Invite Joint Problem Solving. This type of confrontation defines a problem as you see it and asks the other person to work with you to make it better. If the invitation is accepted, you are then in a negotiating mode, which we talk about in Chapter 10. All negotiation starts with this type of confrontation. Here are some ways the invitation can be offered:

- Acknowledge the opportunity to confront an issue and state the issue in neutral terms (e.g., "It seems like we are both motivated to find a better way of dealing with issue X.")
- Set a collaborative tone (e.g., "If you are up for it, let's put our heads together and take some time to share perspectives and find one or more solutions that will work for both of us.")

Once again, considering Dave's confrontation of Alan, Dave could say:

> Alan, I know we both want to make this work group productive, and I think we both realize there have been some problems with morale. If you have time, let's talk about what can be done to fix this situation. I'd like to hear your ideas and I have some I'd like to share.

In the next chapter, Chapter 9, we talk about choosing the most appropriate conflict style for a conflict. In some cases, avoidance or accommodation is the best strategy. However, if competition, collaboration, or compromise is chosen, all three will necessitate some form of confrontation.

Responding to Confrontation. To this point we have focused on how a coach might help a client to confront another. But obviously, there's the other side. What about the client who is being confronted and is responding badly? What if your client were Alan rather than Dave, and Alan's response to Dave's confrontations is to get angry and shut down conversation?

A conflict coach can help a client see confrontation from the point of view of both the confronter and the confronted. Newell and Stutman (1988) offered insights into confrontation involving social infractions. They used four questions for considering whether a confrontation was valid:

- Is the confronter's social rule legitimate?
- Did the person being confronted do the alleged behavior?
- Does the behavior actually violate a rule?
- Does the person being confronted accept responsibility?

In cases where a confronter also proposes a specific solution, the person being confronted may also be encouraged to reflect on the following questions:

- Is the solution achievable?
- Is responsibility for carrying out the solution fairly assigned?
- Can the solution be expected to lead to stated or assumed positive effects?

When confronted by someone who wants to engage in joint problem solving, the following questions may be useful to consider:

- Are the issue of sufficient importance, the relationship of such a quality, and the skills of both parties such that joint problem solving is realistic?
- Are all issues, parties, and interests represented?
- Is there thorough consideration of potentially effective solutions?

CONFIRMATION

In Chapter 4 we talk about the importance of identity in conflict and the ways that identity threats can escalate conflict. In Chapter 5 we continue that discussion by articulating how emotion and identity are linked in conflict. So, it should be no surprise that communication that respects identity—confirmation—and communication that disrespects identity—disconfirmation—are important to conflict coaching.

Types of Confirming Behavior. What kinds of messages are confirming? Kenneth Cissna and Evelyn Seiburg (1981, p. 269) stated, "Confirming behaviors are those which permit people to experience their own being and significance as well as their connectedness with others." Working from R. D. Laing's (1961) thinking, they identified three characteristics of confirming behavior: recognition, acknowledgment, and endorsement.

Recognition. Recognition means that you recognize the other person is there and interested in communicating. Recognition can be either verbal or nonverbal. We often confirm others by seemingly subtle but intensely powerful behaviors like making eye contact with them when they wish to engage us, or touching them when they've communicated a need for support. We can also use verbal communication to recognize the other. A simple "hello" lets others know we see them and welcome them into the conversation.

Acknowledgment. Acknowledgment, which is usually verbal, is a statement about awareness of or interest in the other person's perceptions, comments, or questions. For example, after hearing a person express a strong political opinion, you might acknowledge that by saying, "You seem to feel strongly on this issue," or "You think that he intended to do that?" or "What did you mean when you said you wouldn't support that policy?" The key to acknowledgment is that you can acknowledge the person's perceptions, comments, or questions without agreeing with them.

Endorsement. Endorsement is the strongest level of confirming behavior, because it endorses or supports the way the other person is experiencing the world. Endorsement can be communicated verbally or nonverbally. You can endorse someone's judgments about a situation, feelings about a situation, or identity through supportive or complimentary behavior.

Let's take a look at Max and Dave's conflict and see how Dave could confirm Max. Dave can use any of the following behaviors to communicate that he respects Max. Let's say it's right after the meeting in which Alan has criticized the work group. Dave sees Max in the hall and approaches Max. Dave could do or say the following:

Recognition:

Nonverbal recognition:	(Makes eye contact with Max and waves him into the office to have a seat)
Verbal recognition:	"Hi Max, can we talk?

Acknowledgment:

Direct acknowledgment:	"Hey Max, it looks like you didn't agree with what Alan said."
Clarifying response:	"What did you think about what Alan just said?"
Emotion acknowledgment:	"You seem to be upset about the meeting and the whole credit issue."

Endorsement:

Agreement with judgments:	"Max, I agree that Alan's handling of this situation isn't helping."
Agreement with feelings:	"If I were you I'd be pretty mad about Alan's response."
Supportive response:	"I know it's important for you to have your work and your ideas taken seriously."
Compliment:	"You're an important part of this team and your ideas are a real asset."

All confirming behavior sends at least a message of recognition. This recognition validates identity. Higher order confirming behavior not only recognizes others, it acknowledges their perceptions and experiences. Thus, it is a form of perspective taking. The most confirming behavior is behavior that endorses the experiences, opinions, and feelings of the other. In all of its forms, confirmation is respectful of the other.

Responding to Confirming Behavior. Acknowledging when someone is being respectful may set a collaborative tone and improve the relationship. Although we won't elaborate on this point, we feel it is very important that conflict coaches help clients recognize when others have been confirming to them, and coaches should encourage clients to make an explicit statement that they have seen and appreciate this behavior.

Types of Disconfirming Behavior. Conflict coaches can help clients who are making conflict worse by sending messages of disrespect. When people are in conflict, they may engage in verbal and nonverbal communication that attacks others by suggesting they are unimportant. As Kathleen Ellis says (2000, p. 269), disconfirmation "communicates to the other that he is less than human, . . . valueless and insignificant as a human being."

In this section we talk about intentional disconfirmation. However, it is very important for coaches to realize that clients may perceive they have been disconfirmed even when the "actor" did not intend that. The coach should work with the client to reduce intentional disconfirmation and consider whether the client's behavior may be perceived as disconfirming. For example, Alan may not have meant his behavior to Max to be disconfirming. But if Max sees it as disconfirmation, he will assume that Alan intended it to be so and act accordingly. When it comes to disconfirmation, interpretation is more important than intention, or from the point of view of the disrespected—perception is reality.

There are three ways of disconfirming someone: indifference, imperviousness, and disqualification (Cissna & Seiburg, 1981). All three forms of disconfirmation are intentional in that the user decides he or she doesn't want to deal with the other person and wants to send the message that the other person is not important enough to merit a direct and open reply.

Indifference. Indifference occurs when you ignore the other person.

Imperviousness. Impervious messages deny the other person's self-experience in one of three ways: you deny the feelings of the other person, you deny the other person's perceptions, or you speak for the other person—you answer questions for the person, you put words in the other person's mouth. Impervious responses send the message, "You have no right to define or describe your own experience."

Disqualification. A final way to disconfirm is to disqualify by using equivocal messages (Bavelas, Black, Chovil, & Mullett, 1990). This is the most sophisticated form of disconfirmation. Basically, you give someone a response that looks like an answer, but it really isn't. Many times, others don't realize until later than you didn't give them the proper respect of a direct answer. Janet Bavelas and her colleagues (1990) identify four types of disqualifying responses. (1) You answer by using somebody else's "voice" or opinion. You don't claim the answer as yours. (2) You answer as though the other person just represents a generic type or class of person instead of answering him or her as a unique individual. (3) Your answer is so unclear that it can't be interpreted. You send mixed messages, you babble, or you mumble. (4) You change the topic or answer a question that wasn't asked.

Let's go back to the example of Max and Alan. After the meeting in which Alan antagonizes the work group, Max decides it's time to confront Alan about the situation. Max goes to Alan's office to talk. He knocks on the door of Alan's office and says, "Alan, I want to talk with you about this whole issue of credit for my ideas. I don't think I'm getting a fair shake." Now, let's look at how Alan might disconfirm Max.

Indifference:

Nonverbal indifference:	(Alan pretends he doesn't see or hear Max)
Verbal indifference:	(Alan looks at Max, picks up the phone and starts talking to a colleague.) "No, nothing's going on."

Imperviousness:

Deny feelings:	"You don't really feel this is unfair, Max."
Deny perceptions:	"Nobody is taking credit for your ideas; you are looking at this cockeyed."

Speak for the other:	"Let me guess, you think you should have gotten a big 'thank you' for your ideas and that the company doesn't care enough about worker input."
Disqualification:	
Answer with another's voice:	"Max, the company policy is to not give official credit for worker ideas."
Don't answer the person as an individual:	"Most of the guys in your group would probably like to get credit."
Send unclear responses:	"Oh, I'm sure you're really upset about this (said sarcastically)." (mixed message) OR "It's not really that, well, wait, it might be a little more . . . , but not really. . . ." (incoherent)
Change the topic:	"Is that report done on the Warsaw project?"

Responding to Disconfirmation. One final thought about disconfirmation: If you are being disconfirmed, it is hard to defend against. Think about it from Max's point of view in the example above. Alan is clearly not treating Max as a legitimate person whom he should deal with or has to deal with. If that is Alan's opinion of Max, what can Max do to change it? If Max protests to Alan, will that make Alan treat him as legitimate? Probably not. It may actually encourage Alan to use more disconfirmation. Can Max respond in an aggressive or violent way? Not without seeming to justify Alan's already low opinion of him and drawing condemnation for his behavior from others. Should Max simply avoid Alan to avoid the disconfirmation? How does that help Max confront the issue? Unfortunately, if a client is being disconfirmed, the coach will need to consider advising the client to get some third party involved who can call the behavior for what it is (label Alan's behavior as disconfirming) and initiate a process that will require Alan to take Max more seriously. In this case, that third party could be an ombudsperson, a mediator, Alan's boss, a human resources officer, etc.

COMPREHENSION

Comprehension is communicating for clarity and understanding. It requires communicators to be able to understand others, and it requires communicators to be able to make themselves understood. There are several important communication behaviors that work together to fulfill the general skill of comprehending: listening, questioning, explaining, and providing feedback. Each of these has specific subskills that are important. Comprehension skills overlap to some extent, as we see in the examples below. All of them also overlap with the skills of confrontation and confirmation. We'll draw more attention to that as we discuss each skill.

> *An open ear is the only believable sign of an open heart.*
>
> —David Augsberger

Listening. It's difficult to think of a single communication behavior that is more fundamental for constructive conflict resolution than listening. But most people think they are better listeners than they are (Nichols, 1995). In a survey of managers, for instance, Judi Brownell (1990) found that none of the managers rated their listening skills as "very poor" or "poor," and 94 percent rated themselves as "good" or "very good." These generous self-assessments, however, contrasted with the feelings of their subordinates, whose major complaint was that their bosses didn't listen to them!

It's a simple fact that it is harder to listen well when you are in conflict. A conflict coach can help clients reflect on their listening skills and engage in role plays and activities that increase the appropriate listening behavior.

Types of Listening. There are different types of listening; we listen for different reasons, and these types of listening depend on slightly different skills.

- *Comprehension and critical listening* occurs when our primary goal is to gather information or evaluate what we hear; we need to focus on the *content* of the message.
- *Supportive listening,* which has also been called empathic or therapeutic listening, focuses on helping and expressing concern for another person. When your goal as a listener is to provide comfort, five different listening skills are especially useful (Remland, 2004):
  - *Recognizing distress* (or the need to talk).
  - *Reflecting thoughts and feelings.*
  - *Reaching out and offering assistance.*
  - *Relinquishing control of the floor.* Give the other person the chance to talk and resist the temptation to become the speaker.
  - *Reinforcing speech.* A vital part of the comforting process is getting someone to talk who may be reluctant to do so. We can do this verbally with the use of open-ended and probing questions. Nonverbally, we can encourage someone to speak by being attentive and patient and by using encouraging vocalizations and head nods.

Barriers to Effective Listening. If clients need to improve their listening skills, the coach can start by helping them recognize their barriers to effective listening:

- *Faking it.* We act as though we are listening when we aren't.
- *Letting the mind wander.* We are capable of comprehending speech at rates up to 600 words per minute. Yet the average person speaks between 100 and 150 words per minute (Versfeld & Dreschler, 2002). The result is that our minds may wander while we are trying to stay focused on what a speaker is saying.
- *Situational constraints.* We may not have the time to listen, we may not be in the right mood, and there may be too much noise or too many visual distractions in the surrounding area.
- *Emotional reactions.* Another major listening barrier is becoming too emotional to listen. Something someone says floods us emotionally, and we lose the ability to process information they are giving us.

Questioning. Questions and listening go hand in hand. Good listeners are good questioners, displaying that they've been attentive and continuing the conversation in desired directions. In conflict, a client may not use questions effectively. In order to get the information we need, we must know how to ask for information. Sometimes clients will not ask questions because they don't want to seem ignorant or dependent. Sometimes clients ask questions to look good rather than to get good information. And sometimes a client asks questions that are leading ("Don't you think this is true?") or too directive ("Can't you tell him not to do that?"), which tend to make others defensive.

Clients should understand how to phrase open questions that allow the other person to respond in a variety of ways and that empower the other person to tell the part of the story he or she wants to convey. And clients should understand how to ask more targeted follow-up questions for clarification and additional information.

Questions can be especially important in conflict situations, because there may be an increased need for information sharing. A coach may therefore support a client in identifying types of questions, crafting specific questions, or preparing to answer questions.

Explaining. Explaining typically involves making something known to the other. There are three types of explanations (Brown, 2006). Interpretive explanations answer the question, "What?" Descriptive explanations answer the question, "How?" Reason-giving explanations provide rationales by answering the question, "Why?"

A coach may work with a client to determine appropriate and effective use of explanations by the client. A coach may also act as a sounding board regarding whether it is appropriate and effective to elicit explanations by other parties. A coach working with Alan will likely realize that Alan doesn't do well in offering explanations for his actions and his decisions. Perhaps Alan doesn't want to explain, because he feels it would be showing a weakness to the group. Perhaps Alan doesn't realize that he could explain his decisions in a way that will reduce the conflict and retain his authority.

Providing Feedback. Giving someone feedback can be a sign of respect and an indication of your interest in working through the issue. But, it is essential that you give feedback effectively. Good feedback is specific (it includes a description of the specific event or behavior you are responding to), timely (it is given soon after the event or in time for the person to be able to use the feedback), focused on things that can be changed (as opposed to things that can't), and tentative (offered with a realization that the feedback might not be a good idea).

General Principles for Communication Skills Work With Conflict Coaching Clients

In this section we present some basic principles to keep in mind. In the next section we will discuss some specific approaches for helping your clients improve their communication skills.

Principle #1: Develop awareness that skills are behavioral. Too often our work in communication and conflict is kept at the conceptual level and does not really embrace the behavioral enactment. We talk about skills but we don't help people "do" skills. When you work with clients, help them understand that they need to focus on what they are doing behaviorally and whether the behavior effectively communicates their intent.

Principle #2: Help the client see the interrelation of the three major communication skill areas: confrontation, confirmation, and comprehension. Clients will benefit from understanding that confrontation, confirmation, and comprehension skills are all linked. As we mentioned earlier, concentrating on one skill area without becoming competent in the other skill areas is likely to be ineffective and may even become counterproductive.

Principle #3: Emphasize the importance of context—cultural, organizational, and relational. Help clients appreciate how their contexts influence the needs for certain skills and the ways they are most appropriately performed. All discussions of skills should encourage an examination of the contexts that clients feel are important and a translation of those influences into the best skill enactment in that context.

Principle #4: Emphasize assessment for client skill strengths and challenges. Work toward a variety of assessment methods to help clients identify areas where skills development is most needed and to help them appreciate their strengths. Getting a valid and reliable assessment of communication skill can be challenging, particularly given the importance of context and the fact that skills are very often applied in combination. Assume that your toolbox should include self-assessment instruments, exercises, activities, reflections, and audio or video feedback sessions.

Principle #5. Remember that skill development is usually not immediate. We often make the mistake of assuming that if we explain a skill to clients and show it to them, they should be able to do it right away. This assumption is not only incorrect, it is frustrating. Just as people don't learn to ballroom dance overnight, they don't learn to become good communicators overnight. Work with a client should be based on expectations that there will be a longer learning curve in skill development and incremental improvements.

Principle #6: Make the practice as close to reality as possible. Practicing how to skydive by parachuting off a 20-foot platform bears little resemblance to the experience of jumping out of a moving plane at 5,000 feet. In skills work, practice is most helpful when it takes place in a context that is as close to reality as possible. Coaches should help their clients work through the tricky parts—the aspects of the skill that will be hardest to transfer to real life application.

General Approaches for Communication Skills Work With Conflict Coaching Clients

There are several general approaches you can use when working with a client on her communication skills. These approaches apply regardless of which communication skill area is of most concern. In the next and final section of the chapter, we also add some more specific approaches to work in the three skill areas.

Approach #1: Have the client reflect on which skills are most important to the conflict.

What is it? This is a chance for the client to determine which skills are most important for his conflict. The client's best story highlights the skills which are most necessary for further communicating the story and creating the desired outcomes.

Why is it important? Encouraging the client to reflect in this regard is useful for isolating the "what" of skill development and also the "why."

How do you do it? The client can be supported in determining the requisite skills for each key accomplishment. This can be followed with development, including preparation, of skills. The client can also consider the actions she might take to support appropriateness and effectiveness of the other party involved. In other words, how can the client increase the likelihood that the other will communicate effectively?

Approach #2: Assess skill strengths and challenges by mapping a recent conflict interaction.

What is it? This involves a client recounting a recent conflict interaction to look for times when communication was effective and not effective.

Why is it important? Drafting a transcript, even a recollected transcript, can add richness to the client's exploration of his of her communication abilities.

How do you do it? The client should identify a conflict interaction that is highly relevant. The client can create a transcript of the interaction from memory. If the interaction was long, the client can transcribe one or more key segments. Also, the coach can write the transcript based on the client's dictation. Once the transcription is complete, the coach should invite the client to pinpoint specific skills that he or she demonstrated or would have liked to have demonstrated in the exchange. This discussion can lead into skill development in terms of advancing the best story.

Approach #3: Use self-assessment instruments where applicable.

What is it? There are a number of valid self-assessment instruments (questionnaires, interactive tests, etc.) for most of the communication skills we have discussed. And there are assessment instruments designed to identify people who have a specific deficit in that communication skill.

Why is it important? If valid instruments exist (say for listening effectiveness) they can be taken in private with little or no risk, analyzed quickly, and used as benchmarks for progress throughout the coaching work.

How do you do it? The coach can provide the client with one or more self-assessment instruments and together they can consider the results and use them to plan intervention and skill development.

Approach #4: Use 360-degree feedback to assess skills in context.

What is it? 360-degree feedback involves the coach surveying superiors, colleagues, subordinates and others with whom the client works to assess the client's skills.

Why is it important? 360-degree feedback may be especially appealing because it allows for a triangulated assessment of skills in context.

How do you do it? With the client's consent as well as with the consent of the client's organization and clear pre-established guidelines around access and confidentiality issues, the coach can survey a number of organization members with whom the client interacts. Surveys can take place over the phone, in person, or on e-mail. It is desirable (but not always possible) to include those who are directly involved with the client's current conflict. It is also desirable to include individuals with different relationships to the client and different perspectives on his or her situation. Typically, the coach collects this information, compiles it, and then presents the findings to the client within a coaching session. The client is invited to decide how to proceed, possibly by developing specific skills and/or moving on to another Stage Four conflict coaching opportunity.

Approach #5: Develop one or more specific skills through conversation, written exercises, reading, role play, and more.

What is it? This means helping the client learn how to do the skills that have been identified as most critical to his or her best story.

Why is it important? Skill development is a leading reason why individuals seek and/or are encouraged to take part in conflict coaching. The opportunity for skill development is an important differentiator between conflict coaching and other alternative dispute resolution processes.

How do you do it? Clearly, selection of a particular skill development exercise depends on a number of factors, including the nature of the skill being developed, the context in which the skill will be applied, the client's baseline level of competency, the client's preference for different kinds of exercises, and the coach's expertise and style. Applications of a particular skill can be talked about conversationally between the client and coach. Written exercises can be used, for example, to involve the client in shaping skills to specific circumstances or to reflect on skill applications over time by recording entries in a journal. Clients may be invited to read material that clarifies relevant skills or otherwise helps a client more effectively use skills. Role playing between the client and coach and/or between the client and another party may be beneficial.

Approach #6: Set benchmarks for skills development.

What is it? Benchmarking is defining stages of improvement by clarifying what kinds of things the client should be able to do (what skill he or she should be able to enact) and how he or she can progress over time.

Why is it important? Benchmarking helps the client clarify expectations and "see" success. Benchmarking also helps the coach manage expectations so the client does not assume or expect extremely competent behavior immediately. And, benchmarking helps the coach and client articulate a plan for on-going assessment that will increase the chances they can and will complete the assessment.

How do you do it? The coach and client discuss the kinds of benchmarks that will define skills success and put them on a specific intervention plan and timeline.

Specific Approaches for Confrontation, Confirmation, and Comprehension Work With Conflict Coaching Clients

SPECIFIC APPROACHES FOR CONFRONTATION

Approach #1: Use instruments to measure argumentativeness and aggressiveness.

What is it? The Argumentativeness Scale measures motivation to argue (Infante & Rancer, 1982). The Verbal Aggressiveness Scale measures use of verbal aggressiveness (Infante & Wigley, 1986). Each of these is also available in a condensed format (Infante, Anderson, Martin, Herington, & Kim, 1993).

Why is it important? If a client is prone to argumentativeness or verbal aggressiveness, the coach needs to focus on preparing the client to engage in nonargumentative and nonaggressive confrontation.

How do you do it? After the client completes the instruments, they can be scored by either the client or coach.

Approach #2: Weigh the decision to confront.

What is it? The decision whether to confront is basically the decision to avoid completely, handle the issue indirectly, or handle the issue directly.

Why is it important? Helping the client to apply these choices to a specific situation can be helpful for double checking initial impulses to avoid, communicate indirectly, or confront.

How do you do it? The coach can provide the client with a piece of paper that presents the basic options and gives space for the client to consider the upside and downside of each. Using Table 8.1, the client may weigh all the relevant factors in choosing among these options.

Approach #3: Design and practice client-initiated confrontation.

What is it? The coach supports clients as they select a confrontation strategy, tailor that strategy to a specific situation, and practice the application.

Why is it important? There are many choices for clients to make even after they are confident in the decision to confront. Identifying these choices, designing confrontation, and practicing communication can increase effectiveness.

How do you do it? The client can be invited to consider whether the confrontation should proactively state an assumption, correct a behavior and propose a specific solution, or invite joint problem solving. (Of course, a combination is also possible.) The coach can then support the client as he or she elaborates the strategy and, possibly, practices it with the coach.

Approach #4: Design and practice responses to confrontation.

What is it? This is an opportunity for clients to explore communication possibilities if they are being confronted by the other.

Why is it important? Individuals may not have the same levels of comfort and effectiveness in initiating and responding to confrontation. This activity prepares clients for determining their response to a confrontation from the recent past or in the near future.

How do you do it? The coach can ask clients how comfortable they are when confronted, how they have responded in the past, and whether those responses have been effective. The coach can help the client reinforce current responses or develop different responses that may better fit the situation.

SPECIFIC APPROACHES FOR CONFIRMATION

Approach #1: Help clients consider their confirmation behaviors.

What is it? This approach asks clients to reflect on when they have used confirming behaviors when dealing with the other person in the conflict. It also encourages them to consider whether they are using behaviors that the other may see as disconfirming.

Why is it important? A client may not have considered the identity needs of the other party and how the client's communication is meeting those needs. To reflect on confirming and disconfirming behavior, the client has to take the perspective of the other. This reflection also reminds the client of the various kinds of confirming and disconfirming responses.

How do you do it? One of the most useful approaches is to ask the client to recall a recent interaction with the other person in which the other person seemed to become defensive. The coach can ask the client to recall, as much as possible, the specific behaviors that were exchanged and can get the client to consider which behaviors may have been disconfirming. Conversely, the coach can ask the client to recall a recent interaction in which the other person was defensive and upset but seemed to calm quickly. In this case, recall might focus on the kinds of confirming behaviors that the client used to calm the situation.

Approach #2: Design and practice confirmation.

What is it? This is an opportunity for clients to plan and practice how they can confirm the *other.*

Why is it important? This helps a client consider different levels of confirmation and different ways to enact that verbally and nonverbally. It increases the client's awareness of confirming behaviors and helps him or her assess the impact of context on choosing the best forms.

How do you do it? The coach can ask clients to construct a conversation in which they are intentionally confirming and to role-play that conversation with the coach.

Approach #3: Help the client consider the other party's confirmation and disconfirmation behaviors.

What is it? This is an opportunity for a client to assess the extent to which the other person in the conflict is communicating in a confirming or disconfirming way and how that is affecting the client's attitudes and behaviors.

Why is it important? Clients may not be aware of what is triggering them to be emotional or defensive in a conflict. They may also not sufficiently acknowledge when the other is trying to set a more collaborative and respectful tone. Helping the client consider the confirming and disconfirming behaviors of the other party can provide insight to these triggers and opportunities.

How do you do it? Once again, the client can recall a recent interaction with the other person and remember, as much as possible, the specific behaviors that were exchanged. The client can also be asked to think of triggers that have occurred across interactions with this person to determine whether there is a pattern of disconfirmation that can be identified.

Approach #4: Design and practice responses to disconfirmation.

What is it? This lets clients plan how they will respond if someone is disconfirming.

Why is it important? As we discussed, disconfirmation is difficult to defend against, and if it is allowed to continue, it is debilitating and embarrassing, so some response is needed. The coach can help clients think strategically about whether there are opportunities for them to successfully defend themselves or whether a third party will be needed.

How do you do it? The coach can ask the client to develop several possible responses to a specific example of disconfirmation and talk through the advantages and disadvantages of each. The client can select the most successful response and practice it with the coach.

SPECIFIC APPROACHES FOR COMPREHENSION

Approach #1: Help clients assess their listening behavior.

What is it? Using self-assessment instruments and situation recall, have clients assess their listening ability and listening style.

Why is it important? Poor listening is often associated with a variety of other ineffective or destructive conflict behaviors. And poor listeners often think they are much more skilled than they are, which decreases their motivation to change their listening behavior. Assessment of listening can help the client face reality.

How do you do it? There are good listening assessment instruments that can be used involving both questionnaire and stimulus-response audio materials. The coach can also identify barriers to effective listening that impact the client and what might be done about those.

Approach #2: Design and practice questioning.

What is it? Much as an interviewer constructs a schedule of specific questions for an important interview, the coach can help the client to draft specific questions for conversation with the other party in conflict.

Why is it important? This activity can reveal tendencies the client has to question in particular ways and can help the client craft more effective questions. It also allows the coach and the client to talk about how some questions may be received by the other party.

How do you do it? The coach asks the client to construct a set of questions to be used in a specific and anticipated conversation with the other person.

Approach #3: Help the client practice giving feedback.

What is it? The client learns to give effective feedback on a topic that is sensitive but important to the conflict.

Why is it important? This may help clients to clarify what is bothering them and how to share that in a confirming manner. It can also help clients recognize the kinds of feedback they would like to receive from the other.

How do you do it? The easiest way is for the client to develop the feedback and role-play delivering the feedback to the coach. The client can also give the feedback to someone in the situation who knows the context but is not involved in the conflict to determine whether this third person feels the feedback is appropriate and constructive.

Chapter Summary

Conflict professionals are very aware of the importance of communication in conflict. We can have the best intentions and the most exciting and promising ideas, but we are unable to move the conflict management forward if we are unable to communicate effectively. In too many instances, communication behaviors create unnecessary conflicts that can dominate our personal or professional relationships. In this chapter, we address three functions of communication in conflict: confrontation, confirmation, and comprehension. Coaches can help their clients communicate to announce the need for conflict management (confrontation), to show respect and protect identity (confirmation), and to understand and be understood about the information around the conflict (comprehension).

GENERAL PRINCIPLES FOR COMMUNICATION SKILLS WORK WITH CONFLICT COACHING CLIENTS

Principle #1: Develop awareness that skills are behavioral.

Principle #2: Help the client see the interrelation of the three major communication skill areas: confrontation, confirmation, and comprehension.

Principle #3: Emphasize the importance of context—cultural, organizational, and relational.

Principle #4: Emphasize assessment for client skill strengths and challenges.

Principle #5: Remember that skill development is usually not immediate.

Principle #6: Make the practice as close to reality as possible.

GENERAL APPROACHES FOR COMMUNICATION SKILLS WORK WITH CONFLICT COACHING CLIENTS

Approach #1: Have the client reflect on which skills are most important to the conflict.

Approach #2: Assess skill strengths and challenges by mapping a recent conflict interaction.

Approach #3: Use self-assessment instruments where applicable.

Approach #4: Use 360-degree feedback to assess skills in context.

Approach #5: Develop one or more specific skills through conversation, written exercises, reading, role play, and more.

Approach #6: Set benchmarks for skills development.

SPECIFIC APPROACHES FOR CONFRONTATION, CONFIRMATION, AND COMPREHENSION WORK WITH CONFLICT COACHING CLIENTS

Specific Approaches for Confrontation

Approach #1: Use instruments to measure argumentativeness and aggressiveness.

Approach #2: Weigh the decision to confront.

Approach #3: Design and practice client-initiated confrontation.

Approach #4: Design and practice responses to confrontation.

Specific Approaches for Confirmation

Approach #1: Help clients consider their confirmation behaviors.

Approach #2: Design and practice confirmation.

Approach #3: Help the client consider the other party's confirmation and disconfirmation behaviors.

Approach #4: Design and practice responses to disconfirmation.

Specific Approaches for Comprehension

Approach #1: Help the clients assess their listening behavior.

Approach #2: Design and practice questioning.

Approach #3: Help the client practice giving feedback.

9

Stage Four

The Conflict Styles Opportunity

Quality is never an accident. It represents the wise choice of many alternatives.

—William A. Foster

In the early 1990s, Jesse started as a staff writer with a national news magazine. She boldly stepped out of this position when she proposed to head up initial web development with a small team in the mid-1990s. Her proposal was accepted, and she became the Web site manager. In the early 2000s, she was promoted to director of Web services. In the mid 2000s, she once again broke new ground by instituting a user-powered structure for the organization's website. This meant that her team designed the site in such a way that users' own actions would directly and indirectly build and maintain the site. This fundamental change greatly increased the amount and quality of content available while decreasing oversight costs.

Since moving into the area of Web development, Jesse has regularly operated outside of the formal organizational reporting structure to get her work done. In part, this was a result of working directly under a vice president of information technology who had a hands-off approach. In part, this was the result of working on innovative and highly visible projects. In part, this was the result of her assertive yet disarming way of communicating with some of the most senior leaders in the organization.

While Jesse was completing the initial implementation of the user-powered Web site, Ted, a new vice president of information technology, was hired. Although Ted never directly said as much, Jesse assumed that she would be able to operate as she always had, especially because he basically left her alone for the first few years he was on board. More recently, however, a serious conflict has developed between the two.

In an unplanned, casual conversation between Jesse and the CEO of the organization, she proposed expanding the user-based Web site concept to include the organization's own members. Without incurring major upfront costs or heavily obligating individuals in terms of additional training, each of the organization's writers would have some kind of Web presence that could be collectively marketed as an additional feature of a premium/paid content plan. This new feature may even be linked to the intranet and enhance that information for those with proper access. The CEO loved the idea. Although she requested a full written proposal prior to making a final decision, she also shared that she would very likely back the plan.

Ted heard by way of a trusted colleague, the vice president of marketing, about the plan that Jesse had pitched to the CEO. Ted was furious. He strode into Jesse's office and yelled, "I have given you free rein to implement the user-based Web site. I have juggled our division's budget to make it happen. I am up to my eyeballs in the process of overhauling the organization's intranet as well as negotiating a major hardware purchase for the organization. Your thing, your only thing, is working with your team to maintain the user-based Web site. I manage the hardware, IT security, the intranet, and technological training as well as your area. I manage our relationship with senior leaders. Sure you can force your premium content idea, but get used to fighting for every nickel and dime you spend from this point forward. Get used to the idea of new paperwork. Get used to the idea of being assigned lots of special projects. The one thing you won't be doing is talking to the CEO again without me knowing. If you do, I will force you out of this place."

Although Jesse knew that her Web ideas really amounted to a minor new project that had a minimal net cost for the organization and that she could just as easily undermine Ted's role in the organization (and possibly even assume his position), she was too stunned to respond. As soon as Ted left her office, her impulse was to call the executive headhunter who has regularly reached out to her over the last two years.

A conflict style is a combination of individual motive and general behavioral tendency in conflict situations. The conflict style framework explored in this chapter represents a complete repertoire of individual styles from which a client can draw. Working with conflict styles can provide a client with a road map that he or she can use to make sense of conflict strategy and tactics. An exploration of conflict styles can assist a client in determining his or her style profile and the likely styles of others. A coach can work with a client to recognize strengths and weaknesses of a particular style as well as pinpoint opportunities to select styles more effectively or implement a given style more effectively. Conflict coaching on this topic can also assist in determining whether styles are complementary or incompatible.

Although styles are primarily understood as an individual concern, it is important to consider the styles of both parties in a conflict as well as the style themes of the systems in which the client and other relevant parties are embedded. The use of conflict styles with conflict coaching clients can be very powerful, as they allow the client to see large patterns of behavior or conflict themes for each party and the ongoing conflict conversation. After all, a client may have individual goals and an individual strategy and set of tactics for achieving those goals, but the appropriateness and effectiveness of the strategy and tactics are strongly connected with the goals, strategy, and tactics of the other party and the interactional dynamics between the parties. Therefore, a coach working with a client on the topic of conflict styles is responsible for making sure that the client does not focus on styles in a vacuum and that he or she invites the client to consider the implications of the other's use of styles.

Each of the conflict styles may be seen as a basic option for how to proceed in a conflict situation. They may be used in combination and/or changed within a conflict episode. Conflict styles are also sometimes useful for making sense of larger conflict patterns for self and other.

There are certainly limitations with a conflict styles approach. For instance, perceptions of self and other may be biased, there may be a gap between motivation and behavior, gender differences in stated conflict styles among younger men and women tend to disappear among more mature adults, the use of avoidance may be underreported, use of conflict styles tends to be much more contextual than general, and styles are perhaps more accurately seen as relational and process oriented rather than individual and fixed (Wilmot & Hocker, 2007).

Despite these limitations, many ADR practitioners and clients resonate with the concept of conflict styles and find it helpful in application. They can use conflict styles to gain awareness retrospectively and apply the framework to more deliberately make style choices, especially when they combine these with an awareness of the other's style preferences as well as contextual matters. With respect to the well-known limitations of conflict styles approaches, Knapp, Putnam, and Davis (1988) urge conflict management practitioners to consider organizational and relational factors. In the opening case, Jesse could probably benefit from a consideration of her style patterns leading up to the conflict with Ted as well as her style options moving forward. It makes sense to blend this conversation with a look at Ted's style patterns recognizing that this examination is speculative given that we know less about his actions and point of view.

Conflict styles can be a stepping stone to more specialized topics, especially when it comes to selecting and executing a style in a high stakes situation. While many individuals find the conflict styles typology intuitively appealing and relevant, clients may underappreciate the challenge of knowing when to adopt and switch styles as well as determining how to communicatively enact a particular style. One or more of the other Stage Four chapters might fit well in terms of assisting a client in getting clear about an important style choice or the enactment of one or more styles. For instance, the decision to avoid or engage the other party might be well addressed by considering the confrontation opportunity, while the decision to compete or collaborate could be aided with consideration of the negotiation opportunity.

A Conflict Styles Framework

Conflict styles constitute a widely studied area in the conflict communication literature. Numerous conflict style frameworks have been proposed ranging from the two style model (competition and cooperation) of Deutsch (1949) and Tjosvold (1990) to the eight style model (avoiding, compromising, dominating, emotional expression, integrating, obliging, passive aggression, and third-party help) of Ting-Toomey, Oetzel, and Yee-Jung (2002).

A five-style model is most common. These typically developed out of Blake and Mouton's (1964) two-dimensional model that plotted the five styles of forcing, confrontation, compromise, withdrawal, and smoothing, which varied on dimensions of an individual's concern for people and concern for production. Some of the style models used in organizational settings include those by Thomas and Kilmann (1974), Rahim (1983), Hall (1969), Putnam and Wilson (1982), and Ross and DeWine (1982). While these particular models can all trace their origins to Blake and Mouton (1964), they define conflict styles differently (Putnam, 1988; Womack, 1988). Some assume conflict styles are used consistently, and others assume more situational variability. Models also differ in their relationships to communication (Putnam, 1988; Womack, 1988). For instance, some are concerned with specific communication messages, and others focus on general communication intentions.

The remainder of this chapter draws primarily from the work of Thomas and Kilmann (Kilmann & Thomas, 1975; Thomas, 1976, Thomas & Kilmann, 1974) and the work of Rahim and Magner (Rahim, 1983; Rahim & Magner, 1995). Thomas and Kilmann's conflict styles model consists of accommodation, avoidance, collaboration, competition, and compromise. Rahim and Magner's model consists of avoiding, compromising, dominating, integrating, and obliging. These two five-style approaches will be folded together and elaborated below in terms of basic descriptions, circumstances under which each style is likely to be effective and ineffective, and style-related skills. The five main styles will be plotted along axes of concern for self and concern for other (see Figure 9.1). Subtypes of many of these styles will also be noted by drawing, in part, on the work of Folger, Poole, and Stutman (2005).

AVOIDING

Avoiding means acting in a way that does not address the conflict directly. According to Thomas and Kilmann, avoiding shows a low level of concern for self and other, but this can vary according to subtype. Different subtypes include protecting, withdrawing, and smoothing. Protecting consists of actively working to keep from confronting a conflict with the other party. It can be an assertive, even aggressive form of avoiding. Smoothing is a passive subtype in that it involves emphasizing commonalities and completely avoiding sensitive issues. Withdrawing means removing oneself from the situation to avoid further exposure to the conflict.

There are a number of situations in which avoiding can be a viable option. When an issue is of low importance, and particularly when both the issue and relationship are of low importance, it can make sense to stay disengaged. Avoidance can be effective for a relatively weak party dealing with a highly assertive or even aggressive opponent. More generally, it makes sense when attempts at collaboration, compromise, or competition seem unlikely to work and may even make the situation

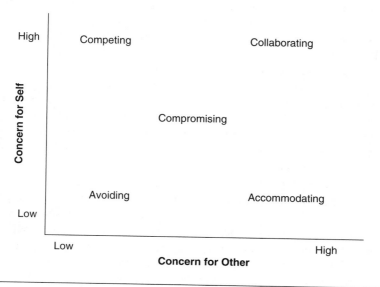

Figure 9.1   A Map of the Conflict Styles

worse. Avoidance can protect a party from embarrassment. It can also be used for buying time to carefully select or plan the execution of another conflict style.

There are a number of reasons why avoiding may not work or may be counterproductive. The motivation to avoid may not be clear to the other party, and there may be a negative misattribution. Avoiding a serious issue may make the conflict situation intensify, possibly causing damage to the relationship. When used excessively, avoidance signals a lack of commitment to the relationship.

It is interesting to note that both Jesse and Ted seemed to avoid one another. This pattern of avoiding was bound to create a problem at some point given that they are dealing with important and overlapping matters. It might be helpful for Jesse to recognize that her impulse to call the headhunter is an avoiding response. This option may or may not make sense for her, but such a decision is almost always best made with a careful consideration of other options as well.

ACCOMMODATING

Accommodating involves accepting the other party's position or interests at the expense of your own. Its use usually indicates low concern for self and a high concern for other. Putnam and Poole (1987) found that accommodating and avoiding are most common styles among workplace peers. Different subtypes include yielding and conceding. Yielding is very passive in that the person gives in to the other's position or interests without even stating his or her own position or interests. Conceding is a little more assertive, because parties give in to others only after stating their positions or interests.

Accommodating may work well when one party is giving in on an issue of modest self-importance, and yet the issue is very important to the other party. It can be seen as an act of generosity, which may set the stage for a better relationship as well as reciprocal accommodation from the other party. Like avoiding, accommodating can be effective for a weaker party who faces a strong competitor.

Accommodating may be counterproductive, because it can be seen as weak, especially when used repeatedly. In a related fashion, it may not garner respect from the other party. Particularly when one or more important and complex issues are involved, accommodating can shut down opportunities to more fully understand and respond to the conflict and, as well, cut short relationship building. Also, the person accommodating may experience increased stress, anger, and frustration if important goals related to self have been sacrificed too quickly or if the other party is not mutually accommodating with related matters.

A major reason for the conflict between Jesse and Ted may be that both parties presumed that Ted had accommodated Jesse over the past few years, but the boundaries of the accommodation were too fuzzy. Retrospectively, it is clear that a more assertive form of accommodating would have been helpful. If Ted was not explicit in his accommodation, Jesse could have used more direct language to probe the matter and possibly have stopped the current conflict from occuring.

COMPETING

Competing may be defined as working to have your position or interests take priority over the other party's positions or interests. This typically shows a high concern for self and a low concern for other. Putnam and Poole (1987) reported that superiors use competition, while subordinates use accommodation or collaboration. Different subtypes of competing include forcing and contending. Forcing refers to using power over others to get your way. It is often aggressive. Contending involves a degree of flexibility although not in terms of sacrificing key goals. It is usually seen as more assertive than aggressive.

Competing may be appropriate and effective when a party has the power and the will to advance a highly valued position. Therefore, it makes sense when the issue is very important and a position is truly inflexible. Competition can take less time than the other assertive styles, especially collaboration. It may be the appropriate choice if assertion is called for and yet compromise and collaboration are not suitable. Sometimes competing leads to good quality solutions.

Competing can require considerable resources and may diminish the user's power over time. It may not work well when attempting to generate multiple solutions, as is often necessary in complex conflict. Also, competing parties often have strained relationships. Leaders who rely on competing may find that those under their control become less willing to speak up and take initiative.

Competition involves crafting and advancing a position. It demands the use of formal authority or informal power. Building coalitions can be important to succeeding in competitive situations. Competition may rely on assertive communication, such as argumentation, or on aggressive means, such as threats and demands. It is important to note that someone can compete while behaving in a very nice way. These individuals are often the best at competition.

The most obvious form of competition in the case consists of Ted's aggressive remarks toward Jesse. He invokes his formal power and the use of a threat to provide backing to his position on the nature of Jesse's work. Notably, Ted's comments come after he learns of Jesse's conversation with the CEO. Jesse may have thought of this conversation as a collaborative act, but Ted probably viewed it as a highly aggressive form of competition.

COMPROMISING

Compromising involves each party giving a little and getting a little in terms of their positions or interests. This generally reflects moderate concern for both self and other. Compromising entails calculating and communicating offers and counteroffers. It incorporates flexibility.

Compromising is sometimes effective because it shows reasonableness. It typically takes less time than collaboration and does not require a high degree of trust. It can work well as a fallback strategy for parties that are locked in competition. It may be a first choice for parties that are evenly matched and dealing with an issue of moderate importance. And compromise is advantageous when the conflict concerns truly finite resources, making a "split the difference" approach most reasonable.

Compromising usually does not work for issues of principle that are not amenable to trade-offs. Also, it may not show enough concern for the relationship to ensure effective solution implementation. More broadly, its use may cut off the opportunities for collaborative problem solving.

Compromising, which relies on clear but not necessarily entirely open communication, seems to be absent prior to the conflict between Jesse and Ted. Although this is an assumption, Ted may have to use this style elsewhere in his work life as he juggles many different responsibilities. It may be a comfortable style for him to adopt in conflict. In any case, Jesse (and Ted) may come to see compromise as a viable option for working through their immediate issues. It does not rely on a high degree of trust and yet allows them to work through fairly complicated details.

COLLABORATING

Collaborating means that parties attempt to meet all or most of the interests underlying their respective positions. Collaborating indicates a high concern for both self and other; it can work very well for generating high-quality solutions for important issues and relationships. Collaboration both requires and advances a high level of trust between parties. This is helpful in terms of supporting the execution of selected solutions.

Collaborating may not be appropriate, because it tends to take considerable time to implement. Also, the trust and good will required for collaboration may not be present. For instance, collaboration may be manipulated by one or both parties but especially by the more powerful party. For example, a more powerful party may appear to be collaborating in order to gain information that can bolster a more competitive shift. Collaboration also relies on the use of considerable interpersonal skills that parties may not possess.

In order for collaboration to work, parties need the ability to identify underlying concerns for self and other. It is also vital to confront issues directly and yet not be threatening to the other party. Additional skills include designing and executing complex and often creative agreements.

It seems that Jesse might collaborate in her job as she works with a successful Web services team and as she maintains constructive relationships with senior leaders. However, she does not have a collaborative relationship with Ted. While collaboration is probably not a likely immediate next step in the conflict with Ted, it may be something that she wants to work.

Focusing on the *Me,* *You,* and *We* of Conflict Styles

Because most clients will focus more on their own conflict styles, it is extremely important that coaches encourage clients to consider the conflict styles of others. The trajectory of conflict is not determined by the style choice of a single individual but by the interaction of style choices by all conflicting parties. A failure to adequately consider the style of others can increase chances of conflict gridlock, because individuals may repeat styles rather than choosing styles in light of combined goals and an awareness of ongoing patterns of interaction.

A major question for a client is the extent to which a personal style choice should be reapplied or abandoned in the face of undesirable behavior by the other party. Wilmot and Hocker (2007) pointed out that conflict research supports the view that dysfunctional conflict with engagement by one or both parties is best addressed with an attempt at collaborative tactics (Pike & Sillars, 1985; Raush, Barry, Hertel, & Swain, 1974). This advice would apply to ineffective compete-compete patterns as well as ineffective compete-avoid patterns.

However, there are times when a client is faced with someone who will not adopt any style other than competing. In these cases, it is critical for the coach and client to consider whether attempts to collaborate are misguided or even dangerous. And similarly, even the most collaborative entrée may not convince an "avoider" to directly confront conflict and engage with the other party.

Conflict Styles and Culture

Ting-Toomey, Oetzel, and Yee-Jung (2002) and Ting-Toomey and Oetzel (2001) provided insight into intercultural communication and conflict styles by building on the five-style model described above. These researchers arranged the five existing styles in terms of self-face concern and other-face concern. They also proposed the three additional styles of emotional expression, passive aggression, and third-party help. Given this expanded conflict style framework, avoidance and accommodation are seen more positively as demonstrating other-face concern. Third-party help is important to note as it shows, in part, a positive face opportunity for the person asked to intervene. Passive aggression and emotional expression are included, because they are common in individualistic cultures.

Collectivistic cultures are likely to use avoidance, accommodation, compromising, collaboration, and third-party help. These show moderate to high other-face concern and low to moderate self-face concern, except for collaboration, which shows high concern for both other and self. Individualistic cultures are likely to use competition (in the sense of dominating), emotional expression, and passive aggression. These show moderate to low other-face concern and moderate to high self-face concern. While these general patterns are important to acknowledge, individual behaviors may show considerable variation. Finally, those who embrace independence and interdependence (for instance, some multiethnic individuals) have been shown to have more options within a conflict situation (Ting-Toomey, Oetzel, & Yee-Jung, 2002) and are more likely to use compromising and collaboration (Ting-Toomey, 2004).

General Principles for Conflict Styles Work With Conflict Coaching Clients

Principle #1: Encourage client identification and elaboration of his or her own conflict styles. This means that the coach might introduce the conflict styles framework as a touchstone but then shift, so that clients are active in applying the conflict styles material to their own situation. This will help to foster client empowerment in terms of learning and orienting to the framework. Because style terms may differ from conventional meanings of the same word, coaching on conflict styles can help clients become better acquainted with the terms' specialized usage and be more engaged in the coaching session.

Principle #2: Emphasize the importance of considering the other person's conflict styles and the interactional nature of conflict communication. Perhaps the biggest danger for conflict coaching clients working with conflict styles is that they feel overconfident with personal insights and fail to adequately appreciate and explore the conflict style preferences of others. Matters of style appropriateness and effectiveness cannot be adequately considered without attention being paid to the other party. Once style preferences of both self and other are recognized, another key step is determining discontinuities between individual preferences and actual communication behaviors.

Principle #3: Encourage the client to take individual cultural backgrounds and organizational culture into account. Exploration of culture helps to further contextualize conflict communication. A conflict style may have different meaning for individuals from different cultures or different organizational positions. Given organizational or cultural realities, style options may be strictly constrained by social rules, such as those concerning power and politeness in relation to social status. It can be very helpful for coaches to raise these issues with clients, as we rarely directly address them in day-to-day life, let alone in relation to conflict situations. Culture-related insights can affect style choices for the client based on self concerns or concerns regarding the other.

Principle #4: Refer to styles as behavioral choices. Describing the individual styles as behavioral choices emphasizes the communication aspect of styles and also supports client empowerment. Coaches should be especially careful to avoid turning the styles into identities. When styles are turned into nouns and referred to as personality types, they take on a rigidity that may unnecessarily constrain clients by limiting their experimentation with other styles.

Principle #5: Focus on developing conflict communication competency by developing breadth and depth of style enactment given situational factors. Two ways that a client can become more effective in terms of conflict styles are to competently draw from a larger repertoire of styles and to more adeptly implement individual styles.

Principle #6: Point out the limits of a conflict styles framework. Conflict styles tend to imply an individualistic and static orientation to conflict. Of course, conflict communication is endlessly fluid and may move in directions unrelated to the preferences of individual actors. Particularly in highly emergent situations, the application of a conflict styles framework may lose relevance.

Specific Approaches for Conflict Styles Work With Conflict Coaching Clients

Approach #1: Help orient clients by using a conflict style survey instrument.

What is it? This involves offering clients an instrument to determine their use of the conflict styles.

Why is it important? Clients find it helpful to get a perspective on their use of the conflict styles. Many times the instrument results intuitively resonate with the client's own experience. Even in cases where the instrument results do not ring true, completion of the instrument gives the client a useful reference point for further exploration.

How do you do it? The coach can create an instrument, possibly drawing from the research of Rahim and Magner (1995), as Wilmot and Hocker (2007) have done. Another option is purchasing a copy of the popular Thomas-Kilmann *Conflict Mode Instrument* from CPP, Inc. Regardless of the exact instrument type, it usually takes the client about 10 minutes to complete it. Scoring typically takes less than five minutes and can be done by either the client or coach. It usually works well to conversationally debrief the results by, in part, inviting clients to reflect on whether the results are consistent with their experience.

Approach #2: Debrief a specific conflict situation.

What is it? This involves getting the client to share the details of an important conflict so that the coach and client can apply a conflict styles framework to promote increased understanding and interaction effectiveness.

Why is it important? Many take the view that debriefing an important conflict situation may offer the most insightful and most practical learning when it comes to selecting and applying conflict styles.

How do you do it? Invite clients to complete a qualitative write-up or verbal debrief of one or more conflict situations (past, ongoing, or upcoming). They could recount a specific episode or a series of related interactions and then be invited to make sense of their actions as well as the actions of the other party given the five conflict styles. Some issues to consider are the appropriateness of the styles selected and the effectiveness of their execution given the context of the situation.

Approach #3: Introduce styles individually, and invite clients to give a lived example of each from across their field of experience.

What is it? This involves introducing the various conflict styles and encouraging the client to give an example of having used each of the styles.

Why is it important? A focus on dominant styles can obscure the fact that virtually everyone uses all of the styles. Clients are empowered to be more flexible in applying conflict styles after they reflect on how they have used each of the five styles in real situations.

How do you do it? Develop general awareness by introducing each style and inviting clients to consider when they used it in the past. If clients cannot recall a relevant time in the past, invite them to speculate as to a possible future application of the style.

Approach #4: Introduce styles individually, and invite clients to apply each style to the same specific situation.

What is it? This involves moving through each of the five styles and having clients apply them to one specific conflict situation. It may be the case that they actually used one or more particular styles in this situation. It is likely that they will need to speculate in some cases about what it would have meant or might mean to use certain styles.

Why is it important? Often, a specific conflict is foremost in the client's mind. This narrow and deep approach to applying conflict styles may be an effective and satisfying way to respond to such a focus.

How do you do it? Develop more specific awareness by introducing each style and inviting clients to consider when they used it or could have used it in a particular conflict situation or when they might use it in a particular future situation.

Approach #5: Invite clients to create a style map that takes into account self style preferences, apparent other style preferences, and organizational climate-related style issues.

What is it? This involves clients generally plotting the landscape of conflict styles within their immediate context.

Why is it important? One of the criticisms of a conflict styles approach is that it is too focused on the individual and does not encourage him or her to consider interactional or contextual matters. This activity incorporates these elements and provides clients with a sense of both freedom and constraint.

How do you do it? Although it is described as a map, it may be most simple and useful to use a table with the various conflict styles along one side and various actors (including the client, subordinates, peers, bosses, and the organization itself) along the other side. The client can use an X to indicate which styles are most relevant for which actors. Another option is for the client to record key points on the relevance of each style for each actor by writing in the appropriate boxes. Once the boxes are appropriately populated, the coach can facilitate a process where the client explores key intersections. For instance, what does it mean that there are similar or different styles across actors? An alternate version of this approach involves diagramming in flowchart style the connection between style choices, specific ways of enacting those choices, likely or possible reactions of others, and subsequent responses. Supply the client with an oversize piece of paper or simply use a letter or legal size piece of paper in landscape orientation. Moving from left to right, begin with the actual or anticipated first conversational turn labeled according to style and tactic. Follow this with at least two or three possible conversational options for the turn of the other party. Turn by turn, develop a number of options that are labeled in terms of styles and tactics and are marked as more or less appealing. Explore what can be communicated verbally and nonverbally in terms of the different styles to make it more likely that the conversation will travel along a productive and desirable path.

Chapter Summary

While a conflict styles approach has a number of limitations, it can be very beneficial for conflict coaching clients as they consider communication patterns, preferences, and the selection of specific messages. The Thomas-Kilmann five-style approach of avoidance, accommodation, competition, compromising, and collaboration is presented. An integrated focus on self, other, and the interaction is encouraged as a way to protect against limitations of a conflict styles framework. Cultural implications of conflict styles are considered.

GENERAL PRINCIPLES FOR CONFLICT STYLES WORK WITH CONFLICT COACHING CLIENTS

Principle #1: Encourage client identification and elaboration of his or her own conflict styles.

Principle #2: Emphasize the importance of considering the other person's conflict styles and the interactional nature of conflict communication.

Principle #3: Encourage the client to take individual cultural backgrounds and organizational culture into account.

Principle #4: Refer to styles as behavioral choices.

Principle #5: Focus on developing conflict communication competency by, in part, developing breadth and depth of style enactment given situational factors.

Principle #6: Point out the limits of a conflict styles framework.

SPECIFIC APPROACHES FOR CONFLICT STYLES WORK WITH CONFLICT COACHING CLIENTS

Approach #1: Help orient clients by using a conflict style survey instrument.

Approach #2: Debrief a specific conflict situation.

Approach #3: Introduce styles individually, and invite clients to give a lived example of each from across their field of experience.

Approach #4: Introduce styles individually, and invite clients to apply each style to the same specific situation.

Approach #5: Invite clients to create a style map that takes into account self style preferences, apparent other style preferences, and organizational climate-related style issues.

10

Stage Four

The Negotiation Opportunity

You can't shake hands with a clenched fist.

—Indira Gandhi

Jared is an associate with a premier international investment bank in New York City. He is in his early 30s and is entrusted with investments totaling hundreds of millions of dollars. While he has consistently earned a strong return for his organization and receives a very generous yearly bonus, his position with his company is on shaky ground.

Jared has struggled in his new role as manager of analysts focusing on government bonds in a major region of the world. Recently, two talented junior analysts left the firm and joined a competitor, because they were not satisfied working under Jared. More troubling for Jared, a respected associate on Jared's team has suggested that the associate was exploring other job possibilities. While Jared may achieve notable financial results, the organization will not tolerate poor leadership that results in employees leaving the company.

Jared is confident in his ability to understand the market, but he recognizes that he needs to learn to communicate with people more effectively. Jared initially thought he must exert dominance to maintain discipline in his group and ensure that they would be effective. This meant that he criticized individuals who made poor buying or selling decisions, often in front of the group. However, Jared tried to make life a little easier for his team by not burdening them with regular briefings on what was taking place higher up in the organization.

Unfortunately, things did not turn out the way that Jared planned. Individuals who bore the brunt of his attacks tended to recoil or leave, and there was poor morale in the team. Jared tried to secure organizational support for increasing the size of his team by replacing outgoing team members, bringing in new team members, and increasing the status and compensation of those already on board. It seemed like a no-brainer that his existing group would support this move, but when he brought in his immediate supervisor to have a round table discussion to explore this possibility, the supervisor was put off by the fact that existing group members were clearly noncommittal about taking on a new direction. As Jared spent more time on managerial responsibilities, he was beginning to find himself less in touch with his core area of expertise. He was realizing that he needed his team members to feed him more information at the same time as they needed him for overall direction.

Although Jared knows that he could get coached in a number of areas, the topic of negotiation is especially important for him. He urgently wants to talk frankly with Dan, the associate who may be looking at moving on, to get Dan to remain with the group. Dan is probably the most important member of Jared's team. Jared has mentioned to Dan that he wanted to have a one-to-one meeting about redefining work roles and forging a better working relationship. Dan expressed a willingness to go ahead with this meeting.

Jared wants to collaborate with Dan but is concerned that Dan might try to take advantage or see Jared's interest in collaboration as weakness. Jared has the ability to greatly influence Dan's fate in the organization, but Jared has no intention of threatening Dan. If Dan left the organization, Jared's own status might be called into question. If Jared left or was fired, he could probably get work in his area of expertise, but he would have serious trouble securing a managerial position and working his way up in investment banking.

Dan is unwilling to lay all of his cards on the table, because he has seen Jared burn others in the past. On the other hand, if Dan is going to remain in the organization, he needs more senior-level information, which Jared has access to, to do his own job effectively. If Jared left the organization, Dan might be a contender for Jared's position but not a guaranteed successor.

Jared and Dan have their team and individual reputations at stake within the company and probably beyond.

Negotiation is central to surviving and thriving in organizations. People routinely talk through and work out expectations in various forms, often without actually describing the process as negotiation. Leaders are regularly engaged in negotiation-based persuasion (Watkins, 2001). In the opening case, Jared is experiencing the challenge of leading in an environment where he depends on the noncoerced cooperation of Dan and others.

Negotiation is a process of joint decision making between parties who share common interests but also disagree about what should be done in a conflict. As joint decision making, the negotiation requires that the parties to the conflict come to some decision together about what will happen. If negotiation is not successful, the parties find themselves at an impasse and need to secure another approach to managing the conflict. Negotiation is important for working through day-to-day and longer-term issues with superiors, peers, subordinates, and clients. As such, negotiations may be informal or formal, public or private, short-term or long-term, dyadic or multiparty, etc. In this chapter the focus is on the relatively informal and private negotiations clients often have in the workplace as a means to resolve conflict.

Assumptions About Negotiation

Although negotiation is a complex process, there are standard assumptions about this critical conflict management process.

Negotiation can be learned. Watkins (1999) wrote that important negotiation skills (such as pattern recognition, mental simulation, process management, and reflection-in-action) can be taught. Watkins (1999) also described a study of the heads of diplomatic training programs that found that, while great negotiators may have inherent negotiation talents (at least some of which are generated through prior life experience), individuals can learn how to become better negotiators. It is therefore reasonable for Jared to assume that he can improve his ability to negotiate with Dan.

Successful negotiation demands preparation. Even someone with a sharp mind and strong communication skills is wise to prepare for negotiations of moderate to high importance. Top negotiators regularly put considerable time and effort into their preparation (Watkins, 1999). Fisher (1983) proposed that a preparation list for negotiation would include skill and knowledge along with a good relationship, a good alternative to negotiating, an elegant solution, legitimacy, and positive commitment. Conflict coaching can provide a good environment to prepare for a negotiation.

Context matters greatly. Context must be taken into account with respect to the study and practice of negotiation, as negotiation is an interpretive process involving the merging and emerging of stories over time (Cobb, 2000). Negotiation is shaped by and gives shape to numerous contextual issues. While it may be appropriate to focus on narrow tactics, it is important to not lose sight of broader issues. Of course, the opposite is also true. Even with big goals in mind, the details still certainly matter. While the remainder of the chapter concentrates on formal or semiformal negotiation opportunities, it is important to remind clients that their day-to-day communications lay the groundwork for the more pointed negotiations in which they will engage in the future. Part of what makes Jared's upcoming negotiation with Dan especially difficult is that he has not laid an effective groundwork in their day-to-day interactions.

The process is vital to the outcome. In negotiation, the journey and destination are thoroughly intertwined. An adversarial negotiation may produce an agreement, but there may not be sufficient goodwill or even basic coordination to ensure that the agreement is put into effect. If principled negotiation is judged to be important, and yet it is difficult for parties to accomplish, it may make sense to have a mediator to increase the likelihood that problem solving will be used (Pruitt, 1983b). More generally, slowing the process down and carefully thinking things through may decrease the likelihood of making regrettable decisions (Watkins, 2001). Even if Jared's conversation with Dan goes well, it is important that their subsequent interaction proceed smoothly. Negotiation is rarely, if ever, a single discrete event.

Collaboration is generally preferable, but there is no universally effective approach. Parties should be cautioned about using a bargaining approach rather than principled negotiation (Deutsch, 1973). If principled negotiation is a viable option, it can keep communication flowing and can foster trust that secures an executable solution and positive ongoing relationship. More pragmatically, negotiation is rarely win-lose or win-win (Watkins, 1999). This view is consistent with the recommendation that even in competitive bargaining situations, threats are counterproductive (Fisher, 1983) and relationships should be maintained (Allred, 2000; Fisher, 1983). While the details of Jared's case may preclude him from using a solely collaborative frame, collaborative potentials are present. Even where Jared finds himself taking more of a bargaining tack, he would be wise to resist using strongly competitive tactics like some of those found in his work team history.

Two Major Approaches to Negotiation

Most scholars identify a competitive and a collaborative orientation to negotiation, reflecting Pruitt's (1983b) dual concerns model and Walton and McKersie's (1965) distributive and integrative approaches to negotiation. Each approach requires engagement with the other party, recognition of the interlinking interests between the parties, and some level of self-assertion regarding interests. Each of these approaches emphasizes the need for relatively sophisticated communication with the other party in order to be successful.

For the remainder of the chapter, these styles will be referred to as bargaining negotiation and principled negotiation, respectively. Overviews of these two major approaches are often instructive to clients like Jared, as most negotiation situations include both competitive and cooperative elements.

THE BARGAINING APPROACH TO NEGOTIATION

Bargaining is concerned with maximizing self-interest through advocacy of certain outcomes or positions. It tends to be used in situations where parties have intersecting interests, some degree of power over one another; and lack the trust, skills, or will to engage in principled negotiation. Jared is probably more oriented to a bargaining approach but could benefit from a thorough and direct consideration of bargaining as well as principled negotiation. This section presents a basic bargaining model before focusing on the special topic of handling decision-making biases. It closes with some general advice for taking part in a bargaining negotiation.

A Bargaining Model. Because bargaining is based on the advocacy of positions, any bargaining model or bargaining strategy starts with some position-based components that will be referred to throughout this section of the chapter. Briefly, bargainers seek to achieve a *target point,* or an outcome that is the best they can anticipate in the situation. But they also recognize that they have a bottom line, or a *resistance point,* which is the worst outcome they'll accept and still make a deal. Both target points and *resistance points* should be based on a great deal of research and thought. And once identified, both should be hidden from the other negotiators, especially the resistance point.

Since bargaining is a process of movement back and forth with offers and counteroffers, a bargainer needs room to move or a *settlement range,* which is the difference between the bargainer's target and resistance points. And, hopefully, the bargainers' settlement ranges will overlap, so there is a *bargaining range* or an obvious set of possibilities that will meet both bargainers' needs.

Last, but definitely not least, is the concept of a *BATNA* or *Best Alternative to a Negotiated Agreement.* A BATNA is the alternative that a bargainer has to get his needs met outside of the bargaining relationship. If Dan doesn't want to negotiate in good faith with Jared, Jared needs to have other ways of getting his needs met regardless of Dan's actions. The more BATNAs and the better the BATNAs, the more power Jared has in this negotiation.

Lewicki, Saunders, and Minton (1999) outline a basic structure of distributive negotiation. It includes the development and communication of opening offers, the counteroffer and concession process, and the closing of agreement. Of course, the process may unfold differently, most notably in situations when negotiation is unsuccessful. For instance, opening offers that are perceived as too extreme may cause parties to walk away very near the start of negotiations, or the use of hardball tactics (such as blatant threats) deeper into negotiations may have the same effect.

Develop and communicate opening offers. Bargaining begins with the development and communication of opening offers. Each party establishes opening, target, and resistance points, although the other party's target and resistance points are likely never to be known with certainty. The opening offer is a negotiator's initial position. It is generally the case that an extreme first offer results in a better final outcome for the person making it; however, taking an extreme position is not without risks. The crafting of the opening offer usually takes into account that concessions will need to be made in order to reach an agreement that is equal to or better than the target point or optimal goal. The opening offer should also be developed with sensitivity to the likely resistance point of the other party. While Jared and Dan may find themselves negotiating in a fairly formal way, the murkiness of their individual and collective situations makes it difficult to determine opening, target, and resistance points. This suggests that if either individual were a conflict coaching client, he should be encouraged to systematically gather and evaluate information in advance of the negotiation. Presuming Jared is the client, he would be helped in knowing Dan's professional intentions in advance of their meeting so long as this information gathering did not threaten Dan. There are many other assumptions that Jared is making and might want to consider in advance of meeting Dan. It may end up being the case that Jared proposes that Dan take on a more appealing role on the team, the acceptance of which entails the protection of Jared's interests. Despite the uncertain nature of the situation, Jared should still be encouraged to determine his resistance point. It might very well relate to a certain level of net status enhancement for himself both inside and outside his organization.

Make counteroffers and concessions. The counteroffer and concession stage involves negotiators moving in the direction of a final agreement that maximizes individual gain and is as close as possible to the other's resistance point. Negotiators do not have to make concessions, although this is typically the case, in part because of their symbolic value. Some flexibility may also be positive, as it can result in learning important information about the other side, and as it simply keeps the negotiation going. This stage can involve numerous rounds of offers and counteroffers (amounting to new positions) that narrow and eventually bridge the initial divide. The counteroffer and concession stage is typically made complex by the fact that most negotiations involve multiple issues or issues that are difficult to quantify. One option for Jared and Dan is to talk through positions with one another regarding their roles and other workplace issues. From a bargaining standpoint, Jared should work to retain information he is receiving from Dan and be careful not to divulge too much about his own situation.

Close agreement. The final stage consists of the closing of agreement. This can be accomplished with the straightforward offer and acceptance of terms. Or it can be achieved with the use of more elaborate tactics such as (1) providing alternatives (a menu of final offers), (2) assuming the close (writing up a contract even though details are not yet finalized), (3) splitting the difference (emphasizing the fairness of a compromise to end the negotiation), (4) exploding offers (giving a tight deadline to force a decision), or (5) sweeteners (providing an incentive to close the deal). The challenge for Jared and Dan might be generating a strong agreement even though there is not a high degree of trust between them. This tension could be managed with the development of clear commitments tied to an immediate timeline which would allow the assessment of success and, in so doing, the building of trust.

Basic Rules for Bargaining. The negotiation literature provides many prescriptions for effective bargaining. The following recommendations draw primarily from the work of Bazerman and Neale (1992), Allred (2000), and Rubin (1983).

Determine BATNAs for each party. Minimally, a coach should work with a client to determine BATNAs prior to negotiation, as the strength of a party's BATNA is closely tied to strength within the negotiation. Jared's BATNA may be working to strengthen his team beyond Dan and seeking opportunities outside the organization. Dan's BATNA may be keeping his head down and doing his existing job well or pursuing one or more outside opportunities.

Determine resistance points for each party. Resistance points should be determined for both self and other. In more complex negotiations, such as those with multiple issues or those with issues that are more difficult to assign numerical value, a client may be encouraged to determine multiple resistance points for both self and other. Resistance points for Jared might include being forced to promise Dan full access to senior-level information or to promise him a more senior role without Dan's commitment to help Jared improve his team performance. Dan might have resistance points of promising increased open allegiance with Jared and promising not to seek Jared's position at any point in the future.

Determine the importance of each issue for each party. This information can be combined with the BATNA and resistance point information to determine the bargaining range and trade-offs. The coach can help the client realize which issues are critical and which are more amenable to compromise.

Develop trust. This can be accomplished by providing information, asking questions, and maintaining a friendly tone. Trust often breeds trust. Even a modest degree of trust can improve a negotiation by decreasing posturing and increasing commitment to agreements. Jared needs to increase trust with Dan for their negotiation to go anywhere.

Demonstrate flexibility. This can be achieved by presenting multiple offers simultaneously and presenting compromises to address the parties' different priorities. Although bargaining may remain competitive, it does not need to become entrenched. The communication of flexibility is important to creating and maintaining productive fluidity. A coach could support Jared in brainstorming different offers if he feels that bargaining is a viable approach.

Maintain a focus on common interests even if the negotiation remains positional. Even when competing, bargainers should be cognizant that they have common interests with each other; if they didn't, they wouldn't be negotiating—they'd be individually dealing with the problem. Even if he took a bargaining approach, Jared would likely find it helpful to consider what his and Dan's common interests are. Both seem to value a good working relationship, professional standing in their organization, professional standing throughout the larger investment banking community, and individual career growth opportunities. Jared is also concerned with having a well-functioning team. Dan may have an additional concern about having more day-to-day control of his work and work environment.

Decision-Making Biases. Bargainers often make poor agreements because they base their decisions on biased perspectives or bad information. Bazerman (1983) and Bazerman and Neale (1992) identified a number of decision-making biases. These can be channeled into a set of six suggestions for negotiators.

Actively work to moderate the conflict climate. Escalating the conflict irrationally can lead to needless polarization, thereby putting desirable agreements further out of reach. Parties should be careful not to publicly state or force others to publicly state adversarial positions, as parties will experience pressure to maintain these visible positions in order to save face. Finally, moderating a conflict means staying open to cutting losses that are connected to courses of action that are not realistically viable despite past investments. Given the tense conflict climate between Jared and Dan, indeed among their entire team, Jared may have to be very deliberate about moderating the climate simply to be successful in initiating his upcoming conversation with Dan.

Focus on the right information. Negotiators tend to underestimate the value of objective information and anchor onto (and get stuck on) the information at hand. Too often they focus on available information rather than good quality information. It is important to consciously assess whether existing information is accurate and relevant. It may be the case that additional or alternative information is needed to determine whether it even makes sense to negotiate. Jared really knows very little about Dan. He should be careful working with unsubstantiated assumptions such as that Dan may be looking for positions elsewhere.

Understand and work with the other's point of view. Understanding the other's point of view does not mean that you have to agree with that point of view. However, taking the other's perspective will allow you to speak more effectively when representing your own interests. Jared will have difficulty working with his own interests, let alone Dan's, unless he is better able to understand Dan's perspective.

Look for opportunities to expand the pie or at least swap desirable pieces. A gain by one party does not require a loss by the other party even in a competitive bargaining situation. Too often bargainers get trapped in the assumption of the fixed pie—the assumption that everything is zero-sum and they can't move on any issue without "losing." Parties may be able to combine cooperative and competitive elements by, for instance, identifying trade-offs. In general, parties do not appreciate the way in which cooperation and competition are intertwined. The case of Jared and Dan is filled with interconnections.

Check your confidence level. Negotiators are often overconfident about the accuracy of their judgments. This can take the form of incorrectly assuming that an entrenched position will pay off or seeking to win even in cases when winning represents an objective loss. While Jared may have been overconfident in the past, it seems that his recent experiences have sobered him. Nonetheless, he may want to be vigilant about keeping his confidence in check, especially if he experiences some success and decides to become competitive.

Recommendations for Effective Bargaining Communication. Knowing what to do conceptually and having a high motivation to perform well are not enough to succeed as a negotiator. Effective communication is also vital.

The following represent some important communication recommendations for client-negotiators who are likely to bargain. They are derived in part from Lewicki, Saunders, and Minton (1999).

1. *Do not communicate your BATNA and/or resistance point.* A client who shares his or her BATNA and/or resistance point with the other party has given up his or her most powerful pieces of information.

2. *Deliberately manage the visibility of communication to third parties.* Negotiating in public is generally a bad idea because parties end up posturing for outside audiences and the negotiation process becomes rigid. This does not mean, however, that involving others is always negative. When holding a completely committed position on an issue and facing intense pressure within negotiation, making a public commitment can bolster one's own sense of strength and communicate the seriousness of the stance to the other party.

3. *Communicate an initial offer that is more in your favor than your target point.* Although it may seem counterintuitive to some negotiators, other parties will typically be more pleased when faced with a negotiator who starts out relatively high and comes down in a series of concessions rather than a negotiator who starts lower and does not offer concessions. In short, concessions are expected and, therefore, the formulation of early offers must allow for them later. Further, extreme initial offers mask the resistance point and target point. However, initial offers should not be so extreme as to be laughable.

4. *Learn multiple ways to communicate and respond to concessions.* Concessions can be made on individual issues, or they can be grouped. Grouping concessions on both sides is known as *logrolling.* A pattern of smaller concessions across time can signal that a party is nearing his or her final offer or resistance point. In terms of responding to concessions, the receiving party may feel pressure to provide a reciprocal concession but should think carefully about the value of the other party's concession, the value of concession options considered as possible responses, and larger metrics such as resistance points and BATNAs.

5. *Send appropriate and effective nonverbal messages.* Negotiation can be so mentally and emotionally consuming that parties lose sight of matters such as verbal-nonverbal fidelity and the strategic use of nonverbal communication by self and other.

6. *Frame and reframe effectively.* Framing and reframing involve setting and changing the perspective on a situation. Negatively framed situations (focusing on losses) are more likely to have parties taking risky all-or-nothing positions rather than finding middle ground. A negotiator can most likely influence the other by talking about the other's gains. If Jared pursued this approach, he could frame the most mutually attractive options in terms of possible gains for Dan.

7. *Ask the right kind of questions.* Effective questions tend to provide substantive clarification for self and other and to enhance the relationship between the negotiators. Ineffective questions tend to coerce the other party into accepting the questioner's position, are obvious as such, and therefore are damaging to the relationship between the negotiators.

8. *Be an active listener.* Active listening is a comprehensive form of listening that includes mentally grasping the content of the speaker, demonstrating acknowledgment with the use of nonverbal and minimal verbal feedback, and having the capacity to paraphrase the speaker's words, including to accurately reflect the speaker's emotion.

9. *Be strategic in communicating your final offer.* Before a client flags an offer as a final offer, he or she should be aware of the commitment this entails. He or she should be sure that finality is desired. A final offer can sometimes be viewed as a threat by the other party.

PRINCIPLED NEGOTIATION

Principled negotiation is a collaborative negotiation process concerned with identifying a solution or set of solutions that meet the interests of all parties. It emphasizes trust so that open communication can take place. It concentrates attention on shifting from positions to interests in an effort to eventually structure collaborative solutions. It tends to be used in situations where parties have a positive relationship with one another and high accountability to constituents (Ben Yoav & Pruitt, 1984). Interestingly, moderately challenging constraints actually foster the pursuit of collaborative solutions (Pruitt, 1983a; Bazerman, Magliozzi, & Neale, 1985).

A Principled Negotiation Model. As most conflict practitioners know, the principled negotiation model was developed by the Harvard Program on Negotiation scholars. The following is a summary of their model adapted from Fisher, Ury, and Patton's book, *Getting to Yes* (1991).

Identify issues. While traditional negotiation often begins with parties stating their opening positions, principled negotiation starts with attention to achieving clarity around the issues that need to be explored. Ideally, parties will refrain from introducing positions during this process as these can generate defensiveness and obscure a complete listing of the issues. As mentioned above, Jared and Dan may face the issues of their respective roles, their relationship, and the future of their work group.

Explore interests. Interests are the basic concerns or desires that lie beneath issues. Preferably, interests are fully developed without emphasis on positions and prior to moving into talk of other possible solutions.

Jared might want to work with a coach not only to develop his own interests but also to develop some hunches about Dan's interests prior to talking with him.

Generate options. A focus on the development of interests sets the stage for generating multiple possible solutions. A possible solution responds to one or more interests. Options should address the interests of both parties. An exhaustive list of solutions should be generated prior to evaluating and selecting options. A coach working with Jared would probably encourage him to focus his attention on fleshing out likely interests in advance of his conversation with Dan. Nonetheless, it might also be beneficial to generate multiple options to emphasize the considerable opportunities that are available to the parties.

Develop criteria. Objective criteria offer a way to systematically evaluate the various solutions that have been generated. Objective criteria may be especially important for working through competitive aspects of largely collaborative negotiations. Criteria often include time, money, and human resource parameters that solutions should respect. Once again, Jared would not want to get too far ahead of the actual negotiation with Dan, but exploration of criteria within conflict coaching might increase his comfort and ability with this important step. Given the uneasy relationship history of Jared and Dan, it may make sense for them to structure time-based performance expectations along with escalating demonstrable commitments, so that compliance with any agreement can be measured relatively quickly and at regular intervals in the coming weeks and months.

Select outcomes. In bargaining, parties start with positions. In principled negotiation, the selection of solutions is ideally held off until the end of a conversation that has deliberately shifted from issues to interests to options to criteria and that culminates in actionable outcomes. It is impossible to define the outcomes that Jared and Dan might ultimately come up with as a result of principled negotiation. However, if they fully engaged their approach, their solutions might very well be uniquely tailored to their individual perspectives and both singular and shared circumstances.

Basic Rules For Principled Negotiation. Just as there are general rules or guidelines for bargaining, there are rules for collaborative negotiation. The following pointers are derived from Fisher, Ury, and Patton (1991).

Seek common ground. A concentration on interests rather than positions helps highlight the overlapping concerns that unite the parties. Emphasis on these shared concerns can prompt the parties to work through their differences. At the very least, it seems that Jared and Dan both value their careers.

Recognize that a position may be a premature solution. Positions should not be dismissed entirely; however, they should be set aside until issues and interests have been fully developed, and then they should be reframed as potential options. There is much that Jared could learn from an initial conversation with Dan that could transform the set of viable solutions.

Note that the optimal solution may be a combination of solutions. Given the proliferation of interests and the complexity of most negotiation contexts, it may make sense to implement more than one solution at a time. In fact, it is common in principled negotiation to decide on a package of solutions that, taken together, provide maximum benefit. The complex circumstances that Jared and Dan face almost lend themselves to a unique and intricate set of solutions so long as sufficient trust is established to develop and implement options.

Make the shift from positions to interests. Shifting from positions to interests is arguably foremost in developing principled negotiation ability, especially for someone who is effective at bargaining. Focusing on interests rather than positions assumes that the negotiator has a solid grasp of the "interest" concept prior to negotiating. It is also helpful to discourage the discussion or presentation of positions. But, if a position is presented by the other, resist immediately countering the position. The other party may deliberately or accidentally employ positional language. And remember to solicit interests—use questions to access interests. An open-ended question delivered with sincerity can be a powerful means of determining important interests. For instance, "What is it about X that is so important to you?" "X" can refer to an issue or a previously stated position.

Recommendations for Effective Communication in Principled Negotiation. As with bargaining, knowing what to do and wanting to do it must be accompanied by the ability to carry it out communicatively. The following are some suggestions for effective communication in principled negotiation:

1. *Develop an opening statement that seeks to establish the negotiation in integrative terms.* Principled negotiation remains an innovative concept in most workplaces. Even when parties are aware of its potential, it may still be challenging to introduce it in actual practice, because it often means changing the pattern of conflict communication in a fundamental way.

   ※ It may be useful to lead with the following, "I do not want to speak for you, but it seems to me that we have been dealing with a challenging conflict. Do you agree? If it is alright with you, I would appreciate hearing your point of view regarding key issues and the positive hopes and expectations that underlie those key issues. I would also appreciate sharing my own point of view. I am hopeful that we can talk about the matter in a future-focused manner that will stay away from blame and concentrate on maximizing what is important for both of us."

2. *Create a situation-specific argument for collaboration.* Particularly if the conflict between the parties is longstanding or intense, or if there is not an integrative precedent, the proposal for principled negotiation may be directly or indirectly challenged. If this occurs, it is helpful to argue for the merit of the approach by addressing joint and/or individual interests.

   ※ The following basic framework may be used by the client to help make the case for principled negotiation when faced with resistance: "You are hesitant about handling this situation in a different manner. That is understandable given all that has taken place in the past. Nonetheless, I think it makes sense now to work together to more effectively meet your needs for X, my needs for Y, and our combined needs for Z."

3. *Demonstrate your understanding of the other's point of view, and note that doing so does not necessarily mean that you agree with it.* Acknowledgment should be separated from agreement. Jared can acknowledge that he hears and understands Dan's interests and concerns without agreeing that these interests and concerns are the only important ones. Through acknowledgment, Jared can learn about what is going on for Dan and also demonstrate that he respects Dan.

4. *Develop tactics for managing defensiveness and impasse along the way.* If the client has interacted with the other party for some time prior to attempting principled negotiation, he or she may be in a strong position to know which issues or interests might be particularly delicate.

   ※ Regardless of the parties' interaction history, defensiveness and impasse within negotiation may be addressed with questions such as the following: "It seems that you have pulled back from our conversation. Is that an accurate assumption? If so, what would it take to make you want to reengage at the level we were at earlier?"

   ※ Another tactic is to acknowledge the difficulty of a particular issue and positively energize the conversation by deliberately confronting it or deferring it: "This is obviously an important and sensitive matter for us to explore. One option is to go into it in more detail now. Another option is to put it aside for the moment and then come back to it. Which do you prefer?"

5. *Generate questions and follow-up language to invite clarification of the other's interests.* Interests—or the parties' needs, wants, concerns, hopes, and expectations, etc.—are the essence of well-crafted solutions within principled negotiation. Questions and follow-up language can include the following:

   ※ Question: "When it comes to issue X, what is most important to you?"

   ※ Response of the other party: "I want Y. . . ."

※ Paraphrase to confirm understanding: "What matters to you is Y. . . ."
※ Confirmatory response of the other party: "Yes."
※ Probe for interest saturation: "Are there needs or wants that are important to you regarding this issue?"

6. *Practice wording self-related interests.* Be clear in terms of giving voice to what is personally important and yet also attempt to communicate it respectfully.
   ※ "When it comes to issue X, what is most important to me is. . . ."
   ※ "My other hopes, concerns, and priorities on this issue include. . . ."

7. *Practice managing the generation of options.* Option generation can be introduced with a summary of self, other, and joint interests. It is also useful to introduce it by emphasizing how parties should refrain from being critical at this point.
   ※ "Given that you need and want A, B, and C, and I need and want D, E, and F, and given that we both need and want G, H, and I, what possibilities come to mind for addressing any one or combination of these interests?"
   ※ "As we brainstorm possible solutions, I would like to recommend that we resist discussing what might be most appealing or achievable, etc. We can get to that, but it makes sense to hold off until we have had a chance to fully develop different options. For creative ideas to flow best, it can help to hold off any type of criticism and even excitement about one particular idea until we feel that all possible solutions are on the table."

8. *Practice handling solution selection and implementation yet remain open to different possibilities.* This stage usually involves developing criteria for effective solutions, applying the criteria to each of the possible solutions, selecting one or more solutions, and clarifying what it means to successfully implement the solutions. Client communication may involve the following:
   ※ Recognition of the completion of brainstorming: "We have developed a considerable list of possible solutions given our interests; are there any other possible solutions? If not, should we move on to consider what solutions will work best?"
   ※ Identification of criteria: "Before we take a critical view of any particular solution that we came up with, let's consider the essential and desirable features of a good solution."
   ※ Implementation of select solutions: "What can be done to ensure the success of the solutions to which we have committed?"

THE NEED FOR A COMPOSITE APPROACH TO NEGOTIATION

Negotiation is rarely win-lose or win-win (Watkins, 1999). It is probably never purely competitive or cooperative. For example, Lax and Sebenius (1986) made the point that even an expanded pie is still one that must be divided. Bargaining and principled negotiation regularly merge together in other ways as well. Good negotiation agreements often result from problem solving that evolved out of competitive beginnings (Morley & Stephenson, 1977). Bazerman, Magliozzi, and Neale (1985) demonstrated that integrative bargaining behavior is learned as negotiators gain experience in a free market. The connection between these different approaches was also seen in Nelson and Wheeler's (2004) finding that those who self-described as strong value claimers also self-described as good value creators.

The attractiveness of shifting between primary approaches indicates additional need for clarifying a composite approach to negotiation. Tjosvold (1985) explained how social context affects how superiors use their power to interact with subordinates. In cooperative contexts, superiors are likely to use their power to facilitate subordinate performance, but this is not likely to occur in competitive contexts. This means that subordinates (and organizations committed to continuous learning) would be aided by prescriptions that allow them to transform contexts from competitive to cooperative.

Recommendations for Using a Composite Approach to Negotiation. The composite approach can be outlined in terms of the following general recommendations. This list represents a good basic strategy for Jared, although it might have to be carried out over days, weeks, or even months rather than over the span of one conversation. If all goes well between the parties, individual knowledge and skill and trust between the parties may develop.

1. Master principled negotiation as well as traditional bargaining.

2. Try to begin by framing the negotiation in collaborative terms.

3. Attempt to reassert collaborative terms if the other person tries to bargain.

4. If the other person continues to bargain, then you should bargain as well.

5. Remain open to taking a collaborative track.

6. Trust is often an indicator of which approach you should take. Collaboration's "cards on the table" style demands a high degree of trust.

Of course, there are plenty of occasions where taking a collaborative approach makes little sense. These include times when one or both parties perceive the issues are of low importance, the relationship is of low importance, there is a low degree of pressure for a solution, or there is a low degree of trust. A negotiator who leads with the collaborative approach in these situations may be weakened as he or she reveals content information that is valuable to the other party or may simply appear weak or incompetent in the eyes of the other party.

Even a negotiator with a strong grasp of the composite approach can find it challenging to respond to someone with an entrenched position or someone who engages in personal attacks or other forms of disturbing behavior. Spangle and Isenhart (2003) compiled various recommendations for these situations. The best approach is to take action by addressing unmet needs before such behaviors become extreme. Other recommended actions include managing your emotions, communicating understanding for the other's interests, calmly but clearly sharing your own interests, and continuing to listen.

Most important, realize that negotiation is not always a good option in a conflict. If you believe the other party is excessively aggressive or that you will endanger yourself in some way by agreeing to negotiate—don't negotiate.

Culture and Negotiation

Responsible efforts to understand culture will almost surely increase the effectiveness of a negotiation. Adair et al. (2004) found that understanding a negotiator's cultural characteristics and practices can be beneficial for planning information exchange and making sense of unusual power strategies. This awareness is necessary, in part, to determine the applicability of the ideas expressed in this chapter. The composite model may or may not be useful in different cultural settings. Based on extensive international cross-cultural negotiation experience, Senger (2002) reported that interest-based negotiation is sometimes applicable, sometimes adaptable, and sometimes not applicable in different cultural settings. Regarding teaching negotiation and culture, Avruch (2000) emphasized the following: (1) Culture should be viewed as context and not a variable, (2) everyone has culture (not just those in traditionally underrepresented groups), (3) it makes sense to learn to negotiate before engaging the challenges of culture, and (4) it is not effective for people to attempt to play the role of those from other cultures.

Spangle and Isenhart (2003) provide a thorough exploration of the ways in which negotiation norms may differ across cultures, including respect for personal space, use of time, level of formality, use of contracts, importance of relationship, use of negotiation styles, displays of emotion, issues of status and hierarchy, and gender issues. These authors organize cultural negotiation preferences in terms of the low-context versus high-context distinction (Hall, 1976; Jandt & Pederson, 1994), and the individualistic versus collectivistic distinction (Hofstede, 1980).

Low-context cultures tend to be more individualistic and are associated with Western countries such as the United States and Canada. People from these cultures typically seek resolution in private, do not incorporate ritual, are comfortable with court settlements, prefer face-to-face negotiation, and rely on the use of individuals involved directly in the negotiation to reach settlement. High-context cultures tend to be more collectivistic and are associated with Eastern countries such as China and Japan. People from these cultures often use methods decided upon by the group, will make conflict public as a means to resolution, employ preventive measures, include ritual, use intermediaries, and view use of the courts as a sign of failure.

Individualistic cultures are focused on autonomy, independence, and self-interest, while collectivistic cultures place considerable concern on group norms, interconnectedness, and in-group interests. Spangle and Isenhart (2003) note the following priorities associated with these cultural orientations.

While conflict coaches may find themselves addressing the cultural influence of nationality in their work with clients, they will certainly need to address organizational and professional cultures when working with clients in workplace conflicts.

Gender as culture is an important consideration when addressing negotiation. Babcock and Laschever (2003) cite numerous studies that demonstrate women's lower tendency to negotiate. These authors also show how women miss out on monetary gains and other benefits as a result of this pattern. Part of the problem relates to cultural norms that view negotiation by men as favorable and negotiation by women as unfavorable. Part of the problem also relates to women not recognizing the

Table 10.1   Priorities of Cultural Orientations

Individualistic Cultures	Collectivistic Cultures
Solution oriented	Relationship oriented
Prefer independent decisions	Prefer group decisions
Approach issues directly	Avoid conflict
Value autonomy	Desire social approval
Emphasize cause and effect	Appeal to authority
Greater interest in personal needs	Greater interest in group needs

SOURCE: Spangle, M. L., & Isenhart, M. W. (2003). *Negotiation: Communication for Diverse Settings.* Thousand Oaks, CA: Sage.

applicability of negotiation. Babcock and Laschever's (2003) own research indicated that men saw negotiation as a more significant and more frequently encountered part of their professional and personal lives. The success that these authors document in training women to identify and overcome real and imagined barriers to negotiation seems to translate well to the arena of conflict coaching. Conflict coaches should routinely check with female clients regarding their tendency to negotiate and their ability to get what they want.

Here are some culture-related questions for clients and coaches to consider:

- *What cultures play a role in this negotiation?*
- *How are the cultural contexts of the various parties to the negotiation similar and different?*
- *How does culture affect communication choices, especially optimal choices, for self and other?*
- *How might culture impact the (mis)interpretation of previous or future communications?*

General Principles for Negotiation Work With Conflict Coaching Clients

Principle #1: Increase awareness regarding when the client negotiates formally or informally. Most professionals probably underestimate the frequency of their negotiation activities. Overlooking negotiation opportunities may mean clients fail to represent important interests or achieve important goals. Of course, awareness of negotiation activities does not have to result in the enactment of negotiation behavior by the client.

Principle #2: Work with the client to determine his or her (pre–conflict coaching) approach to negotiation as well as existing strengths associated with this approach. Many individuals will not have a deliberate approach to negotiation. Even in cases where they have studied or been trained in negotiation, clients may not have a strategic approach or may not have considered that approach for some time. Coaches are encouraged to work with clients to clarify existing negotiation behaviors to determine the client's existing strengths.

Principle #3: Foster the client's appreciation for and ability to apply the composite approach while helping the client identify which general approach to negotiation (bargaining or principled negotiation) is best given the conflict at hand. Clients should be introduced to the fact that the composite approach to negotiation is often necessary. Of course, this issue should not be forced if, for whatever reason, the client is ideologically opposed to this framework. Although an awareness of the composite approach is important, the situation for which the client is being coached may clearly lend itself more to either bargaining or principled negotiation.

Principle #4: Support the client in developing the best alternatives to a negotiated agreement (BATNAs) and resistance points for self and other. It is extremely important for the client to clarify his or her BATNAs before negotiating, as this speaks directly to the person's need to negotiate as well as his or her power within the negotiation. Identification of a strong BATNA may even suggest that negotiation is not necessary. If the client pursues negotiation, he or she should also be encouraged to use his or her BATNA to determine a resistance point. It is also helpful for the client to consider the possible BATNAs and resistance points of the other party as a means of better understanding the other party's power and alternatives to negotiating with the client.

Principle #5: Foster the client's awareness of likely positions or interests, as well as possible solutions, prior to negotiation. This kind of preparation will no doubt increase the quality of the negotiation process and outcomes. Clients should be strongly encouraged to do this for both self and other.

Principle #6: Invite the client to develop specific communication behaviors for advancing his or her positions and interests given the positions and interests as well as likely communication behaviors used by the other party. This prepares the client not only for the "what" of negotiation but also the "how." As part of this process, the client should work to consider the most effective way that he or she can impact the other party's communication in view of the composite approach.

Principle #7: Encourage the client to consider the implications of culture in negotiation. As noted in the chapter, different cultural lenses may mean that specific strategies and tactics are differently understood in terms of appropriateness and effectiveness. While national-level culture may or may not be a feature, other kinds of culture, such as organizational and professional culture, almost always play a role.

Specific Approaches for Negotiation Work With Conflict Coaching Clients

Approach #1: Invite broad consideration of when the client negotiates.

What is it? This is an across-the-board brainstorm of all of the situations in which a client informally or formally negotiates.

Why is it important? Even if a client uses coaching to prepare for a specific, formal negotiation, it may still be helpful to determine how interactions not labeled as negotiation nonetheless play an important role in framing key issues.

How do you do it? The coach can provide the client with a sheet of paper divided in half. One half is for brainstorming informal negotiation situations, and the second is for brainstorming formal negotiation situations. The client should be encouraged to populate each half with written responses. After the client is finished doing so, the client can be invited to verbally share his or her responses. The coach can ask open-ended questions to further expand the categories or prompt consideration of the relationship between the two halves. Clients may find it helpful to draw lines indicating relationships between the different items that they brainstormed. Note that this activity may be focused on negotiation with one particular party or multiple parties throughout the client's professional life.

Approach #2: Perform a negotiation audit.

What is it? This involves moving beyond the question of *when* the client negotiated in the past to consider *how* the client negotiated in the past.

Why is it important? The client may or may not be able to label and describe the main elements of his or her overall approach to negotiation. Whether or not this is the case, it remains useful for many clients to fairly closely recount one, two, or even three past negotiation situations in order to increase awareness of tactics that may or may not fit with an overall approach. Awareness regarding one's approach to negotiation is arguably foundational to developing increased effectiveness in the future.

How do you do it? Encourage the client to identify two or more moderately important negotiations from the past that reflect the client's range of negotiation strategies and tactics. For each negotiation, request that the client recount, in writing if possible, the chronology of the negotiation. Encourage the client to identify patterns within and across negotiations. Invite the client to identify negotiation strengths and opportunities for growth. Have the client consider the extent to which his or her past negotiation behavior reflected a composite approach. After the client has had a chance to respond to each of these subtopics, the coach can share his or her point of view.

Approach #3: Use a decision tree to support effective use of the composite approach.

What is it? A decision tree is an expanding diagram that adds new branches to represent options at a new choice point. Each new branch or option may be elaborated into a series of related branches or options. Branches may converge or remain separate. This activity involves inviting the client to select a past, current, or prospective negotiation situation and consider the relevancy of both collaborative and bargaining orientations based on key choices.

Why is it important? The important and, in many respects, recurring decision in applying the composite approach to negotiation is determining whether to work from a collaborative or bargaining orientation.

How do you do it? One way to do this is to chronologically map interaction in order to determine key collaboration and bargaining intersections and consider whether there are times when the negotiation could be tipped in a certain direction (e.g., collaboration because of its typically larger gains for both parties). The client and coach can chart this exercise on a piece of regular note paper but a larger surface tends to work better (e.g., a white board, large piece of flipchart paper, or even a computer word processing environment that allows for vertical and horizontal scrolling). Start at the left side and work toward the right (representing the passage of time). Add branches to represent specific options at important negotiation choice points. At first, focus on simply documenting chains of possible individual decisions. Once this is reasonably complete, take a wider focus, and consider how various choices are more or less important for taking a collaborative or bargaining orientation. Indicate key choices by circling them or otherwise noting their importance.

Approach #4: Develop the positions and/or interests of both parties.

What is it? This activity involves exploring the positions and interests of both the client and the other party.

Why is it important? Taking time to understand positions and interests prior to actually engaging in negotiation with the other party can enhance the effectiveness of the process and outcomes. In hard bargaining situations, it can be particularly easy to forget to fully consider the other person's situation, especially from the other's perspective. However, even collaborative opportunities can suffer from a lack of prior exploration of interests related to both self and other.

How do you do it? If the client is taking a nonadversarial stance on the negotiation, it may be effective to ask him or her to simply elaborate the underlying needs and wants of both parties. If the client is speaking in positional terms, it may be easiest to begin with the client's own point of view and to ask the following kinds of questions to get at underlying interests: (1) How would you state your position in the negotiation? (2) What is it about your position that is so important to you? (3) What other needs and wants are significant to you in this negotiation? After developing the client's interests, focus can then shift to the other party. The client can be asked the following: (1) How would the other party state his or her position in the negotiation? (2) What is it about this person's position that is so important to him or her? (3) What other needs and wants are significant to this person in this negotiation? Move on to consider common ground and areas of obvious difference. After positions and interests have been elaborated, invite the client to comment on the appeal of the two different negotiation subtypes. Unless the use of a particular subtype is clear-cut, the client and coach may choose to prepare for each eventuality. Regardless of the likely negotiation subtype, it may also be very helpful for the client to consider possible criteria for selecting a good solution.

Approach #5: Identify the BATNAs and resistance points for both self and other.

What is it? A BATNA is the *Best Alternative to a Negotiated Agreement* and, as we have said, a resistance point is the lowest possible outcome you will accept and still settle with the other. In this approach, the coach helps the client identify BATNAs and resistance points for the client and the other in conflict.

Why is it important? As we have indicated, no negotiator should ever sit down to the negotiating table without first identifying at least one (and hopefully many more) BATNA in case the other party does not want to negotiate in good faith. A BATNA is the most palpable source of power in negotiation, whether the negotiation is being approached from a collaborative, competitive, or mixed orientation. If a client plans to bargain, it is absolutely essential that the client give serious attention to the justification for his or her resistance point, because the resistance point is the foundation of the bargaining strategy. If the resistance point is set poorly, the entire bargaining approach is likely to fail.

How do you do it? The coach should start with the discussion of the BATNA and have clients identify specific needs and desires that they are trying to have met through negotiation. For each need or desire, the client should be encouraged to identify at least one alternative outside the negotiation relationship where the client can get that need fulfilled. The coach should encourage the client to identify as many BATNAs as reasonably possible and reflect on each in terms of how easy it would be to achieve that BATNA, how much the other party can or cannot influence the BATNA, and the extent to which the BATNA may provide additional advantages above a negotiated agreement. Once the BATNAs have been identified, the coach can help the client think about how and when to present the BATNA so it will have the most positive influence in the negotiation. In order to establish a resistance point, the client has to be guided in assessing the information that is being used to set the point. The coach should ask the client to list and justify the quality of sources of information used. If the information is lacking or is suspect, the coach can suggest credible information that can be trusted and help the client consider how to secure it. The coach can also test the resistance point by asking a series of questions about whether the resistance point is "livable" for the client and whether it will remain livable in the near future.

Approach #6: Develop communication strategies and skills most vital to success with the composite model.

What is it? Both approaches within the composite model entail specific sets of skills that are important for parties to be successful. This activity has the coach working with the client to develop collaborative and bargaining negotiation skills.

Why is it important? There are various important skills necessary to carry out the composite model. Active learning is probably required to become proficient in the string of skills needed for even a fairly limited negotiation.

How do you do it? A client may choose to concentrate on skill development within one of the subapproaches or across subapproaches. Key bargaining skills include determining bargaining ranges, crafting positions, making arguments, overcoming decision-making biases, and shaping concessions. Key principled negotiation skills include developing interests, shifting from positions to interests, generating options, determining and applying objective criteria, and selecting solutions. Selection of strategies and skills should be done with sensitivity to cultural considerations.

Chapter Summary

One of the opportunities for helping clients make their best story real is by developing their negotiation knowledge, strategies, and skills. The diversity and complexity of workplace interactions often justify a composite approach to negotiation, where individuals are able to use bargaining as well as principled or interest-based negotiation. Bargaining tends to be more positional and is used when trust is limited. Principled negotiation is interest based and works well when the issues and relationship are of considerable importance and there is a high degree of trust.

GENERAL PRINCIPLES FOR NEGOTIATION WORK WITH CONFLICT COACHING CLIENTS

Principle #1: Increase awareness regarding when the client negotiates formally or informally.

Principle #2: Work with the client to determine his or her (pre–conflict coaching) approach to negotiation as well as existing strengths associated with this approach.

Principle #3: Foster the client's appreciation for and ability to apply the composite approach while helping the client identify which general approach to negotiation (bargaining or principled negotiation) is best given the conflict at hand.

Principle #4: Support the client in developing the best alternatives to a negotiated agreement (BATNAs) and resistance points for self and other.

Principle #5: Foster the client's awareness of likely positions or interests, as well as possible solutions, prior to negotiation.

Principle #6: Invite the client to develop specific communication behaviors for advancing his or her positions and interests given the positions and interests as well as likely communication behaviors used by the other party.

Principle #7: Encourage the client to consider the implications of culture in negotiation.

SPECIFIC APPROACHES FOR NEGOTIATION WORK WITH CONFLICT COACHING CLIENTS

Approach #1: Invite broad consideration of when the client negotiates.

Approach #2: Perform a negotiation audit.

Approach #3: Use a decision tree to support effective use of the composite approach.

Approach #4: Develop the positions and/or interests of both parties.

Approach #5: Identify the BATNAs and resistance points for both self and other.

Approach #6: Develop communication strategies and skills most vital to success with the composite model.

11

Stage Four

Coordinating Coaching With Other Conflict Processes

What we need to do is learn to work in the system.

—W. Edwards Deming

June was recently hired as a research professor of bioethics and medicine at a prestigious university. June came to the position highly recommended, with impressive credentials including postdoctoral work with leading researchers in her field. June's initial appointment was negotiated to include assistance on two on-going research teams with the expectation (assuming grant funding was obtained) that she would be promoted to team leader in her second or third year.

June's first year was a disappointment. She was assigned as lowest-seniority and lowest-status member on five research teams. As a result, she spent her work time basically running errands for other teams and was not able to make headway on research initiatives or grant funding.

Faced with this disconnect between negotiated expectations and reality, June went to the department head, Dr. White, to discuss options and request a change. Although Dr. White had been the department head during the hiring process, June had negotiated directly with the dean of the college. June had assumed that Dr. White supported the arrangement with the dean.

June soon learned that Dr. White did not and would not support the initial plans. Dr. White explained to June that June was not the first or second choice for the position, that she was not impressed with June's previous work, and that she did not feel the rest of the department should be reorganized to suit June's needs. Dr. White explained that all new faculty members were given "low-post" duty on several senior researchers' teams for the first 2–3 years.

Junior faculty were not encouraged to write their own grant proposals (as these often competed with proposals from the College and senior faculty) until they had completed this "apprenticeship." Dr. White further explained that, although the Dean liked to be involved in hiring, the Dean was "hands-off" when it came to departmental management. Basically, June interpreted this to mean that she shouldn't depend on the Dean's support in this initiative.

During her second year, June's work situation deteriorated. June could not keep her disappointment and lack of interest from showing. Several of the research team leaders gave her mediocre performance reviews, citing lack of enthusiasm and unwillingness to be a "team player." June was not invited to go with the various research teams to present their work at national and international conferences. She was increasingly left out of meetings where new grant proposals were being discussed. And attempts to gain Dr. White's permission to submit small grants were consistently denied. By the end of the second year June was very dissatisfied, and her relationship with Dr. White had deteriorated to hostile stares and curt memos. Dr. White was overheard in a faculty meeting saying that she was waiting for June to get the hint and just leave.

But June couldn't just leave. If she left a position at a prestigious institution without clear evidence of success in the first two years, she was very unlikely to get a lateral move and certainly would not get a better position. And a lateral move depended on fairly strong recommendations from her current job, which June knew Dr. White would not give. June talked with her earlier mentors in graduate school and they confirmed what she feared—she needed to make it much better where she was if she wanted a chance to get out, go elsewhere, and salvage a once-promising career.

On the recommendation of the human resources department, June began conflict coaching with an external coach hired by the university. During the conflict coaching sessions, the coach suggested that June should "get system savvy" and learn about other dispute resolution policies and procedures that she might want to use depending on the trajectory of this conflict.

June, despite her current work woes, is fortunate to have a coach who understands the need to "think systems." In this chapter, we explain how conflict coaching can and should be used in conjunction with larger systems of conflict management and dispute resolution found inside and outside the workplace. This chapter encourages coaches to think in terms of systems by introducing the literature on organizational dispute system design, illuminating some of the components of those systems that are likely to be well coordinated with conflict coaching, and suggesting some basic principles of accessing and using these systems. Obviously, conflict coaches need to be well informed about systems of dispute resolution and their components in order to provide optimal guidance for clients planning to engage these systems. Throughout the chapter, we'll return to June's example for illustration of these points.

Organizational Dispute Systems

The dispute resolution field has seen an explosion of workplace processes and an increasing emphasis on organizational dispute system design in the last several years. In one of the first books on conflict management system design, Cathy Costantino and Christina Merchant (1996, p. xiii) stated in their preface:

> Increasingly, however, given today's economic, political and social realities, executives, managers, organization development (OD) consultants, human resource (HR) personnel, conflict management systems designers, and attorneys are seeking more creative and improved methods to manage conflict. They are being asked to devise processes that constructively draw conflict to the surface and channel it: these are the sluices and viaducts of effective conflict management.

Their statement is even more fitting now than when it was written, and conflict coaching is one of the newest and most promising tools in the dispute system designer's set of options.

While we will not review the literature in organizational dispute system design (ODSD), we will trace the high points of the literature from the earliest conceptualizations to the most elaborate systems models. From this, we can discern principles and components of ODSD that will guide the application of conflict coaching as a valued component.

The initial foray into ODSD was *Getting Disputes Resolved: Designing Systems to Cut the Costs of Conflict* (1988) by William Ury, Jeanne Brett, and Stephen Goldberg. Among several novel ideas introduced in this book were the distinctions among interest-based, rights-based, power-based, and avoidance methods of managing conflicts. These insights have served as the foundation of all subsequent ODSD models.

Interest-based approaches, which Ury and colleagues advocate and lament as less used than they should be, are approaches that emphasize an interest-based negotiation of the conflict between the disputing parties. Our discussion of negotiation and conflict styles for conflict coaching has already introduced you to ideas about interest-based orientations to conflict management. Interest-based approaches involve direct negotiation between the parties as well as intervention by a third party facilitator, conciliator, or mediator who does not remove decision-making authority from the parties.

Rights-based approaches involve the use of external arbitration or adjudication to determine whether individuals' rights (provided to them under law, policy, or practice) have been violated, by whom, and with what consequence. Rights-based approaches usually include fact-finding, binding and nonbinding arbitration, adjudication, and litigation.

Power-based approaches are generally more difficult to identify because they don't manifest as easily in terms of discrete dispute resolution processes (like mediation or arbitration). Instead, power-based approaches include all means by which conflicts are managed through the exertion of physical, social, economic, or psychological power against the other. Thus, power-based approaches may include physical confrontation, sabotage, strikes, lockouts, media campaigns, boycotts, and civil disobedience, to name just a few.

Avoidance approaches involve the use of physical and/or psychological avoidance of a conflict in order to escape confrontation, de-escalate the conflict, or provide time to gather additional resources for confrontation. Interestingly, scholars often omit discussion of the avoidance approaches when designing systems.

In addition to clarifying these approaches to conflict management, Ury, Brett, and Goldberg argued that dispute system designs should follow some basic principles, including encouragement of interest-based approaches, development of low-cost rights-based and power-based approaches, and loop-back systems that enable the conflict to be brought back to the lowest level of processing (that nearest to and most dependent on the parties in the dispute).

The next important work in ODSD was Costantino and Merchant's book, *Designing Conflict Management Systems: A Guide to Creating Productive and Healthy Organizations* (1996). This book emphasized the need to understand organizations and dispute systems in organizations from a systems theory perspective with the attendant discussions of boundaries, uncertainty, equifinality, wholism, feedback, inputs, outputs, transformation, etc.

Costantino and Merchant also significantly extended the identification of conflict management and dispute resolution processes that were associated with interest-based, rights-based, and power-based approaches presented by Ury, Brett, and Goldberg. Costantino and Merchant added discussion of preventive ADR processes, including consensus building and negotiated rule making. They distinguished two types of interest-based processes, negotiated ADR and facilitated ADR; the latter involves a third party without decision-making authority. They significantly elaborated on rights-based processes by detailing fact-finding ADR, advisory ADR, and binding ADR.

Costantino and Merchant supported the same basic principles of ODSD presented by Ury and colleagues but added an emphasis on needs assessment to appreciate operative organizational culture. They argued convincingly that ODSD designers should respect organizational culture in ODSD design and provide infrastructure support for the dispute system. Their model was a more complex rendering of the many processes one might make available for organizational members to deal with their disputes.

In 1998, Karl Slaikeu and Ralph Hasson contributed their volume, *Controlling the Costs of Conflict: How to Design a System for Your Organization*. Slaikeu and Hasson reintroduced Ury and colleagues' (1988) four approaches to conflict management (with slightly different labels). Their contributions are in three areas.

First, they provided a template that they argued any organization can use to design a dispute system. The template is predicated on the use of internal and external systems coordinated such that initial site-based resolution, which relies strongly on interest-based approaches involving the parties, is followed by internal support processes (ombuds, HR, internal mediation services, etc.) in which some third party becomes involved in the dispute but with an emphasis on interest-based intervention. If these internal mechanisms don't work, the next step in the process and template is referral to external ADR mechanisms, including external mediation, arbitration, minitrial, and fact-finding. And finally, if that does not resolve the dispute, the last process step is to external higher authority (courts, hearings, etc.). This model creates an expectation that internal processes will be heavily interest oriented and that rights-based procedures are largely external.

Second, Slaikeu and Hasson introduced the idea of seven critical subsystems that must be properly developed, implemented, and maintained in order for the ODSD to function: policy, roles and responsibilities, documentation, selection, training, support, and evaluation. They describe each of these subsystems and provide insights into best practices.

The third contribution is actually their discussion of the seventh subsystem—evaluation. These authors made the strongest and most practical case for good evaluation techniques as a constant component of ODSD.

The latest contribution to the literature is David Lipsky, Ronald Seeber, and Richard Fincher's *Emerging Systems for Managing Workplace Conflict: Lessons from American Corporations for Managers and Dispute Resolution Professionals* (2003). As the title indicates, this book assumed the reader had a more sophisticated knowledge of organizations and the field of dispute resolution than the earlier works assumed. The authors provided a lengthy and valuable discussion of the historical, social, political, and economic contexts that promoted ADR in the workplace. They dutifully re-presented the earlier models and work in the area. They introduced a new taxonomy of conflict management strategies: contend, settle, prevent. There was a much stronger labor relations thread running throughout their discussion of systems design and the examples they provided of organizations with dispute systems. And they did an excellent job of reviewing the barriers they saw to growth of ADR in the workplace as well as what they anticipated to be the future of ADR in the workplace. Their discussion of specific processes is the most updated, but the processes are presented as freestanding components rather than elements within a system template.

As we know, the interest-based and rights-based procedures detailed in the ODSD literature have analogues outside the workplace as well. Clearly, the external rights-based processes of courts and agency hearings exist for processing workplace and nonworkplace disputes. It has always been held that access to these systems is the prerogative of an individual who feels his or her rights have been violated and who has the economic resources to pursue their use. Similarly, a variety of external interest-based procedures are available through governments and community organizations that provide mediation, conciliation, and facilitation services.

The Role of Conflict Coaching in Leveraging Dispute Systems

Let's return to June, the young research professor in our example at the beginning of the chapter. June has been connected with a conflict coach who understands organizational dispute systems. How can the coach help June access and use the system? We suggest that conflict coaches can fulfill six functions in this regard: investigation, explanation, preparation, selection and timing of system access, reflective analysis, and future planning.

INVESTIGATION

The coach can begin by helping June investigate the current state of internal and external dispute resolution options available to her. Many organizational members are unaware of their organization's dispute resolution policies, procedures, and systems (if they exist). A recent study of MBA students representing a wide variety of fields suggests that most do not know about the potentials for ODSD and are wary of using the traditional HR procedures of which they are aware (Jameson, 1998). The coach can help June put together an investigative protocol like the following:

- What types of conflicts regularly occur in this workplace? To what extent is the kind of conflict you are experiencing a typical or common conflict?
- To what extent are these conflicts considered serious or in need of intervention by organizational leadership? What evidence do you have for that?
- How do members of the organization perceive these conflicts? How concerned are they about these conflicts? What makes you assume this?
- Have there been recent incidents of similar conflicts in your workplace? If so, how have they been handled? What was the end result for the person or persons in a situation similar to yours?
- What conflict management and dispute resolution policies currently exist in the organization? (Seek formal policy statements.)
  - Are these policies directly relevant to the kind of conflict you are experiencing?
  - How well do these policies address the types of conflicts you have identified as problematic?
  - If these policies do not address your type of conflict well, are there umbrella policies that may pertain in a general sense?
- How well are these policies known and understood by organizational members?
  - Were you aware of these policies prior to this incident?
  - Are your co-workers aware?
  - Are you familiar with incidents when the policies have been used?
- What information dissemination practices are used to inform organizational membership of these policies?
- What kind of education and training is available to help organizational members deal more effectively with these conflicts?
  - Is this training available to all organizational members?
  - Is this training perceived as effective?
  - Has this training been suggested or made available to you or others involved in this conflict? Why? Why not?
- What internal dispute resolution processes are available for use by organizational membership?
  - What specific processes are available?
  - How easy and accessible are they?
  - How well does the organization make these processes available to people experiencing serious conflicts? What mechanisms do they use?
  - How well are these processes understood by organizational members? Do they know what they are, why to use them, and how to use them?
  - What level of support (publicity, staffing, etc.) is provided for these processes?

※ Are the dispute resolution processes operating as a coordinated system?
   ※ Is there a clear trajectory of steps by which one can move through the coordinated system? Is this trajectory well explained and easily understood?
   ※ Does the logic of the system make sense in terms of its ability to deal well with disputes?
※ Is the internal dispute resolution process linked to external dispute resolution procedures in some coordinated fashion?
   ※ If so, does the organization help a member access these external procedures?
   ※ If so, does the organization provide support of any kind to members as they access these procedures?
   ※ If not, does the organization have basic information about external dispute resolution procedures that a member may wish to access and use independently?

One of the reasons that a conflict coach is potentially so helpful in the investigation function is that he or she knows about ODSD and can direct a client to seek commonly used processes and commonly developed policies.

In June's case, the investigation may yield very valuable information like the following: (1) These conflicts have been increasingly common at this institution over the past decade; (2) the conflicts have resulted in at least two other assistant research professors leaving the institution; (3) there was some discussion after the most recent similar case to put together a task force to review the problem and suggest policy, but that action was never taken; (4) the university does not have a dispute system design, but it does have an ombudsperson office that deals with faculty-administration conflicts; (5) there is a mediation program in the law school at this institution that offers free mediation services for a variety of faculty and staff conflicts; and (6) this problem has become significant enough in the field that one of the leading professional associations offers facilitation/mediation services for people just like June.

EXPLANATION

What is the difference between mediation and arbitration? What is early-neutral evaluation? What does an ombudsperson do? How can fact-finding help me or hurt me? If you've worked with clients in designing and using ODSD, these are questions you've heard before. Many conflict consultants are all too familiar with the general lack of information that the public has about dispute resolution and possible processes. Thus, an important role for the conflict coach is to explain ADR to the client. Essentially, the coach can provide a primer on common ADR processes by explaining the nature of the process, the advantages and disadvantages of the process, and the resources (time, money, and expertise) needed to engage the process. The conflict coach can also explain how internal versus external processes work, for example, the differences between using an internal mediator and using an external mediator provided by a government agency or community mediation center.

Two processes that vary a great deal in form and function are mediation and the use of ombudspersons. Conflict coaches can help the client understand the range of behaviors and approaches that one might expect from an ombudsperson in order to help the client select that resource carefully. For example, June may learn that the university has an ombudsperson but may be unsure whether that ombudsperson will serve as a shuttle mediator in this dispute. A coach can help June in drafting questions for a conversation with the ombudsperson.

June has learned that there is a mediation program at the law school and a mediation program in her professional association. But June does not understand different styles of mediation and how those may impact what mediation can mean to the resolution of a dispute. The conflict coach can explain the various styles of mediation and help June understand that the transformative style mediation practiced by the professional association's mediation program is not as likely to emphasize problem solving as the facilitative style used in the law school mediation program.

PREPARATION

Most of us learned about the idea of a coach in the context of sports. A coach was someone who taught you skills and techniques to be used in a sporting event or contest. The coach was the person who knew which skill was most critical for a certain level of performance.

In just the same way, a conflict coach should help prepare a client to get the optimum from whatever dispute resolution process is being used. Throughout this book we have talked about how a conflict coach can help a client identify and perfect skills for strategic avoidance or strategic confrontation. The emphasis has been on preparing the client to deal with the other disputing party directly in some fashion, as the conflict coach in the case has done for June, to help June in preparing to deal directly with Dr. White.

But June has tried to negotiate with Dr. White and the outcome has not been to June's satisfaction. June has now worked with the coach to investigate the other options that are available and realizes that she is likely to use the ombudsperson, some form of external mediation, and possibly arbitration. Now the coach's contribution is to prepare June to participate as effectively as possible in each of these processes.

Preparing for Ombudspersons. The role of ombudsperson is one of the least understood roles in the dispute resolution field, even though ombudspersons have been used in American organizations for decades (some would say longer) and most large organizations have an office of the ombudsperson. As Tyler Harrison (2007, p. 350) explains,

> While ombuds are historically a government position, ombuds offices have seen tremendous growth in both the academic and corporate world, largely as a result of the civil rights movement of the 1960's (Robbins & Deane, 1986). Ombuds, and other internal dispute resolution processes, were seen as a way to respond internally to complaints, with the hope of reducing litigation costs and demonstrating organizational concern (Edelman, Erlanger, & Lande, 1993; Shapiro & Kolb, 1994).

Ombudspersons are designated neutrals within an organization who usually report at or near the top of the organization but often outside of ordinary management channels. As a result they have the ability to engage in discussions about disputes and possible actions to remediate disputes in a private, diplomatic, and powerful way. An ombudsperson may serve the internal staff and clients of the organization and is responsible for a variety of functions including confidential information resource, intervener, and protector of the less powerful (Rowe, 1987).

Earlier we mentioned that a coach can help explain the various roles an ombudsperson might perform to prepare a client, like June, to interview or initially engage a particular ombudsperson about a particular dispute. There are other ways that a coach can help clients maximize their interactions with an ombudsperson:

Learning more of the political context of the organization. An ombudsperson is not going to air the political peccadilloes of an organization. But the ombudsperson often understands political undercurrents that make conflict management attempts more or less workable or risky. The coach can help prepare the client to ask the ombudsperson about the political landscape.

Testing reality for dispute resolution processes. The coach can suggest how the client can get information from the ombudsperson about the likelihood of success of various dispute resolution procedures. Again, the ombudsperson is likely to have intimate knowledge of this company and how it tends to respond and exercise possibilities. While a conflict coach can give a client a general expectation for certain procedures (like mediation), the ombudsperson can provide information about how that procedure tends to work in this context.

Testing alternatives for outcomes. An ombudsperson is a good sounding board for ideas about how best to solve this problem or manage this conflict. But a sounding board is only as effective as the ideas that are bounced off it. A conflict coach can work with a client to brainstorm a variety of options for resolution and see what the ombudsperson thinks of their potential.

Assessing costs for actions. An ombudsperson may have considerable insight into what an action might cost a client, either personally, professionally, or economically. The coach can help the client prepare for this conversation with the ombudsperson. For example, the coach might help June draft questions for the ombudsperson about the damage to her long-term career if she continues to pursue this conflict with Dr. White.

Preparing for Mediation. Mediation is a common dispute procedure that is still misunderstood by the majority of workers. It can take a great many forms depending on the orientation and ideology of the mediator and the mediation program (Moore, 2003). The conflict coach can help clients decide whether to use mediation and then help them utilize mediation well.

Understanding the mediator/mediation approach. The conflict coach can help clients develop a short interview that will enable them to them discover whether this mediator uses an approach or adheres to a style that the client is comfortable with. Perhaps the mediator has an ideology that the client considers essential to working through this conflict. Or maybe the mediator believes only in multiple-session, lengthy mediations to which the client does not want to commit.

Preparing the narrative for mediation. In this book we have placed a great emphasis on helping the client understand and assess the narrative of his or her conflict experience. Here, the conflict coach can help the client to prepare how to share this narrative in mediation. Perhaps there is a "better" way for June to tell the story of this conflict, a way that will make it more likely that Dr. White will adopt a more collaborative stance. Conversely, perhaps there are parts of the story that are better left untold, at least in joint session. The conflict coach can discuss these possibilities with the client.

Clarifying interests and criteria. Granted, we are emphasizing an interest-based framing in this discussion, but efforts to help a client examine and articulate underlying interests and criteria that will make a good resolution are rarely wasteful. The coach can fulfill this quasi-mediator role and let the client reflect on these insights before mediation takes place.

Brainstorming options. The more a client considers possible options for resolution, the more he or she can consider how well the options suit his or her needs. Again, the coach can help the client play with ideas in a safe and relaxed environment.

Determining limits. Sometimes the collaborative tone and flow of mediation can encourage clients to make agreements that they later regret—agreements that they believe did not uphold certain limits or standards. This is more likely when clients are responding to an idea for the first time without carefully considering their comfort level with it. For example, in mediation Dr. White might suggest that June agree to remain in her position with the same basic duties for one more year before taking further action. June may initially agree only to realize after the mediation that emotionally and professionally she can't remain in this situation without it continuing to do increasing damage.

Preparing for Arbitration. Workers are often less knowledgeable about arbitration than mediation. They probably have a general understanding of the process but are ill-equipped to participate in an arbitration hearing. Too often workers think that arbitration, like a relaxed version of court, will have certain process protections. They may not understand that the arbitrator has great latitude to control the process, including how to elicit testimony, whether to hear witnesses, etc. The conflict coach can help the client prepare for arbitration in a variety of ways:

Thinking about selection of the arbitrator. The coach can help the client consider how arbitrators are selected for this arbitration process and whether the client is comfortable with that. In labor arbitration the convention is for both sides to select from a supplied list by striking unwanted names until the top one or two options that suit both sides are left. One is selected to arbitrate. However, in various forms of workplace arbitration, the arbitrator may be selected by the program rather than by the participants. If there were an internal arbitration system at the university, June could find herself agreeing to be arbitrated by an arbiter who has a long career in academic administration (much like Dr. White).

Preparing testimony and evidence. This is similar to preparing a narrative, but there is an important difference. Coaching and mediation are processes in which preparing the narrative helps to clarify the conflict for self and other. Arbitration is a process of advocacy in which the disputants are trying to convince the arbitrator that they have a better case. A conflict coach can help the client prepare testimony, choose the most persuasive evidence, and consider how to present it to best advantage.

SELECTION AND TIMING OF SYSTEM ACCESS

When the client understands the nature of the ODSD and has talked with the coach about the components of the system, the coach and client will eventually come to key questions.

1. *What level of intervention (ombudsperson, mediation, arbitration, fact-finding, litigation, etc.) is most beneficial for the client at this point in the conflict?* This is the million dollar question. It requires the coach and client to understand the system well enough to predict whether engaging in one level of intervention (e.g., mediation) will best address the client's needs. It requires that the coach and client understand whether engaging that intervention will enhance or inhibit further use of the system in this particular situation. Though most organizational dispute system designs are created to establish loop-back procedures, the reality is that it is more difficult to go from a rights-based back to an interest-based procedure than vice versa. Thus, the question of where to begin and why is strategically critical.

2. *At what point is it optimal for the client to engage the dispute system?* Does it make more sense for the coach and client to focus initially on skills development and application outside of the dispute system? Does entering the dispute system restrict in any way the flexibility of the coach and client to manage aspects of the conflict outside of the system? There are no general guidelines that can be developed, because the answers to these questions are so situated in the unique aspects of a specific dispute. But failing to ask these questions can result in an otherwise good system and set of options becoming destructive, because the decisions to access were based on poor timing.

3. *How can conflict coaching be best coordinated with active interventions in process through the dispute system?* Again, this question has no simple answers, but it does suggest that the coach and client must be vigilant and converse regularly about whether the conflict coaching process is impeding the successful use of the component in the dispute system. And it suggests that the conversation should include relevant members of the organizational dispute system. For example, perhaps the ombudsperson that June goes to is not comfortable having an external conflict coach in constant conversation with June while the ombudsperson is attempting to work with her. Perhaps the ombudsperson would prefer, and for reasons very much in June's interests, to have the coaching postponed until after the ombudsperson's interventions have been completed.

REFLECTIVE ANALYSIS

As Louis Pondy (1967) noted in his famous essay on conflict, one of the most important stages of the conflict process is the conflict aftermath, in which a sophisticated conflict manager reflects on his conflict behavior and analyzes how well he managed the conflict. Reflective analysis is very helpful when clients are evaluating how well they engaged and used organizational dispute systems. Conflict coaches can guide clients through reflective analysis as they complete various stages of the dispute system or after the entire experience. Reflection can lead to an assessment of better options for the future. In this way, reflection is part of the overall learning assessment process discussed in Chapter 12.

FUTURE PLANNING

This is straightforward. The conflict coach helps the client look at possible next steps and chart a course for future action.

General Principles for Coordinating Conflict Coaching With Other Conflict Processes

The preceding discussions have introduced a number of implicit principles about coordinating coaching with other dispute systems. But here are some additional, more general principles.

Principle #1: Help the client adopt a systems orientation to potential dispute resolution and conflict management options. The more clients can understand the system of options for dealing with the conflict, the more empowered, confident, and strategically successful they will be. As the old adage goes, "You can't work the system if you don't know the system." Clients, especially in the heat of conflict, are usually thinking about immediate action and short-term consequences. The conflict coach has to help them pull back, lift their heads, and take the larger and longer view.

Principle #2: Develop multiple options for using the dispute system. A cardinal principle of all systems thinking is the notion of equifinality—or the idea that there is more than one way to achieve a desired outcome (or as a more colloquial saying suggests, "There's more than one way to skin a cat") (Katz & Kahn, 1976). The power of systems thinking is that it enables clients to understand that all components of the system are interrelated, which means there are an infinite number of ways to affect the system. People who are systems savvy, as June's coach encouraged her to be, are people who understand the components and connections within the system well enough to know how to strategically manipulate the system. Just as backup plans are critical for negotiation strategies (as we discussed in Chapter 10), alternate approaches are critical to maximizing the utility of a dispute system. The coach and client should map out a variety of plans for accessing and using the dispute system.

Principle #3: Encourage the client to consider interest-based, rights-based, power-based, and avoidance-based approaches to resolving conflict. Too often clients focus on one basic approach to dealing with the conflict rather than being ready to embrace all of the approaches. Clients may be predisposed to be collaborative and feel that interest-based approaches are their only options. Clients may be angry and in search of justice and consider only rights-based approaches as a possibility. Clients may distrust the system and want to use power-based approaches, particularly when clients feel powerful and assume they can marshal resources to successfully influence the outcome. And conversely, clients may be emotionally and mentally fatigued and in serious doubt that they have any power, thus wanting to think only about avoidance-based approaches. A conflict coach must help clients understand how any and all of these approaches may be useful. In fact, the coach should help clients develop plans for the utility of each of these approaches, even if one approach is clearly superior.

Principle #4: Promote the client's awareness of dispute resolution processes inside and outside the organization. The client's organization may not have a well-designed dispute system, or the system may be subject to politics or bureaucracy that severely limit the system's ability to serve the client. In many cases, the client may also have access to external dispute systems through community and government organizations that should be explored.

Principle #5: Encourage the client to strategically select dispute resolution processes, even if that means discontinuation of conflict coaching. The client needs a game plan, and the best game plan may not include the continuation of conflict coaching. This should be an open point in the conversations and one that the coach is willing to encourage if it serves the interests of the client.

Specific Approaches for Coordinating Conflict Coaching With Other Conflict Processes

Approach #1: Explore the client's current knowledge of, attitudes about, and experiences with alternative dispute resolution.

> *What is it?* This is a basic survey of the background that the client has with a variety of basic ADR processes like mediation, arbitration, and ombudspersons.

> *Why is it important?* This survey can be helpful in several ways. It can provide information about how much the client already knows and understands ADR processes and, as a result, how much the coach may need to

explain. This approach may uncover some biases that the client has about specific processes, for example, mediation, because of personal experience with the process. In these cases, the coach may need to explain that the person's previous experience was not necessarily common or typical. It may be that the client had or heard of a bad experience with a good process and needs to be encouraged to consider the process in the current situation.

How do you do it? The coach can ask clients to describe ADR processes and share their previous experiences with the process. This exploration can be done at the level of general approaches (i.e., interest-based, rights-based, etc.) or specific interventions (i.e., mediation, ombudsperson).

Approach #2: Solicit the client's expectations for ADR processes to set goals and manage expectations.

What is it? This approach would naturally follow the first, but it is distinct in that the coach asks clients to talk about what expectations they have for what can be accomplished through each ADR process.

Why is it important? Clients may have unrealistically low or high expectations of various processes, like mediation, and those expectations need to be managed before a client can select or participate in that process effectively.

How do you do it? Again, the easiest way is for the coach to ask clients what they expect from each process and what would be "success" in each process.

Approach #3: Consider the direct and indirect consequences of system access.

What is it? This approach asks the client to forecast what positive and negative consequences may occur for the client and for others (co-workers, other organizational members, family members, etc.) if an ADR process is used.

Why is it important? Any conversation that asks the client to forecast potential consequences is valuable, even if the consequences are not likely, because such forecasting raises possibilities and allows the coach to be certain that these possibilities have been surfaced. It is also helpful because it requires clients to consider consequences for others in addition to themselves.

How do you do it? Using a simple worksheet for each ADR process, the client can complete a matrix that identifies positive and negative consequences for self, important co-workers, and important others (defined as desired). Having the client write down the positive and negative consequences is more helpful than having the client simply state these. Writing thoughts down takes more time and will encourage a more comprehensive analysis.

Approach #4: Demonstrate ADR processes with which the client is unfamiliar.

What is it? This is a way of showing the client what a specific process is and what to expect from it.

Why is it important? Sometimes a picture is worth a thousand words, and a description is worth a hundred. Even if the coach can define the ADR process for clients, they may not really understand what the process is like (e.g., mediation) unless they "see" it.

How do you do it? One of the best ways is for the conflict coach to have videotapes of portions of or whole sessions of basic processes like mediation or arbitration that the client can view at home or on a Web site at the client's leisure. The coach may also have taped interviews with ADR professionals, like ombudspersons, talking about their work and how it is done. Finally, the coach may have an "ask the experts" panel of ADR professionals who are willing to engage in phone interviews, etc., with a client to deepen the client's understanding of the process.

Approach #5: Role-play an ADR process with a client.

What is it? The coach (and other confederates) participate in a role play of an ADR process, so the client has a better sense of what to expect from the process and how to participate in the process.

Why is it important? If a client is particularly concerned or insecure about a process like mediation, experiencing that process in a realistic role play can help the client decide whether to pursue or avoid the option. If the client likes the idea of the process but is unsure whether she or he can participate well, the role play can also provide opportunities for skill development (for example, how to get the most out of a caucus discussion or how to best present a solution for consideration in mediation). And, if the client is basically secure about the process and knows what to expect, the role play can focus on tricky parts and responses to difficult situations. For example, a client may like mediation and feel comfortable in mediation but may wonder how to respond if the mediator seems to be favoring the other party. The role play can provide an opportunity to test these skills for difficult situations.

How do you do it? The more realistic the role play, the more valuable it will be for the client. If the organization's dispute system uses a transformative model for the internal mediation the role play should also employ a transformative model. The other participants in the role play should be given enough information about the conflict to enact a realistic portrayal of their characters. And, if possible, the role play should be audiotaped or videotaped for later review by the client.

Chapter Summary

In this chapter, we explained how conflict coaching can and should be used in conjunction with larger systems of conflict management and dispute resolution found inside and outside the workplace. We introduced you to the literature on organizational dispute system design, illuminated some of the components of those systems that are likely to be well coordinated with conflict coaching, and suggested some basic principles of accessing and using these systems. We discussed that conflict coaches can fulfill six functions in this regard: investigation, explanation, preparation, selection and timing of system access, reflective analysis, and future planning.

GENERAL PRINCIPLES FOR COORDINATING CONFLICT COACHING WITH OTHER CONFLICT PROCESSES

Principle #1: Help the client adopt a systems orientation to potential dispute resolution and conflict management options.

Principle #2: Develop multiple options for using the dispute system.

Principle #3: Encourage the client to consider interest-based, rights-based, power-based, and avoidance-based approaches to resolving conflict.

Principle #4: Promote the client's awareness of dispute resolution processes inside and outside the organization.

Principle #5: Encourage the client to strategically select dispute resolution processes, even if that means discontinuation of conflict coaching.

SPECIFIC APPROACHES FOR COORDINATING CONFLICT COACHING WITH OTHER CONFLICT PROCESSES

Approach #1: Explore the client's current knowledge of, attitudes about, and experiences with alternative dispute resolution.

Approach #2: Solicit the client's expectations for ADR processes to set goals and manage expectations.

Approach #3: Consider the direct and indirect consequences of system access.

Approach #4: Demonstrate ADR processes with which the client is unfamiliar.

Approach #5: Role-play an ADR process with a client.

12

The Parallel Process

Learning Assessment in Conflict Coaching

Learning is not attained by chance, it must be sought for with ardor and attended to with diligence.

—Abigail Adams

Michael was recently hired by a large medical center to provide conflict coaching to Joan, a middle-level nurse manager who works on the pediatrics ward and oversees cases of minor to severe illnesses among children ages 6 months to 18 years of age. The medical center is in a large northeastern urban center and is noted for its affiliation with a well-respected teaching institution.

Joan worked as a ward nurse in the same ward for 10 years before being promoted last year to the position of nurse manager. Many of the nurses that she now manages were her peers, and they have had a tough time accepting her in this new role. As a result, Joan has tried to become more forceful in implementing her decisions—especially revisions in work and vacation schedules needed to save money and maintain current staffing of part-time nurses.

When Joan first implemented these changes, the full-time nursing staff thought she would back down if they resisted. Several of the nurses approached Joan and threatened to quit, noting that they could easily find other jobs with other area hospitals. They expressed concern that Joan was more focused on controlling costs (e.g., loading the schedules with more inexperienced part-time nursing staff) than with quality of nursing. They argued that they should be given the more desirable schedules because they had seniority in the field and seniority in the hospital. They further argued that if Joan pursued these policies, she would find herself on the wrong side of the nurses union.

Joan consulted her director, Robert, who advised her to hold her ground rather than give in to pressure. Robert explained that the nurses were testing Joan and relying on her previous personal relationships with them to sway hospital policy. He reminded Joan that the union had no right to control scheduling processes.

Joan held the line and told the nurses that her policies would be implemented. She expected tension but not revolt. In the six months since Joan held her ground she has had fifteen grievances filed against her with the union. This is three times as many as any other nurse manager at the hospital. Her nurses have had a number of "blue flu" incidents, resulting in the highest absenteeism rates of any nursing unit in the hospital. To make matters worse, the nurses with the most increased absenteeism have been the most senior nurses, and the absenteeism has been steadily increasing despite Joan's addressing the issue in recent staff meetings.

Physicians have started complaining to Robert that they have to deal with "a revolving door of new nurses" they can't count on and to whom they have to explain basic things. The physicians are concerned about the quality of the care their patients are receiving, and they are concerned with the additional time they have to spend instructing newer nurses.

Joan and Michael have analyzed the conflict situation in terms of Joan's identity needs, her power dynamics with the nurses and physicians, and the emotions motivating her and others. They have crafted a plan for the constructive management of the situation and have been working on improving Joan's communication skills and her negotiation abilities. They have discussed the possibilities for Joan to interact more effectively with the grievance procedures under the union contract. Joan has begun to use some of the recommendations for communication and negotiation behaviors with her senior nurses.

Joan and Michael have talked with Robert about how to tell whether the conflict coaching is making a positive difference. Robert is very interested in being able to monitor the impact of the conflict coaching in order to justify its use to his superiors. And both Joan and Robert are interested in improving the general atmosphere and operation of the pediatrics unit.

Michael, Joan, and Robert share a common interest; they want to know whether conflict coaching is making a positive difference. They want to be able to demonstrate its value and determine whether and how to continue. We believe, as they do, that assessment is essential. In this chapter, we focus on learning assessment. In the next chapter, we'll discuss the need for broader program evaluation.

At the outset, we want to emphasize that learning assessment is not something that happens only at the end of conflict coaching. Learning assessment is a process that is interwoven with the conflict coaching from the beginning. In this chapter we will define learning assessment, relate it to foundations in adult learning theory, and discuss the components of learning assessment and how they parallel stages of conflict coaching.

Far too often, conflict consultation and dispute resolution practices are not carefully examined in terms of their need, their impact, and their effects on other persons or systems. When a new process, like conflict coaching, is introduced, it may be even less likely to be evaluated than more established processes. Many conflict consultants are not trained in evaluation and assessment and are reluctant to attempt them (Jones, 2006).

In this chapter, we strongly suggest that a conflict coach become proficient with learning assessment. Learning assessment examines the learning process and outcomes of an individual client in a coaching process. It is Joan's central concern—is she learning knowledge and skills that are helping her respond more constructively to her conflicts? How can Joan continue to focus on what she is doing well and emphasize those strengths as she moves forward?

Learning Assessment: Did the Conflict Coaching Work?

Think about this question, "Did you learn something useful?" It is at the heart of all learning assessment processes. It is deceptively simple on its face. But when you unpack the question, you find a number of questions implied—none of which are easy to answer. "What does it mean to learn?" "What is the 'something'? Is it knowledge, skill, attitude, or some combination?" "How do we determine 'useful' and does that change over time and context?" "How can you know or prove this was learned?" "How can you know or prove this was 'useful'?"

How might Joan answer the same questions? She may feel that she has learned something useful because she has gained a keener awareness of how to establish a new identity with the nurses in order to have credibility in her position. Perhaps she was unaware how her guilt (about succeeding where her peers had not) made her reluctant to negotiate effectively or to be directive when needed. She may feel that she has learned a great deal in terms of negotiation strategies that she did not know before.

A conflict coach works with a client to identify strengths that should be continued and to learn new approaches and skills. To do that well, the coach needs to think through, obviously with the client's input, the answers to these questions. But, as a beginning, the coach should be aware that adult learners, like the client, learn differently than younger counterparts. Adult learning theory has illuminated some of the needs and strengths of the adult learner that are helpful to consider in devising learning assessments.

ADULT LEARNING THEORY AS A GUIDE

Adult learning theory began with an idea called *andragogy* (Knowles, 1990), the art and science of how adults learn. As Addor, Denckla-Cobb, Dukes, Ellerbrock, and Smutko (2005, p. 210) summarize as follows:

> Learning by adults is enhanced when they: 1) are valued for the wealth of life experiences and expertise they bring to the learning environment and acknowledged for how their experiences enrich and inform the curriculum and learning; 2) have autonomy and self-direction with respect to individual interests; 3) perceive the learning is goal oriented with established expectancies; 4) perceive the learning is relevant and has direct personal benefits to them both personally and profession-ally; 5) are ready to receive and apply lessons to deal with real-life sit-uations; and 6) are supported, inspired and motivated by internal goals and pressures to enhance professional and personal development.

Other fields, including social work, business, and medicine teach practitioner-trainers to adopt andragogical approaches (Bartz, Calabrese, & Kottkamp, 1991; Cartney, 2000; DeWitt, 2003; Shannon, 2003; Vaughn, Gonzalez del Rey, & Baker, 2001). In fact, many training initiatives for human service professionals are designed to be andragogical given the unique needs of adult learners.

What are the characteristics of training that is designed with andra-gogy in mind? Speck (1996; as reported in Galbo, 1998) argues that effective training or professional development design for adults should follow these guidelines:

- *Adults need real-world applications.* Adults learn best when they are con-centrating on real situations and engaging in real interactions with real consequences. Abstract and exclusively theoretical information is not as valuable to them.
- *Adults need some control over the specifics of the what, how, why, when, and where details of their learning.* Adults learn best when they are empow-ered to design the training or learning experience.
- *Adult learning opportunities should be structured to allow support from peers and to reduce the fear of judgment while participants are learning to apply new skills.* Adults learn best in a collaborative, nonjudgmental learn-ing environment. Support from peers and emphasis on strengths and improvements rather than failures and inabilities bolster confidence and learning.

✎ *Adults need constructive feedback on their efforts to learn and apply new skills.* The more feedback adult learners can get, especially when the feedback is strengths-based rather than deficit-based, the more they can learn.

✎ *The transfer of learning must be facilitated.* Support is needed to help adult learners transfer learning into daily practice so that it is sustained. Adult learners benefit from incremental steps in applying their new learning to the context of application. Continuing support for transfer of learning helps the adult learner succeed with the skills in a variety of contexts.

Diana Dempwolf's research (1993) found that activities should be planned that deal with the change process. Learners should participate in needs assessments, help determine learning processes, and participate in the self-evaluation of their professional growth experiences. In other words, the more that adult learners can participate in planning the assessment of their own learning, the better.

Adult learning theory suggests that Michael approach the conflict coaching and the assessment process as a partner with Joan. Of course, this would make sense as an extension of the coach-as-facilitator model that we have encouraged throughout this book. In order for Joan to maximize her learning, she needs to be a full partner in all of its aspects.

Context is extremely important as a tenet of adult learning. As Joan and Michael identify possible strategies and skill development, these must be grounded in the workplace relationships and realities that Joan faces. To talk in abstracts and speak of generic skill development without reference to Joan's daily situation simply will not work. Appreciating context is part of the initial needs assessment that occurs in concert with discovering Joan's story and looking at it from the perspectives of identity, emotion, and power. Context is critical when Joan and Michael create the "best" story and identify skills that can be enhanced to support that vision. The best story is that which maximizes Joan's strengths and outcomes in Joan's context.

Practice and feedback are critical in adult learning, especially when the adult is trying to develop new skills or patterns of response and interaction. As Joan and Michael discuss new skills, they can design a variety of feedback processes that Joan can use as she learns. Perhaps she can videotape her negotiation skills and give herself feedback (as well as get feedback from Michael) using video playback. Joan may be able to try out new strategies and skills with other nurse managers or colleagues outside her hospital—colleagues who are willing and able to give her feedback on her efforts. And when Joan is ready to use her new strategies and skills with nurses in her unit, there she should be able to monitor and discuss with Michael and Robert when things are working well and when things are not.

THE PROCESS OF LEARNING ASSESSMENT

These insights about adult learning form the basis of the process of learning assessment that we articulate: (1) needs assessment, (2) goal setting, (3) reflection and feedback, and (4) learning transfer. Each component builds upon the previous ones, and together they form a continual learning cycle, as the last component leads naturally into a new iteration of the entire process (see Figure 12.1). We are going to discuss each of these elements in learning assessment, and following that, we will discuss how these elements are integrated as a parallel process in the CCC model.

Needs Assessment. Needs assessment concerns how conflict coaching will meet the needs of the client and/or the client's organization. Why is this client coming to coaching at this time? What are the needs or issues that are motivating the consultation? Effective needs assessment should be made from multiple perspectives, based on evidence when possible, and flexible and ongoing. Let's look at Joan as an example. When Michael and Joan first consider the conflict coaching process, they should identify the felt needs that bring Joan to this possibility.

There are *multiple perspectives* that should be considered. First, and perhaps foremost, Joan's needs should be discussed. Is she coming to coaching because she believes she needs to learn different approaches to conflict to maintain a more productive case management relationship with physicians and allied health professionals? Does she feel her interpersonal relationships with valued co-workers are being harmed? Or perhaps she is experiencing stress in her family relationships, because she's bringing home conflict-related stress from the hospital? The more Joan understands her motivations and possible gains, the more committed and focused she is likely to be.

Other critical perspectives include Robert's perspective; Robert is Joan's supervisor. He may see problems that Joan does not, and he may have feedback from others in Joan's unit that she does not. Perhaps Robert is aware that there will be a downsizing in the health care system, and he wants to protect Joan by making her less vulnerable to criticism. Of course, there are also the perspectives of the co-workers in Joan's nursing unit and her team members in the case management teams. They can provide an understanding of how Joan's behavior is impacting their personal and professional behavior.

Realistically, the conflict coach and client are likely to have limited time for needs assessment and will want to concentrate on the perspective of the client, the person responsible for the referral (in this case, Robert, who hired Michael to help Joan), and other parties to the conflict.

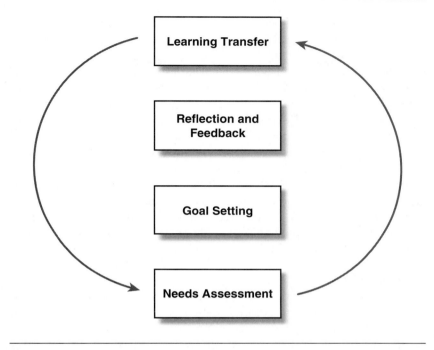

Figure 12.1   Learning Assessment Process

It always helps if you can look at hard evidence when considering the nature and extent of a problem. *Evidence-based assessment* may consist of relatively simple facts. For example, Joan has had 15 grievances filed against her; that is twice as many as any other nurse manager. Joan's unit has had increased absenteeism, higher tardiness, late paperwork, and more frequent failure to file necessary case documentation than other units. Hard indices of the problem can define measurable outcomes to be assessed during and after conflict coaching to determine coaching success.

Certain needs bring a client to coaching, but needs change; thus, conflict coaching should use needs assessment that is *flexible and ongoing*. Especially in coaching situations that extend over several weeks or months, the coach should revisit the discussion of needs to make sure the coaching is focused on the most important issues at the time. Michael and Joan have worked together for eight weeks. At the beginning of the coaching, the most critical needs for Joan were to understand her patterns of behavior that had resulted in several grievance filings. At this stage in the coaching, the needs are different—now Joan and Robert are most concerned with her ability to rebuild constructive relationships with those she has alienated. Just as conflict scholars realize that goals in conflict can be transitional (Wilmot & Hocker, 2007), needs also change.

*Goal Setting.*What do you want to accomplish in the conflict coaching? This is another way of asking, "What do you want to learn?" Setting learning goals not only clarifies what changes you want to see, it narrows the types of learning experiences that are more likely to be effective in producing the change. So, this aspect of learning assessment is very helpful for determining coaching techniques and processes as well as assessment.

In an excellent article on training efficacy in Middle Eastern conflict contexts, Abu-Nimer (1998) articulated a taxonomy of training models and strategies that can be used to discuss learning goals. Citing Havelock and Havelock's (1973) model of training, Abu-Nimer describes three basic goals of any learning endeavor: (1) provide new attitudes, skills, or knowledge; (2) reinforce existing attitudes, skills, or knowledge; and/or (3) remove or eradicate existing attitudes, skills, or knowledge.

A good first step in conflict coaching is to determine which of these is most important. Perhaps in Joan's case she needs to remove existing attitudes before she can learn new negotiation skills. And using this approach reminds the coach and client to consider goals in the areas of skills, knowledge, and attitudes. Perhaps Joan needs to gain knowledge about conflict escalation. Perhaps she needs to change her attitudes about the value of de-escalation and a healthy conflict climate. Perhaps she already knows these things and holds these attitudes, but she doesn't have the skills to send confirming messages or articulate interests in a negotiation.

Simple goal-setting worksheets can be used to identify goals, and they also point to desired outcomes that can be used in further assessment. Knowing you want to change an existing attitude raises the question of how you will know when and to what extent the attitude has changed. Good goal setting always involves clearly defined and measurable objectives. If you can't determine when the change has happened, you can't know whether your work is making a positive difference.

Just like needs assessment, goal setting and articulating measurable outcomes should have primary input from the client but may benefit from secondary review by others. And, as discussed earlier, we know that goals change throughout a learning process (as well as throughout a conflict process), so periodic revisiting of goals and goal achievement is a must for any lengthy conflict coaching.

Feedback. Feedback is perhaps the most critical aspect of learning, but it may be underemphasized—especially in conflict consulting. Reflection is a form of feedback in which the client thinks about what she has learned and how that has made a difference.

Tim Hedeen (2005, p. 191), in a thoughtful essay on contributions of Maria Montessori, John Dewey, and Paulo Freire to the design of conflict education, heralds Dewey's advocacy of experiential learning coupled with *reflection* and the importance of context as a factor in educational design and process:

> Dewey held that individuals *can* learn from experience, but only when they undertake the task of connecting experiences to consequences or to related information or ideas. Trainings and courses in conflict resolution routinely ask participants to recall experiences of conflict or crisis, and to consider how the application of given theories or approaches might have led to different conclusions. Doing so involves the two principles that constitute Dewey's "theory of experience": continuity and interaction.

Continuity is the principle that past experiences influence future ones, while *interaction* represents the interplay between a present condition and the individual's past experience. Dewey believed that learning occurs when learners engage with experience. There is learning when the consequences of the experience are seen, but there is further learning when the student reflects upon the experiences and consequences. The student then may apply this new understanding to future actions.

As a coach, it is essential to encourage clients to reflect on their past and present experiences and the extent to which those are connected. A variety of techniques can be used that are borrowed from the reflective practice literature in our field, for example, Schön's *The Reflective Practitioner* (1983), which has inspired the reflective-practice writings of Kressel (1997) and Lang and Taylor (2000), as well as Picard's related "insight mediation" (2003). Self-interviews, journaling, video review, and consultation with peers all serve as techniques that heighten our ability to see ourselves and our behavior as contexted, dynamic, and impactful.

However, there is a cautionary note. Coaches cannot take for granted that their clients will be able to engage in reflection and self-assessment easily or well.

There are numerous challenges to effective self-assessment. As Cantillon and Jones (1999) found, different learners resonate with different forms of assessment and feedback. As Reiter, Eva, Hatala, and Norman learned (2002), many adults are not facile at self-assessment, often unable to accurately identify their own strengths and weaknesses in knowledge or behavior. Similar deficits have been reported and addressed in sister fields like social work (Council on Social Work Education, 1988; Gleeson, 1990). The coach may need to try a variety of reflection techniques before finding one that works well with a particular client.

Feedback given to the client is critical according to all adult learning theories. Of course, one important source of feedback is the coach, who should be providing regular, specific, and constructive feedback throughout the coaching process. (See Chapter 8 for more guidelines on providing constructive feedback as a communication skill.) A tension in conflict coaching is maintaining a critical stance while operating as a paid consultant to the client or organization. A coach may be tempted to soften feedback to maintain the coach-client relationship. If Michael sees that Joan is continually making hostile attributions about her co-workers and is acting aggressively toward them based on those attributions, he must give Joan that feedback. How he gives Joan that feedback is the key. According to tried and true guidelines for effective feedback, it should be specific (focusing on specific behaviors or expressions), timely (provided as quickly as possible after the behavior), constructive (focused on what can be better rather than just articulating what is wrong) and provisional (recognizing that it may not be the only way of seeing this behavior).

In addition to feedback from the coach, the coach and client should discuss other sources of important feedback. Perhaps those sources will include supervisors, co-workers, family members, direct reports, etc. In other parts of the book we've talked about different feedback processes common to the workplace—gap analysis and 360-degree feedback. These techniques can be used to elicit feedback from others, but first you need to agree on who should provide feedback and what you want to know from them. For example, asking Robert, "How do you think it's going with Joan?" may start a conversation that is a waste of time and creates frustration. Asking Robert, "Can you think of a specific instance in the past week where you have seen Joan respond more positively in a conflict situation and can you tell about that incident?" provides much clearer and more useful feedback.

Feedback from the client should be encouraged throughout the process. Negotiation and conflict theorists have promoted the use of assessment models from Kirkpatrick (1976) (reported in Susskind, 2004), who suggests there are five possible levels of assessment:

- *Level 1: Reaction.* Was the coaching enjoyable? Was it useful?
- *Level 2: Learning.* If I test you on the concepts or skills, will you know more than you did before you had the coaching?
- *Level 3: Application.* Do you know how to apply the coaching?
- *Level 4: Impact.* What is the impact of the coaching on important business or organizational outcomes?
- *Level 5: Return on Investment.* What is the ratio of direct and indirect costs of coaching to the benefits yielded from it?

Clients can be asked to provide feedback on all of these levels, other than perhaps level 5. The most useful feedback will be that which is provided in response to specific aspects of coaching at the time that the learning is taking place. A healthy coach-client relationship should foster easy conversations that provide this feedback on a regular basis.

Looking at these levels of feedback, it is obvious that some clients will not have answers at certain levels (particularly levels 4 and 5) until some time after the coaching has ended. A coach should plan for this and build in follow-up feedback processes that will allow a long-term perspective on the coaching efficacy.

Learning Transfer. Learning transfer facilitates the learner's ability to apply what has been learned. As Addor et al. comment (2005, p. 210),

> Caffarella (1994) suggests three important elements of planning for successful learning transfer: knowing when to initiate effective learning transfer strategies (before, during, and after the learning experience for reinforcement and retention); knowing which strategies to apply (strategies such as self-designed action plans or mentoring); and identifying who should support learning transfer (learners willing to make personal changes, peers and supervisors willing to support the change).

LEARNING ASSESSMENT AS A PARALLEL PROCESS

Integration of learning assessment components in the CCC model will vary depending on the complexity of the conflict, the length of the coaching relationship, and the desire of the direct and indirect clients. There are logical connections between components of learning assessment and stages of the CCC model, which we present here.

Needs Assessment. This begins with the preparatory conversation, but is most connected with the first two stages of the coaching model. With the initiation of the coaching relationship, the coach talks with the direct and indirect clients about why coaching is a valuable alternative. In the preparatory conversation, the coach and clients identify the broad areas of need that they see. And, in some situations, the areas of need identified by the direct client (for example, Joan) and the indirect client (for example, Robert) will be different, suggesting to the coach that needs assessment discussions should be given priority as the parameters of the coaching relationship are established.

During Stage One, the client and coach work together to discover and refine the story of the conflict. By so doing, they are articulating what is wrong or what needs to be fixed in the conflict situation. When Joan tells her story of discomfort with her relationship with her nurses and the poor performance indicators of her department, she is signaling things that she needs to have changed.

Yet, it is in Stage Two, as the coach and client examine the conflict from the perspectives of identity, emotion, and power, that they complete the most significant aspect of needs assessment. As we have discussed in Chapters 4, 5, and 6, the client comes to terms with her identity needs, her emotion needs and her power needs.

Needs assessment is replaced by goal setting, feedback, and learning transfer through the latter stages of the model. However, in lengthy conflict coaching relationships, it is a good idea to periodically revisit needs assessment to make sure that the conditions in the workplace have not shifted to such an extent that previously identified needs are no longer relevant.

Goal Setting. Goal setting is emphasized through Stage Three and Four of the conflict coaching process. As clients craft their best story, they describe a vision of what they want to see happen. Joan's best story may be that she has a very successful relationship with her nurses, that she is regarded as one of the best nurse managers in the health system, and that her department has the highest performance indicators of any department. Her vision is one way of identifying broad-level goals and beginning to articulate measurable objectives for those goals.

The intensive goal setting is concentrated in Stage Four, when the coach and client focus on knowledge, skills, and attitudes to be developed or improved for the client to be able to enact their vision. Michael and Joan realize that for Joan to accomplish her vision, she needs to learn much more about negotiation. Joan also needs to develop the skills to analyze a situation and determine which negotiation orientation is the best fit. And once she has selected an orientation, Joan needs to be able to behaviorally enact the various negotiation skills that Michael can teach. Moreover, Joan may need to change her attitude about competitive negotiation, becoming more comfortable with bargaining in order to accomplish her vision.

As with needs, the longer the period over which conflict coaching occurs, the more likely it is that goals will change, because the larger context of the conflict has changed. Even if Joan has achieved her goals in Stage Four, she will need to think about what goals she will set for learning transfer and for the period beyond the initial application of her newly acquired negotiation expertise.

Feedback. Feedback occurs throughout conflict coaching, but it takes different forms at various stages. In the preparatory conversations, the coach may give clients feedback about their competency to engage in coaching. The client will also have received feedback from others in the organization, often indicating their perception that coaching is needed.

But we are most concerned with feedback in terms of information the client receives from herself or others about what she is learning and how she is performing in areas of learning. During Stages One, Two, and Three, the client receives feedback from the coach about the client's perception of the situation. As coaches test the initial story or the best story, they are indicating that there are other ways of seeing the situation or deeper analysis that is needed. Especially during Stage Two, clients will provide considerable reflection and self-feedback as they engage in self-assessment and self-analysis to get a clearer understanding of identity, emotion, and power needs.

The feedback generated in Stage Four concerns the degree to which clients are able to learn knowledge and skills that are important to achieve their vision. Joan and Michael concentrate initially on feedback about Joan's understanding of negotiation and her ability to enact negotiation strategies. Perhaps Joan can role-play a negotiation and, through videotape or audiotape, reflect on her performance. She may also engage in negotiations with others outside her workplace to test her comfort level and skills. She may request feedback from her negotiation partners. And, when Joan believes she has enough skill and knowledge to confidently negotiate within her workplace, she can discuss with Michael strategies to obtain feedback on that negotiation.

The more elaborate the skill development plan in Stage Four, the more important it is that the coach and client establish a comprehensive feedback system. A comprehensive feedback system has several characteristics:

It provides feedback in the area of knowledge, skills, and attitude.

It provides feedback proportionate to the needed improvement. If the most critical improvement is the development of a better attitude about bargaining and the ability to enact bargaining strategies, the majority of feedback should be concentrated there.

It provides feedback from multiple sources (the client, the coach, and others—preferably those outside of and inside the conflict context).

It provides feedback immediately after the performance or learning.

It provides feedback over time; as skills develop, there should be incremental feedback.

Learning Transfer. While we present learning transfer as a final component in our learning assessment process, it can and does take place at various levels throughout the coaching experience. Joan may be learning skills of integrative negotiation that she tests during the coaching as well as applies more fully after coaching. Still, the preponderance of learning transfer takes place after skills development and at the end of the coaching sessions.

In the initial stages of coaching, learning transfer is mainly about applying new knowledge and insight as an analytic tool to the conflict experiences in context. Can Joan look at conflicts happening in her workplace and see when a certain negotiation approach would make sense and why? Does Joan understand how her identity needs and emotion needs are influencing her potential response to this conflict?

In the skills development stage, the emphasis on learning transfer is on applying the skills in a context other than that of the presenting conflict. By doing this, the client can think about how to apply the skills and learn from that application without creating disruption or escalating the conflict. In this way, learning transfer is much like the out-of-town opening for a Broadway show. It can provide excellent information without jeopardizing the final effort.

If conflict coaching has been successful, learning transfer comes with the effective application of the new conflict knowledge, skills, and attitudes in the conflict context. How well can Joan analyze the conflicts with her own nursing staff and her peers in the hospital? How successfully can she negotiate with them to achieve the outcomes she has determined are important? How well can she see changes in the workplace that necessitate large or small alterations in her conflict approach?

Learning transfer is an ongoing process. As participants in this process, the client and conflict coach should develop a process by which they can stay in touch and check in about how well things are going. They should identify very specific outcome measures that they want to track to determine success. And they should discuss these indices of success with indirect clients and other stakeholders.

General Principles for Learning Assessment

Principle #1: Involve the client as much as possible in designing the learning assessment strategies. As adult learning theory suggests, the more involved and empowered clients are in setting learning assessments, the more they will be committed to the learning assessments and the information the assessments provide. The client has a better understanding of the context in which the learning will be applied and, as a result, has an important voice in designing valid learning assessments.

Principle #2: Design learning assessments that are positively oriented and strength based. People learn much better by concentrating on what they are doing well than by being reminded what they are doing poorly. Just as we embrace an appreciative inquiry orientation in crafting the best story, we embrace a positively oriented and strength-based learning assessment model.

Principle #3: Link learning assessments to reward and evaluation systems in the larger context when possible. If your clients know that they will ultimately be judged by some assessment system in the workplace, it behooves the coach and client to consider whether that external assessment system should be included in the learning assessments used in conflict coaching. If there is not a good fit between the learning that is taking place and the external assessment, the coach and client have an opportunity to articulate why that is a poor fit and why the external system should be de-emphasized during learning transfer.

Principle #4: Update learning assessment strategies as the conflict coaching progresses. As people learn, they need to have learning assessments that become more reflective of the level of learning. This doesn't mean that the coach and client completely discard learning assessments from earlier stages of learning. But it does mean that they need to continually update learning assessments to guarantee that the newer skills, knowledge, and attitudes are being assessed.

Principle #5: Attempt to gather multiple types of feedback from multiple sources throughout the learning assessment process. While not all feedback is equally valuable, a general rule is to seek as many reasonable forms of feedback from as many important sources as possible. This provides the coach and client with more information to guide refinement of skills and abilities. And especially when the client will be engaged in learning transfer in multiple contexts, it is useful to know how stakeholders in each context perceive the client's skills. It is also critical to generate feedback from the client, the coach, and external others. Without all three forms of feedback, essential information is missing.

Principle #6: Clarify the termination of the learning assessment process. Like all good things, learning assessment must come to an end. There is a risk that a coach and client will not want to or know when to let go and will continue assessing learning after the point at which it is beneficial or informative. One of the explicit discussions that a coach needs to have with a client is how to determine the point at which learning assessment has been completed.

Specific Approaches for Learning Assessment

Approach #1: Record and reflect on needs in initial stages of conflict coaching.

What is it? The client keeps a record of needs that are articulated in the preparatory conversation and initial stages of coaching. This record becomes a focus for reflection leading to goal setting.

Why is it important? In the initial stages of conflict coaching, it is easy to forget or miss some of the needs that have been identified. Having a record of the need, who identified the need, and how the need relates to others gives the client a memory aid as well as a means of organizing thoughts. When the client reflects on the needs, either through conversation, journaling, or using worksheets, the client becomes clearer on which needs are critical and why.

How do you do it? The coach can keep a record through initial conversations and ask the client to respond. Or, after each session, the client can complete a needs worksheet. Clients can complete reflection writing assignments; these are particularly useful after the completion of Stages One and Two.

Approach #2: Construct a goals chart.

What is it? A goals chart is a device that lists specific goals, defines them by behavioral objectives, and indicates the kind of evidence one would see to prove the objective had been met.

Why is it important? Most people have difficulty setting goals, because the goals are too abstract and general—they can't seem to bring it down to the level of specific behaviors and measures. The goals chart pushes the client to be able to do that. And, in so doing, the goals chart becomes not only a record but a tool that helps identify goals that are poorly conceived and perhaps not really important. A goals chart is also very helpful as a first step in planning feedback processes.

How do you do it? At the end of Stage Three, the client is asked to complete a goals chart, such as the one provided on the CD-ROM. The client can elaborate on the goals chart by obtaining feedback on the goals from others or by considering both positive and negative consequences if those goals are achieved.

Approach #3: Plan a feedback support system.

What is it? A feedback support system is a list of people who are willing and able to provide clients feedback about their learning in a safe and nonjudgmental way. The feedback support system may include members from the conflict context or not.

Why is it important? The feedback support system helps define an operative network of support for the client and, at the same time, makes it clear where there are gaps in the client's ability to get certain kinds of feedback from "safe" others. Having a supportive feedback network will encourage the client to seek feedback rather than shun it. And it provides a means of ongoing encouragement and enthusiasm about the client's progress.

How do you do it? The client identifies important feedback that is related to each of the goal areas identified. For each area of feedback, the client lists one or two people who are qualified to provide feedback and who the client trusts to be positive and supportive but still honest and direct. The client then asks those individuals whether they are willing to serve as feedback providers, and those people are called upon to do so when appropriate as the process moves forward.

Approach #4: See the tricks in the transfer.

What is it? This activity asks the client to think about the difficult or tricky aspects of applying his or her new skills and knowledge to the real world.

Why is it important? By identifying what will make learning transfer of a specific skill difficult, clients allow themselves to think about what will need to be done to reduce that difficulty. Perhaps more skill practice to build confidence is needed. Perhaps applying the skill to an easier situation before using it in the real conflict will help. If clients can articulate what makes the application tricky, they can approach the problem logically. If they can't say why an application may be tricky, they may not have thought enough about what the goal should be and why it will be important.

How do you do it? The client and the coach can first talk through the assumptions about what makes learning transfer difficult. Or the client can attach a worksheet to earlier statements of goals—basically the "add a column" approach, and indicate the tricky parts for each.

Approach #5: Develop a learning transfer timetable and follow-up plan.

What is it? The client and coach create a timetable for when learning transfer will take place and when they will periodically meet to review how the learning transfer is going.

Why is it important? At the end of conflict coaching there is a tendency to move to the next challenge and forget about follow-through. Both the coach and the client may be pulled unconsciously in these directions. By articulating a timetable for transfer and follow-up, they are making it easier to stay in touch and to chart progress and success. Of course, this also means that they are creating a process by which they can more formally evaluate the success of the coaching and tweak the work if necessary.

How do you do it? The process is the same as action planning used in many project situations. The coach and client complete a chart in which the goal to be transferred is listed, the timing of the transfer is indicated, and the means of evaluating success is stated. The action plan then indicates at what intervals the coach and client will gather this information and when they will meet to discuss it.

Chapter Summary

Learning assessment is a parallel process that flows throughout the conflict coaching experience. It is composed of four components: needs assessment, goal setting, feedback, and learning transfer. Although these components can take place at any time, there is a general pattern of priority. Needs assessment tends to be emphasized in the initial stages of the coaching. Goal setting is often highlighted in Stages Three and Four. Feedback is fairly constant throughout, but feedback on skills development is most emphasized in Stage Four. And learning transfer is usually greatest at the end of coaching and beyond.

GENERAL PRINCIPLES FOR LEARNING ASSESSMENT

Principle #1: Involve the client as much as possible in designing learning assessment strategies.

Principle #2: Design learning assessments that are positively oriented and strength based.

Principle #3: Link learning assessments to reward and evaluation systems in the larger context when possible.

Principle #4: Update learning assessment strategies as the conflict coaching progresses.

Principle #5: Attempt to gather multiple types of feedback from multiple sources throughout the learning assessment process.

Principle #6: Clarify the termination of the learning assessment process.

SPECIFIC APPROACHES FOR LEARNING ASSESSMENT

Approach #1: Record and reflect on needs in initial stages of conflict coaching.

Approach #2: Construct a goals chart.

Approach #3: Plan a feedback support system.

Approach #4: See the tricks in the transfer.

Approach #5: Develop a learning transfer timetable and follow-up plan.

SECTION 3

*Integrating Conflict
Coaching Into Your Practice*

13

Needs Assessment and Program Evaluation for Conflict Coaching

Believe one who has proved it.

—Virgil

Michael, like many conflict consultants, offers a variety of dispute resolution and conflict consulting services. He would like to be more certain that his conflict coaching practice is fitting well with his clients' needs and is adding value to his practice. He wants to evaluate when and how conflict coaching is most effective for his clients and overall business.

Michael struggles with being stretched too thin. His practice has five full-time consultants including himself, and they work in a relatively rural region. As a result, they provide services to several small towns and cities and a variety of individuals and organizations within the region. For Michael to direct energy and resources to conflict coaching (rather than other services like mediation, conflict training, facilitation) he needs proof that this direction makes good business sense for his practice and delivers good results for his clients.

Michael was recently approached by a large medical center to provide conflict coaching to middle-level nurse managers. In the initial meeting the vice president of human resources asked Michael to provide evidence that conflict coaching, in general, delivered positive outcomes for the organization. The vice president also asked Michael whether he had specific evidence that his firm's conflict coaching had made a positive difference for other employers in the area.

Michael needs to gather information to evaluate the quality of his decision to conduct conflict coaching and to determine whether the conflict coaching is making a positive difference for his clientele. To paraphrase Dr. Phil, Michael is asking himself, "How's this working for me?"

In earlier chapters we concentrated on presenting and explaining the CCC model of conflict coaching. In this chapter we shift the focus to needs assessment, program evaluation, and marketing. We encourage the prospective conflict coach to ask the needs-assessment question, "Is conflict coaching a valuable addition to my practice?" If the decision is made to engage in conflict coaching, we strongly encourage the coach to ask the program evaluation question, "How well is conflict coaching achieving desired outcomes for my clients and my practice?" And if the data from program evaluation and needs assessment are positive, we suggest the coach consider the marketing question, "How can I use this information to market my conflict coaching practice?"

Needs Assessment: Will Conflict Coaching Meet My Needs?

The first step in deciding to implement a conflict coaching program is determining what you hope or expect to get from the endeavor. What do you want the program to do? Or, put another way, what is wrong with the current state of affairs?

Imagine you want to use conflict coaching to support your mediation practice. Do you want to attract clients who are not already coming to you for possible mediation? Do you want to increase the number of clients who ultimately decide to use mediation? Do you want to expand to another context of practice, for example, more workplace conflict management consulting, and you believe conflict coaching would be attractive for that context? Do you want to increase your skills to add coaching to your other areas of practice expertise? Are you interested in generating more revenue and having a larger return on your investment? Any of these may be needs that you have identified that support your decision to use coaching.

Perhaps you direct an internal dispute system in a larger organization. Your needs assessment may be guided by different questions. For example, you may be interested in how conflict coaching could help organizational members currently underserved by other components of the dispute system. Perhaps you have a need to introduce tools that will increase the loop-back processes in your system, and you believe that conflict coaching is one such tool. Or possibly you see conflict coaching as an important management skill and wish to train all managers to add this to their conflict management repertoire.

You may be the director of a community mediation center that is struggling to maintain staff and programming in this era of tight resources and changing funding patterns for conflict programs. You may see conflict coaching as a fee-for-service option that can help generate revenue. Or perhaps coaching is a way to reenergize your volunteer base by offering new training to enhance their experience. Possibly you are branching into online dispute resolution (ODR) and you see conflict coaching as a powerful outreach tool that is economically advantageous compared to other ODR options.

ASKING STAKEHOLDERS

How do you identify and assess your needs? Of course, you can start by thinking of your personal needs and the information you have available to you. But you wouldn't want to end there. You also want to consider asking stakeholders about their perceptions of needs for conflict coaching.

Broadly defined, stakeholders are people who have an interest in your program. They may be people who will be involved in its day-to-day implementation and operation, or people who will be affected by the program, or people who feel they have a connection or link with the program and an interest in its activities. For a conflict consulting firm, stakeholders may include trainers, consultants, staffers, and existing clients. For an organization, the stakeholders may include organizational members, leadership, stockholders, and internal and external clients. And for a community mediation center, stakeholders may include center staff, the board of directors, community members, the volunteer base, and community organizations who support or use the center.

Knowing who the stakeholders are allows you to identify their interests and design the conflict coaching program in a responsive and responsible fashion. Have all stakeholders had the opportunity to voice their needs about the program? If not, how can you give them this opportunity? A good place to start is to survey or interview the stakeholders. Use fairly open-ended questions, and keep the survey or interview brief. The purpose is not to find out everything the stakeholder thinks, but to identify the significant concerns and goals. Some sample questions that you could ask of stakeholders include the following:

- What kinds of conflicts are occurring that are a good fit for conflict coaching?
- How common are these conflicts?
- Who tends to be involved in these conflicts?

❦ Why does the (practice, organization, community mediation center) need a conflict coaching program?

❦ What would you like to see such a program accomplish? What are your goals for the program?

❦ What are your concerns about having this kind of program?

❦ Who should we talk to before proceeding with the development of such a program?

ASSESSING RESOURCES

Let's say that you have decided there is a strong need for a conflict coaching program. Now you face the question of whether there are adequate resources to begin program development or implementation. Consider the availability of the following:

Commitment of stakeholders. You should have at least a majority of stakeholders who have expressed a strong commitment to actively supporting the program.

Conflict coaching experts. Do you have access to training organizations and experts in the area who can provide training and program implementation guidance?

Staffing. Do you have people in the organization/firm/center who can be trained as conflict coaches? Who can oversee or monitor the conflict coaching program activities?

Money. Do you have the money to pay for training support and to buy curriculum, instructional materials, etc.?

Time. Do you have the time, or does someone in the organization have the time, for needs assessment, program evaluation, and marketing?

Assume that Michael has conducted a strong needs assessment to determine whether conflict coaching makes sense. He surveyed and interviewed his stakeholders and discovered that his staff were very interested in exploring conflict coaching and felt that they saw significant need for it and significant opportunity. Client organizations consistently reported to Michael that conflict coaching would be a positive approach to helping them address certain kinds of conflicts and provide more support to some workers. And Michael learned from several of the municipal governments he consults with that they saw potential benefit from coaching to address worker burnout in human services. As Michael considered the issue of resources, he concluded that adding viable conflict coaching to his practice was workable but would definitely mean shifting resources from one program area to another, at least for the short term.

Program Evaluation: Is Conflict Coaching Working for You?

In this chapter, we strongly suggest that a conflict coach become proficient with program evaluation. In the last chapter we discussed learning assessment that examines the learning process and outcomes of an individual client in a coaching process. And we explained that learning assessment is typically the clients' central concern—are they learning knowledge and skills that are helping them respond more constructively to conflict? Program evaluation has several components that determine systems-level impacts rather than individual growth or change. Program evaluation is concerned with the enterprise of conflict coaching rather than the experience of a client going through conflict coaching. Of course, both learning assessment and program evaluation are linked and should be considered together for the coach to have a comprehensive understanding of coaching effectiveness. In the CD-ROM accompanying this book, we have suggested resources that can provide a general overview of program evaluation approaches.

Conflict coaches need to evaluate whether their coaching practice is working for them. Like all consultants, they should be concerned with questions of fit, quality, impact, and profitability. Michael is an independent consultant who needs program evaluation to make sure he can get and keep clients. However, Michael could be the director of a larger consulting firm, or the head of an internal conflict consulting function within an organization, and if he were, he would want to know how well conflict coaching is fitting in the system and whether it is delivering a strong return on investment.

Evaluation is a means of getting feedback for two general purposes: (1) to summarize the nature and impact of the coaching and (2) to change or alter the coaching to better serve the consultant and the client (Fitzpatrick, Sanders, & Worthen, 2003; McDavid & Hawthorn, 2005; Wholey, Hatry, & Newcomer, 2004). When you use the evaluation information as a basis for change or improvement in the coaching program, the links between program implementation and evaluation are clear. While the two processes may be distinct, they can be and often are used in conjunction. We feel strongly that it is important to use these processes together.

Good program evaluation answers the questions: "What happened?" "How did it happen?" and "Why did it happen?" In order to know, or have evidence about why something happened—why a certain outcome was observed or not—you need information about the "what" and "how" of the coaching process. This is especially important if you are trying to avoid problems or failures in the next program implementation or want to increase the chances of success in newer coaching approaches.

WHY EVALUATE YOUR CONFLICT COACHING PROGRAM?

The main reason to do program evaluation is to see if the program works. But that is a deceptively simple statement. When you actually contemplate a program evaluation, you are assuming what "works" means and why it may be important to you. As you progress through this manual and develop realistic assessments of your program evaluation needs and strategies, your purposes for evaluation will be tailored to your needs and hopes. But, as a general starting place, let's consider some of the typical reasons that program evaluation is wanted and warranted.

Monitoring a program to make sure it is operating as planned. The program is developed to meet specific needs or goals. One of the most compelling reasons to evaluate a program is to determine whether those needs have indeed been addressed or whether the goals have been achieved.

Improving a program by identifying strengths and weaknesses. A second reason for program evaluation is to be able to identify things that are working and things that are not in order to know what to repeat and what to fix. Sometimes we approach program evaluation with an eye for the negative, or the things that aren't what we'd like to see. It's important to remember that assessments of both strengths and weaknesses are helpful. A good program evaluation will help you identify strengths that were expected as well as those that were not. Sometimes, the reasons a program works are unanticipated, and program evaluation helps us recognize and perpetuate those. Just as with the investigation of strengths, not all weaknesses are recognized in advance. Program evaluation can be very helpful in uncovering previously unsuspected sources of difficulty. In some cases, program evaluation finds that the training material or curriculum used, materials that had previously been assumed to be of high quality and appropriate for use, just do not meet the needs of clients. Perhaps the material is not sensitive to the cultural diversity in the organization, or the coaching is not sensitive enough to the kinds of challenges the client faces.

Expanding a program. Expansion may be a result of an initially positive program evaluation. The program is expanded by introducing it to new clients, more client organizations, etc. Or it can be expanded by adding more components to the program. Whenever program expansion is a possibility, and certainly when it is a goal, program evaluation provides a means of forecasting needs and planning for strengths. For example, program evaluation can provide a good estimate of the staff support necessary for maximum impact of the program. This information is crucial for effective planning and resource allocation in new programs.

Gaining additional resources. People love a winner. This is an old maxim but a true one when it comes to decisions about where to put already scarce resources. In business, there is little reason to throw good money after bad, especially when a lot of good programs vie for limited funding.

Thus, one of the main reasons to do program evaluation is to make the strongest case for why you should continue to receive support for your efforts. All decision makers want to make sure that the resources they allocate make a difference. If you have solid program evaluation, you can provide this evidence and prove that you have the competence to continue overseeing the processes and outcomes of the conflict coaching program.

Your program evaluation also makes it easier for these decision makers to compare programs in terms of efficacy and efficiency. How can you help a decision maker realize that she or he will help achieve more by going for your conflict coaching program than by using an alternative touted to address the same issues with the same or superior impact?

PROCESS AND OUTCOME EVALUATION

Program evaluation is usually discussed in terms of process and/or outcome evaluation. Although we resist the temptation to treat these two processes as dichotomous, they are different in general focus. Process evaluation is concerned with the process of implementing the program and whether that process is enhancing or inhibiting the success of the program. Thus, good process evaluation tells the story of the program as it unfolds. It helps you focus on the techniques and events that made a difference—whether for good or bad.

Process Evaluation. What are some of the processes that one might be interested in monitoring in conflict coaching?

Assessment Process. The more elaborate the program model, the more complex the assessment process should be.

- How well were the needs for the program assessed prior to program development and implementation?
- Were key stakeholders identified?
- Were all relevant voices heard?
- Were needs clarified and well articulated?

Planning Process. Processes of planning are critical to program success. Strategic planning ensures that you are projecting difficulties and planning for them instead of being caught unaware.

- What planning processes were used to identify program goals and objectives?
- What planning processes were used to secure needed resources?
- What planning processes were used to develop an implementation strategy?
- Did planning consider how the program would be integrated into existing activities or systems?

※ For more complex program models, did planning deal with problems of coordination between program components (for example, how coaching is used as an adjunct to mediation)?

Orientation Process. Once the assessment and planning are completed, the program needs to be introduced to the client or client organization. Process evaluation can focus on how well the orientation was accomplished. Perhaps the vice president of human resources is hesitant to use conflict coaching because Michael was not able to clearly explain the process and potential benefits.

※ How extensive was the explanation of program content and purpose?
※ How was it presented?
※ To whom was it presented and in what forum?
※ What processes, if any, were used to secure and assess the degree of resistance or commitment to the program?
※ How was feedback handled, and how were suggestions for change negotiated?

Selection Process. This is the issue of who is chosen to directly participate in the conflict coaching program.

※ Was participation voluntary?
※ Did organizational members working with the coaching client (as boss, co-worker, direct report, etc.) have a chance to refuse participation?
※ What processes were used to recruit participation, and how well did these work?
※ Were interested parties not allowed to participate for some reason?

Coaching Training Process. Assuming that Michael has a large consulting firm with several consultants trained as conflict coaches, one aspect of process is the quality of training provided to conflict coaches.

※ How long did the training last?
※ Who delivered it?
※ Were the trainers qualified?
※ What kinds of pedagogical approaches were used?
※ What instructional or supporting materials were involved?
※ What was the quality of those materials?
※ What reflective practice and learning assessments were done?
※ How effective was the learning assessment overall?

Coaching Program Implementation Process. Up to this point, all activity has been preparatory. Now, the organization and key personnel have been oriented, the clients or departments have been selected, the training has taken place, and the coaching is ready to begin.

▓ What procedures are used to refer cases to coaching, and how well are organizational members using the referral mechanisms?

▓ How do issues of referral and publicity relate to how the program is used?

▓ What processes are used to link mediation to other dispute resolution processes in the organization?

▓ What happens if coaching is not successful? What aftercare or follow-up contingencies are available?

▓ How well was learning assessment conducted?

▓ What conflict coaching materials are being used?

▓ How were the coaching materials and approaches selected and why?

▓ How comfortable are coaches with using the materials and the techniques?

▓ How well are they using the materials and techniques?

▓ What changes, if any, were made to the coaching model or materials to better meet client and organizational needs?

▓ How often is coaching being used? With what client populations?

▓ What is the length and involvement of the coaching processes?

▓ Are client or organization rewards or accountability structures linked to conflict coaching participation and success?

▓ How are clients reacting to the conflict coaching? What is their level of satisfaction, their perceived utility of the material?

▓ What are the successes and challenges with learning transfer?

Program Maintenance Process. If a program is long-lasting it will have to face the issue of turnover in personnel and participants. Again, the more complex the program, the more turnover opportunities exist and the more possibility there is that change can disrupt an effectively functioning program. Some questions that can be asked of program maintenance include the following.

▓ What is the degree of client and coach turnover that is experienced in the program?

▓ How are the selection, initiation, and orientation of new members or participants handled?

▓ How is record keeping used to maintain a working history and continuity of the program?

Context/Environmental Factors. No matter how well a consultant plans for and tries to oversee a conflict coaching program, the reality is that the larger context or environment can influence what happens, sometimes beyond our control.

▓ How are changes in the departmental or unit environment enhancing or inhibiting conflict coaching?

▓ How are changes in the organization enhancing or inhibiting conflict coaching?

Outcome Evaluation. Outcome evaluation focuses on whether and to what extent specific, tangible goals and objectives established for the program are achieved. The emphasis is on the outcomes of the program and the evaluator's ability to document them. The crux of outcome evaluation is twofold: (1) to document what happened in terms of utility or frequency (as opposed to how it happened in process evaluation) and (2) to document what changed as a result of the program. In the first area of outcome evaluation, people attend to questions about the extent of involvement or activity. For example, how many clients were coached? How many coaches attended training sessions? How many times was conflict coaching used as an adjunct to mediation?

In the second area of outcome evaluation, the notion of proving change requires that you have some way to compare the situation prior to the program with what happened during and/or after the program. Most of us are familiar with pretest and posttest designs and the use of control groups that are necessary for this kind of outcome evaluation.

Outcomes can be monitored on a short-term or a long-term basis. Some outcomes—for example, satisfaction with conflict coaching sessions—are more helpful if measured in the short-term, immediately following the coaching session. Long-term assessment of satisfaction doesn't make as much sense, because most people forget the process and focus more on the results being achieved. But, various outcomes concerning improved relationship with the other party, or decreased incidents of conflict with the other party, are better evaluated both short-term and long-term. The conflict coach and client want to see an immediate and lasting effect in these areas. And finally, an outcome like increased likelihood to be promoted can only be evaluated in the long term; it will take time for the client to work through a career path and for the coach to evaluate whether clients in coaching have achieved more promotions than clients who did not use coaching.

The types of outcomes that can be evaluated are as varied as the types of coaching programs and applications that exist. However, we can talk about five general kinds of outcomes that most programs are interested in at some level.

Skills/Abilities Learned. Conflict coaching has as a central focus the teaching of foundational abilities necessary for the enactment of constructive conflict management. Thus, outcome evaluation may focus on questions about how well clients learned the skills of active listening, perspective taking, empathic response, generation of alternatives, anger control, etc. The key is to clearly specify the skills and abilities that you are trying to coach and to make sure that these are being evaluated in terms of how well the program developed these skills or abilities in participants.

Attitudes Changed. Many conflict coaches are interested in helping clients adopt more prosocial attitudes. Pretest and posttest attitude surveys are often used and useful in determining this type of change.

Behaviors Changed. Many would argue that changes in attitudes or skill development are relatively irrelevant if the client does not apply the new knowledge in the form of changed behavior in the workplace. It doesn't help the vice president of HR for the nurse managers to learn more about the roots of passive aggression if they continue to act in a passive aggressive manner.

Program Utility. Questions of program utility have to do with the extent to which conflict coaching has been used in the organization. In many programs this is the most common form of outcome evaluation. As mentioned above, this focus often assesses how frequently coaching is used, by whom, and with what outcome.

Resources Created. Sometimes outcome evaluation can focus on resources that are created as a central or peripheral purpose of the conflict coaching. These resources fall into three categories: First, there are the *tangible economic resources.* For example, sometimes a program outcome is that a program receives a financial award based on effectiveness or secures additional funding for continued work. Second, there are the *instructional products.* Training manuals and instructional material developed or modified for use in the program can be seen as valuable outcomes. Finally, there are *relationships and infrastructures* that are formed. Especially in programs that link departments, units, organizations, and communities, an important area of outcome is how well the program helped develop relationships between key players.

SUMMATIVE AND ACTION RESEARCH EVALUATION

One of the decisions a program evaluator will have to make concerns when and how to use the information gained from program evaluation. Once again, there are two general approaches: (1) summative evaluation and (2) action research evaluation. Summative evaluation waits until the end of the evaluation period to report findings. Action research evaluation assumes that information gained from the evaluation should be fed back to the program as a relatively immediate feedback mechanism that allows the program to be revised and altered in midstream in order to maximize performance (Carruthers, Carruthers, Day-Vine, Bostick, & Watson, 1996).

Both approaches have advantages. Summative evaluation is advantageous when the highest priority is to demonstrate the impact that the program had on certain outcomes, and strong change indices are needed as evidence. For example, assume that you have gotten funding for the program on the condition that you can prove that the conflict coaching can produce a 25 percent reduction in absenteeism and a 10 percent reduction of grievance claims in a year. In this case, you may need to forgo altering the program in mid-course in order to be able to assess, or "prove" impact due to the program. Action research evaluation is advantageous because it allows you to make improvements quickly that can prevent wasting resources and effort. Proponents of action research often argue that it makes little sense to know you are doing something wrong but to continue to do it in order to be able to better document the degree of the problem. Realizing that organizations are dynamic entities, action research allows you to monitor and adjust quickly.

Our view is that both summative and action research evaluation are useful. The important point is that you know why you are selecting one or the other. And it is imperative that you realize the kinds of information necessary to collect in one approach versus the other. Finally, in an effort to escape the either-or nature of this discussion, we argue that a long-term evaluation process can include components of both summative and action research evaluation. In the initial stages of the program, action research makes more sense. This allows you to monitor, tinker, and adjust until you have the program running at strength. At this point, it may make sense to use summative evaluation strategies for specific periods (say one to two years) to assess impact and change.

TYPES OF INFORMATION TO COLLECT

Many conflict practitioners do not have a background in program evaluation, data collection and data analysis. This section won't provide that background, but it outlines some kinds of data useful in program evaluation. If the need is to conduct a sophisticated summative evaluation it is wise to consult a program evaluation expert, perhaps at a local university.

Qualitative Measures. Qualitative measures are data you collect that are not numeric. The most common kinds of qualitative data are interviews, observations, and documents.

Interviews. There are several different types of interviews and interviewing styles; most involve the querying of one or more persons by another person or persons in a face-to-face setting. However, interviews can also take place over the phone or via e-mail. Furthermore, interviews can be formal and structured or casual and spontaneous, and each can provide information useful to evaluation. We'll briefly overview two types of interviews and their best uses, discuss logistical concerns, and finish with some of the pros and cons of each.

Structured interview. This type of interview is basically the same thing as a written, closed-ended questionnaire with a set of limited response options, but it is read to the respondents by an interviewer who uses a tally sheet to record responses. The goal is to be as systematic as possible and for the interviewer to be as neutral as possible. This is a good method to use following coaching sessions, when the goal is to keep a basic record of a party's perceptions of the process and satisfaction with the outcome. However, coaches should not conduct these, as clients may be hesitant to reveal negative information.

Semistructured interview. As you might guess, in this type of interview, interviewers have a set of predetermined questions they ask of everyone, but they are able to encourage the participants to elaborate on their responses in order to get richer, more detailed information. The upside to using a semistructured interview is that it tends to be more casual and generate more information. You can also more easily conduct these types of interviews in group settings (sometimes called *focus group interviews*), especially if the goal is to generate ideas.

Document Analysis. Documents relative to the coaching process, also called archival data, are documents produced for the purpose of record keeping, for example, a performance review record for a client. Because archival data already exist, they are a relatively easy form of information to use in evaluation research. However, the coach may not be given access to the information if it is considered sensitive or proprietary.

Observation. Sometimes, just observing clients in their natural context can shed enormous light on what progress is being made and what actions are still needed. Note-taking is important so the observations are recorded and not left to memory.

Quantitative Measures. Quantitative measures are data that are turned into numbers for statistical analysis.

Surveys. Literally volumes have been written about good survey methods. Again, we are not going to try to recreate that wisdom, although we do encourage you to seek additional information on constructing and administering surveys if this is going to be your main form of measurement. If surveys are an important part of your evaluation, it is worth the time to have an evaluation expert construct the survey for you. You can administer surveys using easily accessible internet programs (for example, surveymonkey.com), where clients or others can log on and take the survey, and the data are saved and analyzed for you by the program.

Behavior Coding. Counting incidents of certain kinds of behavior (e.g., fights, arguments, collaborative behavior) may be an important measure. Good behavioral coding is clear about exactly what behavior is being observed. For example, if you are counting each time an individual makes an interest statement, it's important to define specifically what an interest statement sounds like.

Questionnaires. Some people consider questionnaires a form of survey instrument. Questionnaires are measures that ask clients or others about their attitudes and opinions. Written questionnaires vary widely in their form and function. They can have closed-ended (forced choice) or open-ended (free response) items, and they can be used to ask questions of opinion (like survey interviews) or represent validated indices and scales used in research to measure attitudes, beliefs, and behaviors (e.g., indices of aggressive behavior). Questionnaires usually require more sophisticated statistical analysis than surveys or behavioral coding.

Using Needs Assessments and Program Evaluation to Market a Conflict Coaching Practice

How can you use the information gathered from needs assessment and program evaluation to market or publicize a conflict coaching practice? Needs assessment provides data about whether conflict coaching is a good idea and for which stakeholder groups. It helps a coach define the kind of coaching practice to be developed. And, by so doing, the needs assessment information defines the target market area you want to approach. Good needs assessment identifies potential clients and how conflict coaching can serve their needs. The next step is to put that insight into marketing communication tools that are distributed to the target client group.

Program evaluation data provide evidence that conflict coaching works for the client group. And program evaluation also sends an implicit message of confidence—that a coach is confident enough in his coaching work to document it and make the data available for public review. Whether in executive coaching or conflict coaching, the lack of program evaluation data is cited as a weakness (Valerio & Lee, 2005). Coaches who can provide program evaluation data will definitely stand out.

The following are some quick suggestions for the kinds of information from needs assessment and program evaluation that may be most effective in retaining and attracting a client base (Mosten, 2005). The key is "seeing the difference that makes a difference."

What is confirming? If a need and a goal is to have clients learn more constructive conflict behaviors, solve conflicts, and receive higher feedback ratings from peers and superiors as a result of conflict coaching, note examples of when data confirm these achievements. You can present numbers or a compelling story of success.

What is new or unexpected? Perhaps the data suggest a new accomplishment that is positive and important. Perhaps clients in coaching experience increases in work productivity that were unanticipated. The program evaluation data may uncover unexpected positive consequences of coaching. For example, direct reports of an executive receiving conflict coaching may demonstrate better conflict skills after watching the client interacting.

Chapter Summary

Conflict coaches need to gather information to make decisions about whether to engage in conflict coaching, how to engage in conflict coaching, and how to prove that they have positive results from conflict coaching. To accomplish this, coaches should conduct needs assessments and program evaluation.

Needs Assessment. In needs assessments, stakeholders are contacted to determine their interest in and to consider their available resources for the conflict coaching practice.

Program Evaluation. Conflict coaches need to evaluate whether their coaching practice is working for them. There are several reasons to evaluate a conflict coaching program: (1) monitoring a program to make sure it is operating as planned, (2) improving a program by identifying strengths and weaknesses, (3) expanding a program, and (4) gaining additional resources.

Process evaluation can focus on how well key processes are being conducted including the (1) assessment process, (2) planning process, (3) orientation process, (4) selection process, (5) coaching training process, (6) coaching program implementation process, (7) program maintenance process, and (8) context/environmental factors.

(Continued)

(Continued)

▨ *Outcome evaluation* focuses on whether and to what extent specific, tangible goals and objectives established for the program are achieved. The crux of outcome evaluation is twofold: (1) to document what happened in terms of utility or frequency (as opposed to how it happened in process evaluation) and (2) to document what changed as a result of the program. There are five general kinds of outcomes that most programs are interested in at some level:

- ▨ Skills/abilities learned
- ▨ Attitudes changed
- ▨ Behaviors changed
- ▨ Program utility
- ▨ Resources created

Needs assessment and program evaluation data are important tools in marketing the nature and success of a conflict coaching practice.

14

The Future of Conflict Coaching

The best way to predict the future is to invent it.

—Alan Kay

Conflict coaching is a relatively new technique and one that we believe holds great promise for the field of conflict management and dispute resolution. In this book, we've presented our Comprehensive Conflict Coaching model based on a variety of existing research and theory from social scientific analysis of conflict. We have suggested a diverse array of intervention tools that conflict coaches can use. And we have provided a process of learning assessment and evaluation to monitor the benefits and challenges of conflict coaching. But we realize that this is just the beginning of the possibilities for conflict coaching.

In this chapter, we consider where we should go in terms of future research, training and delivery mechanisms, and policy implementations of conflict coaching. We begin with research because we believe that our decisions about training and policy/program implementation depend on our learning a great deal more about conflict coaching and what factors affect its success or failure. We continue with questions for training and delivery mechanisms because we anticipate that this area will be of utmost interest to the majority of the field. And we end with discussion of policy and program implementation because, as we have learned from previous experience with other conflict interventions (e.g., mediation, arbitration), the manner in which the intervention is institutionalized and constrained through policy dictates the trajectory of the field. We invite you to consider the following and participate in the conversation about the future of coaching.

A Research Agenda

As social scientists, we are committed to investigating the impact of conflict interventions. As developers of the Comprehensive Conflict Coaching model, we have a vested interest in seeing that research is conducted that demonstrates the efficacy of conflict coaching. The following are areas of research that we advocate and plan, at least in part, to initiate.

Qualitative action research on the process of conflict coaching. As we mentioned in Chapter 13, action research allows you to look at aspects of a process and use the insights to alter the process for the better. One of the first research projects that we plan to undertake is a comprehensive qualitative action research investigation of utilization of the conflict coaching model in a health care context.

With any new intervention, it is important to assess how it is working and whether there are aspects of the model or process that need revision. The best way to do this is to train a cadre of coaches and follow them as they implement the coaching experience. What learning processes are most effective in training coaches? What aspects of the model seem to have the most value for coaches as they apply the model in their workplace? What aspects of the model are unclear or difficult for coaches to use? What aspects of the model are too lengthy or raise practical difficulties that require alternate processes?

Most of these questions deal with the extent to which the coaches are well trained and able to implement the conflict coaching model. A related and equally important matter is how clients respond to conflict coaching. Through observation and qualitative interviews, we can ascertain the clients' comfort with the model and the extent to which they use the knowledge gained through conflict coaching to handle conflicts differently. Essentially, we anticipate using the learning assessment processes and approaches discussed in Chapter 12 to evaluate the learning process and success of clients in our qualitative research project.

Survey of conflict coaching activities and characteristics. We would not have written a book on conflict coaching if we did not believe it was a growing and increasingly important component in the field of conflict management and dispute resolution. As we discussed in Chapter 1, the related field of executive coaching is huge. And the specific interest in conflict coaching is evident in the development of conflict coaching courses and presentations at professional association conferences. But there is no catalog of the extent of conflict coaching in the field. We need a better understanding of the nature and extent of current practice as well as related challenges and opportunities.

There are some obvious places to start in such a widespread survey, for example, contacting all members of professional associations and inviting them to complete an online survey about their knowledge and use of conflict coaching. One question on the survey could ask them to identify additional professionals who may also be involved in conflict coaching—and this could lead to the generation of additional samples. The survey could gather information from people actively involved in coaching about the professional associations they look to for guidance and support in their coaching efforts. And, of course, it is important to survey major organizations and government agencies in which ADR has been used or mandated to see whether conflict coaching has been added to their list of possible or actual interventions.

Ultimately, we need to develop a directory of professionals who are active in conflict coaching. This database can serve the field in a variety of ways; it would give us the ability to monitor growth of the field, longevity of individual practices, context of practice, nature of client bases, interfaces with other alternative dispute resolution mechanisms, and degree of overlap with other fields of practice such as executive coaching.

Dosage. One of the questions that is rarely researched in the conflict management field is how much of an intervention it takes to make a difference. With conflict coaching, this question of dosage level is perhaps more germane than for other interventions, because conflict coaching is inherently more elastic in application. In other ADR processes, like mediation and arbitration, the amount of exposure to the process is limited by some characteristics of the process, i.e., when agreement is reached, when a decision is made, or when one party refuses to continue with the process. But conflict coaching is more like a therapeutic intervention in that there is an open-ended ability of the coach and client to determine when and how much coaching takes place.

This raises the question of efficiency mixed with effectiveness. In short, we need to engage in research that helps us discover the minimal amount of coaching that yields the maximum impact. We are in search of the parsimony principle for conflict coaching. Evidence on dosage, an issue raised in other areas of conflict education (Aber, Brown, & Jones, 2003), would be extremely helpful in planning training agendas and monitoring program implementation.

Impact of Coaching Training and Delivery Factors. Many scholars and practitioners have recently bemoaned the lack of research on training effectiveness in the field of conflict. And it is worth reminding ourselves once again of how little attention has been paid to this central question. As Lewicki (2002, p. 1) states, "With 20 plus years of history contributed from multiple disciplines, cross-disciplinary dialogue on theory and problems, eclectic teaching method, and a rich panoply of instructional tools, we still don't know if conflict resolution teaching and training methods are really effective."

There is a rich research literature in the fields of education and organizational training that provides answers to questions about what components of training are effective in producing which outcomes. Wade (1984) reports on a meta-analysis of 91 studies of in-service teacher training. More recently, Winfred Arthur and his colleagues (Arthur, Bennett, Edens, & Bell, 2003) published a massive meta-analysis of hundreds of studies examining training design and assessment in organizational training.

We can use this research to investigate the impact of different training and coaching delivery modalities on learning. This suggestion also relates to some of our thoughts about expansion to online modalities discussed in the second section.

Characteristics of Effective Trainers and Effective Coaches. Are there common qualities shared by the best trainers of conflict coaches? Are there common qualities that define the best coaches? Are there qualifications that clearly increase one's ability to coach or train conflict coaches? We know very little empirically about qualifications for trainers in the field of conflict. The field tends to operate on an assumption that "those who can do it, can also teach and train," but we don't have any research that compares trainers of different qualifications in terms of training effectiveness.

Similarly, we have a number of assumptions about what makes a good mediator or a good arbitrator, and there are strong logical arguments to support these assumptions; but again, we know little or nothing about what characteristics would make a good conflict coach. Offhand, we would argue that a good conflict coach is one who has a thorough understanding of conflict analysis and intervention. Yet, we can't say whether someone with a human resources or ombuds experience would be better than someone with a counseling background or someone active in community mediation. We need research that begins to reveal the characteristics associated with effectiveness—especially if the field wants to move in policy directions that involve standards for conflict coaching.

Efficacy of the Train-the-Trainer Model. Many conflict coaching programs will take place in organizations that depend on train-the-trainer approaches to build capacity; an approach in which a group of trainers are trained with the expectation that they will do "turn-around" training for a group of participants in the same or similar context. Once again, we simply don't have research that supports the efficacy of train-the-trainer programs in the conflict field (Jones, 2006). We do have varying degrees of support from people in the field who rely on anecdotal evidence, but no firm empirical conclusions. And this evidence may be more necessary for a process like conflict coaching than a process like mediation. We posit that the more flexibly the intervention can be implemented, the more questionable the efficacy of train-the-trainer approaches. For a very flexible process like conflict coaching, it will be helpful to ascertain whether quality of training and practice is lost with a train-the-trainer approach.

Learning Benefits for Coaching Clients and Affiliated Parties. Conflict professionals talk about the ripple effects that conflict interventions can have on participants and related parties. Some, like Robert Harris (2005), study whether involvement in a conflict intervention can change people; can they learn through modeling and observation? To what extent can someone learn to deal with conflict more effectively by watching a client who has learned through conflict coaching? Especially in situations where coaching is used as an attempt to create more positive and constructive conflict climates, examinations of indirect learning processes would be useful.

Indirect Effects of Conflict Coaching on Systems and Clients. This area is related to the one just discussed, but it deals with broader conceptualizations of impact at both the systems and individual levels. In terms of the systems level, there are many questions about unplanned or indirect effects of conflict coaching. Does conflict coaching increase the utilization of other ADR programs in the workplace? Does conflict coaching decrease the incidence of litigation or reliance on external rights-based arbitration or adjudication processes? Does conflict coaching influence organizational climate to the extent that we see reverberation effects on related indices like absenteeism, morale, and job satisfaction? Does conflict coaching enhance team development in organizations that emphasize team structures and operation? And in terms of indirect effects on clients, are there unplanned benefits for conflict coaching clients in terms of general competence, perceived credibility, promotability, resilience, etc.?

Best Methods for Integrating Conflict Coaching With Organizational Dispute Systems or External Dispute Systems. Systems thinking brings us to questions of systems integration. And, we acknowledge that there will never be only one right way to integrate conflict coaching into existing organizational or community/social dispute systems. Yet, it would be valuable to collect case studies describing alternate models of integration and gleaning integration best practices from those cases. Are there ways to integrate conflict coaching that enhance the benefits of the coaching as well as other aspects of the system? Are there types of integration that negatively impact either the conflict coaching or the larger dispute system?

Impact of culture on conflict coaching. The issue of culture is so expansive and overwhelming that it is difficult to research in meaningful ways. As we discussed in Chapter 8, when we deal with issues of culture, we must recognize that everyone is influenced by a complex layering of cultural influences. Research on cultural effects in conflict management often takes a reductionist approach in which the complexity (and reality) of culture is sacrificed for the ability to explore one aspect of culture operating in the situation (Avruch, 2003). The fact that we can't easily explore the influence of culture on conflict coaching doesn't mean we shouldn't try. We could advocate an entire research agenda on this area alone, one that looks at how cultural influences on the coach, client, and context differentially affect conflict coaching and its outcomes.

Training and Delivery Mechanisms

As the field of conflict management and dispute resolution grows, it becomes ever more creative in the ways that it is applied to contexts and the means by which conflict professionals do their work. In this section, we consider some possible training and delivery mechanisms for conflict coaching.

Online Dispute Resolution Formats for Conflict Coaching. Online dispute resolution (ODR) is the fastest growing area of practice in the field. As Melissa Conley Tyler and Susan Raines (2006, p. 332) commented,

> The figures alone should convince some that ODR is worth watching. So far, there have been more than 115 ODR sites and services launched worldwide (Conley Tyler, 2005) with services now available in all regions. ODR has been used to resolve disputes as varied as family, workplace, e-commerce, insurance and political conflict.

The delivery of conflict coaching in a distance learning or online forum makes a great deal of sense but should be investigated in terms of effectiveness. There is no more reason for coaching to have to occur in person than for mediation to have to occur in person, if the right safeguards are taken to retain critical elements of the process. There may be opportunities for ODR systems to add a conflict coaching component (albeit a simplified version) to help prepare disputants who are planning to use their online mediation or arbitration services.

Multimedia Training Programs (software, videos, Web sites). In this age of technologically enhanced learning, an obvious next step for conflict coaching is the development of multimedia instructional materials. There are three that are very high priority. The first is the development of a Web site related to conflict coaching and its approaches (see www .conflictcoaching.org). The second is the development of instructional videos and streaming video segments for use in training. And the third is creation of a conflict coaching software program that people could use for self-instruction.

Expansion of Conflict Coaching to Youth Populations. Throughout this book we have discussed conflict coaching in terms of adult clients in workplace settings. But we do not mean to suggest that conflict coaching is appropriate only with adult clients.

Conflict coaching is a natural application for youth conflict resolution education, which we are defining as K–16. As we noted in Chapter 1, the earliest conflict coaching models were developed as components of campus mediation programs to provide a conflict education service to students who wanted to mediate but who had a conflict partner who didn't want to mediate. Coaching provided these students with a way of learning more options for handling the conflict without having to depend on others.

Looking at the current state of conflict resolution education reveals several additional reasons why conflict coaching would be an excellent addition to this area of work. The same advantage of conflict coaching for campus mediation would apply to peer mediation programs at elementary, middle, or high schools. An ongoing difficulty for peer mediation programs is the inability to generate sufficient cases; lack of cases puts the peer mediation program in jeopardy (Jones & Compton, 2003). For those students who want or need mediation but cannot force the other party to participate, coaching makes great sense.

Conflict coaching could be done by teachers, counselors, or peers. Each population of coaches would offer various advantages. Teachers could use coaching to supplement the other conflict education they are already doing in the classroom, just as counselors could add coaching to their repertoire of social skills interventions. Peer coaching would have the advantage of developing the conflict analysis expertise of the peers, and it would probably increase the chances that students would seek conflict coaching if it were offered by a peer rather than an adult.

Finally, conflict coaching is very flexible and can be tailored to the specific needs of the student. Coaching is more flexible than curriculum-based or program-based conflict resolution education. In coaching, students can work at their own pace, they can focus on skills that are most relevant for them rather than having to attend to the "skill of the week" in the curriculum, and they can build a relationship with their peer or adult coach that increases their sense of connection at the school.

Development of Undergraduate and Graduate Coursework in Conflict Coaching. In concert with the provision of conflict coaching programs at college campuses, coaching should continue to be a topic for development of conflict coursework at the undergraduate and graduate levels. Currently, most if not all of the conflict coaching courses mentioned in Chapter 1 are at the graduate level. Institutions like Columbia University, Kennesaw State University, Salisbury State University, and Temple University offer conflict coaching courses for students in their graduate programs in dispute resolution (and Salisbury State University also offers a conflict coaching course at the undergraduate level). Conflict coaching courses in undergraduate conflict and peace studies programs could also provide an academic support for campus mediation and conflict education programs.

Development of a Template for an Elastic Model of Conflict Coaching Training. Ever since Frank Sander's famous suggestion that we "fit the forum to the fuss" (Sander & Goldberg, 1986, p. 49), the dispute resolution field has been concerned about how to match specific conflict interventions with specific needs in conflict. Conflict coaching is no different than interventions that have preceded it. We have considerable work to do to develop an intervention schema that articulates how best to emphasize aspects of the conflict coaching model given certain characteristics of the conflict presented. The conflict coaching model we present is not intended as a one-size-fits-all approach. While we have developed the model with a solid internal logic, we have continually articulated, as in Chapter 2, that flexibility of application is a cardinal principle. But the flexibility must be reasoned rather than random. And for that, we need more information about discriminating factors and coaching component effectiveness.

We should also examine whether different conflict contexts require different conflict coaching training processes and implementation. For example, we may find that divorce mediation and family conflict cases require much more emphasis on the emotional components of the CCC model. Or we may discover that workplace conflicts need a deeper approach to power analysis within a systems framework. Community conflicts may benefit from conflict coaching training that places emphasis on issues of identity, particularly on issues of cultural identity. Once we have that knowledge, we can tailor training models to meet the needs of the context of conflict as well as the factors that influence coaching effectiveness.

Research on the optimal interface between conflict coaching and executive coaching. In Chapters 1 and 2 we talk about executive coaching as a context for conflict coaching and as a potential lever for increasing the use of conflict coaching. However, we also allude to the tension between conflict coaching as a component of executive coaching and conflict coaching as separate from executive coaching. The reality is that executive coaching is a huge and growing area of practice that we would be foolish to disregard. The challenge is to better understand how conflict coaching and executive coaching can be combined without losing identity or integrity of practice.

Policy/Implementation Agenda

What are the rules or policies that will guide our development and utilization of conflict coaching? In this section we consider policy and implementation issues that will need to be addressed as conflict coaching takes its place among the prominent practices in dispute resolution.

Standards for Conflict Coaching. The question of standards is usually reserved for processes like mediation that have reached a certain level of utility and prominence. Conflict coaching is not at that stage, partly due to novelty but also due to a lack of basic research about how it works and to what extent. Ultimately, if conflict coaching fulfills its promise, there will be a need to articulate what differentiates good conflict coaching from bad. As we develop the subfield of conflict coaching, we should be mindful of what implicit standards of performance we are working from and try to make those more explicit so they can be challenged and revised if necessary.

Issues of Confidentiality, Ethics, and Conflict Coaching. One area of coaching practice that will be problematic, as it has been in many other areas of the field, is the question of confidentiality. Confidentiality is easy to promise if the client is a private client seeking help from a private coach in a process removed from the workplace or community context of the conflict. But we anticipate that the majority of conflict coaching will happen in workplace contexts where the external coach or internal coach is known and hired by the management of the company or one of their representatives. In these situations, questions of confidentiality become much more problematic. To what extent should coaches offer the assumption of confidentiality? To what extent can confidentiality, if promised, be protected? What is the impact on conflict coaching process and effectiveness if confidentiality cannot be promised to any degree?

The orientation to confidentiality is an element of the larger question of ethical practice in conflict coaching. As this area of practice develops, we encourage an ongoing conversation about what ethical standards are essential. To that end, we begin the conversation here with an initial listing of ethical standards that we believe are important.

❧ A conflict coach must always be open with all parties about who are the direct and indirect clients in a coaching situation. If the indirect client is paying for the conflict coaching or in some other way controlling whether conflict coaching can happen, that information must be transparent to all parties but especially to the direct client.

❧ A conflict coach must clarify with the direct client if the coach perceives a conflict of interest between the direct client and the indirect client who is financing or controlling the coaching. The ethical responsibility of the coach is to the direct client—to make sure the direct client understands when the indirect client is advocating in a way that can be perceived as clearly against the interests of the direct client.

❧ A conflict coach must not accept a coaching contract where there is serious doubt about the competency of the direct client to engage in coaching (e.g., for reasons of mentality instability, substance abuse).

❧ A conflict coach must not accept a coaching contract where there is a question or appearance of conflict of interest involving the coach and the direct or indirect client. Exceptions to this rule would include situations in which an internal conflict coach working in an organization is coaching clients within that organization. But even in such instances, the conflict coach should adhere to earlier stated principles that the direct client is the primary concern of the coach.

When Conflict Coaching Should Not Be Used. As conflict scholars and dispute resolution practitioners, we are always concerned about the misapplication of any conflict intervention. We assume that there are a variety of conflicts in which an intervention may not be appropriate and that it is the responsibility of the field to articulate those limitations clearly. We assume that conflict coaching has these same limitations and that it will be our duty, as we move forward in this work, to always keep in mind the need to draw clear boundaries that demarcate the appropriate and inappropriate use of conflict coaching. For example, we have already mentioned that conflict coaching is questionable when there are concerns about client competence or coach bias. There may also be instances where coaching is used by an indirect client to discriminate against members of nondominant groups (e.g., services are not given to certain workers because of their race or ethnicity, or conversely, only workers of a particular race or ethnicity are sent to coaching).

Conclusion

Throughout this book we have suggested the power that we see in conflict coaching. If we envision the future of the field, we anticipate that conflict coaching will shortly parallel mediation as a core intervention in our field. Just as mediation swept the country in the 1980s, we believe that conflict coaching has the same momentum in the coming decades. We believe we will see a time, in the not so distant future, where conflict coaching courses are taught in every graduate and undergraduate conflict analysis, conflict education, management and business, human resources, and organizational development program. We assume that conflict coaching will be incorporated as an essential intervention and area of practice in community and workplace dispute resolution systems. And we fervently hope that we see conflict coaching become an expected skill area for youth and peer educators working in conflict and peace education.

> *Change is the law of life. And those who look only to the past or present are certain to miss the future.*
>
> —Winston Churchill

Chapter Summary

In this chapter, we consider where we should go in terms of future research, training and delivery mechanisms, and policy implementations of conflict coaching. We begin with research because we believe that our decisions about training and policy/program implementation depend on our learning a great deal more about conflict coaching and what factors affect its success or failure. We continue with questions for training and delivery mechanisms because we anticipate that this area will be of utmost interest to the majority of the field. And we end with discussion of policy and program implementation because the manner in which the intervention is institutionalized and constrained through policy dictates the trajectory of the field.

A RESEARCH AGENDA

- Qualitative action research on the process of conflict coaching
- Survey of conflict coaching activities and characteristics
- Dosage
- Impact of coaching training and delivery factors

(Continued)

(Continued)

- Characteristics of effective trainers and effective coaches
- Efficacy of the train-the-trainer model
- Learning benefits for coaching clients and affiliated parties
- Indirect effects of conflict coaching on systems and clients
- Best methods for integrating conflict coaching with organizational dispute systems or external dispute systems
- Impact of culture on conflict coaching

TRAINING AND DELIVERY MECHANISMS

- Online dispute resolution formats for conflict coaching
- Multimedia training programs (software, videos, Web sites)
- Expansion of conflict coaching to youth populations
- Development of undergraduate and graduate coursework in conflict coaching
- Development of a template for an elastic model of conflict coaching training
- Research on the optimal interface between conflict coaching and executive coaching

POLICY/IMPLEMENTATION AGENDA

- Standards for conflict coaching
- Issues of confidentiality, ethics, and conflict coaching
- When conflict coaching should not be used

References

Aber, J. L., Brown, J. I., & Jones, S. M. (2003). Developmental trajectories toward violence in middle childhood: Course, demographic differences, and response to school-based intervention. *Developmental Psychology, 39*(2), 324–348.

Abu-Nimer, M. (1998). Conflict resolution training in the Middle East: Lessons to be learned. *International Negotiation, 3*(1), 99–116.

Adair, W., Brett, J., Lempereur, A., Okumura, T., Shikhirev, P., Tinsley, C., et al. (2004). Culture and negotiation strategy. *Negotiation Journal, 20,* 87–111.

Addor, M. L., Denckla-Cobb, T., Dukes, E. F., Ellerbrock, M., & Smutko, L. S. (2005). Linking theory to practice: A theory of change model of the Natural Resources Leadership Institute. *Conflict Resolution Quarterly, 23*(2), 203–224.

Adler, R. S., Rosen, B. & Silverstein, E. M. (1998). Emotions in negotiation: How to manage fear and anger. *Negotiation Journal, 14,* 161–179.

Allred, K. G. (2000). Distinguishing best and strategic practices: A framework for managing the dilemma between creating and claiming value. *Negotiation Journal, 16,* 387–397.

Anderson, D. L., & Anderson, M. C. (2005). *Coaching that counts: Harnessing the power of leadership coaching to deliver strategic value.* Amsterdam: Elsevier, Butterworth & Heinemann.

Arthur, W., Bennett, W., Edens, P. S., & Bell, S. (2003). Effectiveness of training in organizations: A meta-analysis of design and evaluation features. *Journal of Applied Psychology, 88,* 234–245.

Avruch, K. (2000). Culture and negotiation pedagogy. *Negotiation Journal, 16,* 339–346.

Avruch, K. (2003). Type I and Type II errors in culturally sensitive conflict resolution practice. *Conflict Resolution Quarterly, 20,* 351–372.

Axtell, R. (1998). *Gestures: The do's and taboos of body language around the world.* New York: Wiley.

Babcock, L., & Laschever, S. (2003). *Women don't ask: Negotiation and the gender divide.* Princeton, NJ: Princeton University Press.

Bachrach, P., & Baratz, M. (1962). Two faces of power. *American Political Science Review, 56,* 947–952.

Bacon, T. R., & Spear, K. (2003). *Adaptive coaching: The art and practice of a client-centered approach to performance improvement.* Palo Alto, CA: Davies-Black.

Barge, J. K. (2001). Creating healthy communities through affirmative conflict communication. *Conflict Resolution Quarterly, 19,* 89–101.

Bartz, D. E., Calabrese, F. L., & Kottkamp, R. B. (1991). Improving graduate business school programs by strengthening the delivery system. *Journal of Education for Business, 66*(3), 147–151.

Bavelas, J. B., Black, A., Chovil, N., & Mullett, J. (1990). *Equivocal communication.* Newbury Park, CA: Sage.

Baxter, L. A., & Montgomery, B. M. (1996). *Relating: Dialogues and dialectics.* New York: Guilford.

Bazerman, M. H. (1983). Negotiator judgment: A critical look at the rationality assumption. *American Behavioral Scientist, 27*(2), 211–228.

Bazerman, M. H., & Neale, M. A. (1992). *Negotiating rationally.* New York: Free Press.

Bazerman, M. H., Magliozzi, T., & Neale, M. A. (1985). Integrative bargaining in a competitive market. *Organizational Behavior and Human Decision Processes, 35*, 294–313.

Ben Yoav, O., & Pruitt, D. G. (1984). Accountability to constituents: A two-edged sword. *Organizational Behavior and Human Performance, 34*, 283–295.

Bendersky, C. (2003). Organizational dispute resolution systems: A complementarities model. *Academy of Management Review, 28*(4), 643.

Berglas, S. (2002). The very real dangers of executive coaching. *Harvard Business Review, 80*(6), 86–92.

Blake, R. R., & Mouton, J. S. (1964). *Managerial grid.* Houston, TX: Gulf Publishing.

Blitman, B., & Maes, J. (2004). Visioning and coaching techniques in mediation. *Dispute Resolution Journal, 59*(2), 20–23.

Blumer, H. (1969). *Symbolic interactionism: Perspective and method.* Englewood Cliffs, NJ: Prentice Hall.

Brinkert, R. (1999, July). *Challenges and opportunities for a campus conflict education program.* Paper presented at the Conflict Resolution in Education Network (CREnet) Conference, Boston, MA.

Brinkert, R. (2000, October). *ADR plus one: Developing ADR practice by advancing conflict coaching models.* Paper presented at the University of Massachusetts Conflict Studies: The New Generation of Ideas Conference, Boston, MA.

Brinkert, R. (2006). Conflict coaching: Advancing the conflict resolution field by developing an individual disputant process. *Conflict Resolution Quarterly, 23*, 517–528.

Brown, B. R. (1977). Face-saving and face restoration in negotiation. In D. Druckman (Ed.), *Negotiations* (pp. 275–299). Beverly Hills, CA: Sage.

Brown, G. (2006). Explaining. In O. Hargie (Ed.), *The handbook of communication skills* (3rd ed., pp. 195–228). New York: Routledge.

Brown, M. H. (1990). Defining stories in organizations: Characteristics and functions. In J. A. Anderson (Ed.), *Communication yearbook 13* (pp. 162–190). Newbury Park, CA: Sage.

Brown, P., & Levinson, S. (1987). *Universals in language usage: Politeness phenomena.* Cambridge, UK: Cambridge University Press.

Brownell, J. (1990). Perceptions of effective listeners: A management study. *Journal of Business Communication, 27*, 401–415.

Brunner, J. (2002). *Making stories.* New York: Farrar, Straus, and Giroux.

Buck, R. (1984). *The communication of emotion.* New York: Guilford Press.

Burgoon, J. K., Johnson, M. L., & Koch, P. T. (1998). The nature and measurement of interpersonal dominance. *Communication Monographs, 65*, 308–335.

Burleson, B., & Goldsmith, D. (1998). How the comforting process works: Alleviating emotional distress through conversationally induced reappraisals. In P. A. Andersen and L. K. Guerrero (Eds.), *Handbook of communication and emotion: Research, theory, applications, and contexts* (pp. 246–281). San Diego, CA: Academic Press.

Campbell, J. (1972). *The hero with a thousand faces.* Princeton, NJ: Princeton University Press.

Campbell, J. R. (2001). Coaching: A new field for counselors? *Counseling and Human Development, 34*, 1–14.

Cantillon, P., & Jones, R. (1999). Does continuing medical education in general practice make a difference? *British Medical Journal, 318*, 1276–1279.

Carruthers, W. L., Carruthers, B. J. B., Day-Vines, N. L., Bostick, D., & Watson, D. C. (1996). Conflict resolution as curriculum: A definition, description, and process for integration in core curricula. *School Counselor, 43*, 345–373.

Cartney, P. (2000). Adult learning styles: Implications for practice teaching in social work. *Social Work Education, 19*, 609–626.

Cavanaugh, M., Larson, C., Goldberg, A., & Bellows, J. (1981). Power and communication behavior: A formulative investigation. *Communication, 10*(2), 81–107.

Chapman, T., Best, B., & Casteren, P. (2003). *Executive coaching: Exploding the myths.* New York: Palgrave Macmillan.

Cissna, K. N., & Seiburg, E. (1981). Patterns of interactional confirmation and disconfirmation. In C. Wilder-Mott & J. H. Weakland (Eds.), *Rigor and imagination: Essays from the legacy of Gregory Bateson* (pp. 253–282). New York: Praeger.

Clegg, S. (1989). *Frameworks of power.* London: Sage.

Clegg, S. R. (1993). Narrative, power, and social theory. In D. K. Mumby (Ed.), *Narrative and social control: Critical perspectives* (pp. 15–45). Newbury Park, CA: Sage.

Cloke, K. (2001). *Mediating dangerously: The frontiers of conflict resolution.* San Francisco: Jossey-Bass.

Cloke, K., & Goldsmith, J. (2000). Conflict resolution that reaps great rewards. *Journal for Quality and Participation, 23*(3), 27–30.

Cobb, S. (1992). *The pragmatics of empowerment in mediation: Towards a narrative perspective.* Report for the National Institute for Dispute Resolution. Washington, DC: NIDR.

Cobb, S. (1993). Empowerment and mediation: A narrative perspective. *Negotiation Journal, 9*, 245–259.

Cobb, S. (1994). A narrative approach to mediation. In J. P. Folger & T. S. Jones (Eds.), *New directions in mediation: Communication research and perspectives* (pp. 48–77). Thousand Oaks, CA: Sage.

Cobb, S. (2000). Negotiation pedagogy: Learning to learn. *Negotiation Journal, 16*, 315–319.

Cobb, S., & Rifkin, J. (1991). Neutrality as a discursive practice: The construction and transformation of narratives in community mediation. In A. Sarat & S. Silbey (Eds.), *Studies in law, politics, and society* (Vol. 11, pp. 69–91). Greenwich, CT: JAI Press.

Cody, M. J., Greene, J. O., Marston, P. J., O'Hair, H. D., Baaske, K. T., & Schneider, M. J. (1986). Situation perception and message strategy selection. In M. L. McLaughlin (Ed.), *Communication yearbook 9* (pp. 390–420). Beverly Hills, CA: Sage.

Conley Tyler, M. (2005). 115 and counting: The state of ODR 2004. In M. Conley Tyler, E. Katsh, & D. Choi (Eds.), *Proceedings of the Third Annual Forum on Online Dispute Resolution.* Melbourne, Australia: International Conflict Resolution Centre in collaboration with the United Nations Economic and Social Commission for Asia and the Pacific (UNESCAP). Retrieved June 1, 2005, from www.odr.info/unforum2004

Conley Tyler, M., & Raines, S. (2006). The human face of on-line dispute resolution. *Conflict Resolution Quarterly, 23*, 333–342.

Cooperrider, D., & Srivastva, S. (1987). Appreciative inquiry into organizational life. In R. Woodman & W. Pasmore (Eds.), *Research in organizational change and development* (Vol. 1, pp. 129–169). Greenwich, CT: JAI Press.

Cope, M. (2004). *The seven Cs of coaching: The definitive guide to collaborative coaching.* Harlow, UK: Pearson Education.

Costantino, C. A., & Merchant, C. S. (1996). *Designing conflict management systems: A guide to creating productive and healthy organizations.* San Francisco: Jossey-Bass.

Council on Social Work Education. (1988). *Handbook of accreditation standards and procedures* (Rev. ed.). New York: Council on Social Work Education.

Cupach, W. R., & Canary, D. J. (1997). A competence-based approach to interpersonal conflict. In W. R. Cupach & D. J. Canary (Eds.), *Competence in interpersonal conflict* (pp. 20–35). New York: McGraw-Hill.

Cupach, W. R., & Metts, S. (1994). *Facework*. Thousand Oaks, CA: Sage.

Cuthill, M. (2004). Community visioning: Facilitating informed citizen participation in local area planning on the Gold Coast. *Urban Policy & Research, 22*(4), 427–445.

Dahl, R. A. (1957). The concept of power. *Behavioral Science, 2*(3), 201–215.

Dempwolf, D. H. (1993). *The utilization of principles of adult learning in California staff development programs*. Unpublished doctoral dissertation, University of La Verne, La Verne, CA.

Denzin, N. (1984). *On understanding emotion*. San Francisco: Jossey-Bass.

Deutsch, M. (1949). A theory of competition and cooperation. *Human Relations, 2,* 129–151.

Deutsch, M. (1973). *The resolution of conflict*. New Haven, CT: Yale University Press.

DeWitt, T. G. (2003). The application of social and adult learning theory to training in community pediatrics, social justice, and child advocacy. *Pediatrics, 112*(3) Supplement, 755–757.

Diedrich, R. C. (1996). An iterative approach to executive coaching. *Counseling Psychology Journal: Practice and Research, 48*(2), 61–66.

Dillard, J. P., Kinney, T. A., & Cruz, M. G. (1996). Influence, appraisals, and emotions in close relationships. *Communication Monographs, 63,* 105–130.

Dillard, J. P., Segrin, C., & Harden, J. M. (1989). Primary and secondary goals in the production of interpersonal influence messages. *Communication Monographs, 56,* 19–38.

Edelman, L. B., Erlanger, H. S., & Lande, J. (1993). Internal dispute resolution: The transformation of civil rights in the workplace. *Law and Society Review, 27*(3), 497–534.

Ellis, K. (2000). Perceived teacher confirmation: The development and validation of an instrument and two studies of the relationship to cognitive and affective learning. *Human Communication Research, 26,* 264–291.

Fairclough, N. (1989). *Language and Power*. London: Longman.

Fisher, A. (1976). *Perspectives on human communication*. Mahwah, NJ: Lawrence Erlbaum.

Fisher, R. (1983). Negotiating power: Getting and using influence. *American Behavioral Scientist, 27*(2), 149–166.

Fisher, R., Ury, W., & Patton, B. (1991). *Getting to yes: Negotiating agreement without giving in* (2nd ed.). New York: Penguin.

Fisher, W. R. (1984). Narration as human communication paradigm. *Communication Monographs, 51,* 1–22.

Fisher, W. R. (1985). The narrative paradigm: An elaboration. *Communication Monographs, 52,* 347–367.

Fisher, W. R. (1987). *Human communication as narration: Toward a philosophy of reason, value, and action*. Columbia: University of South Carolina Press.

Fisher, W. R. (1989). Clarifying the narrative paradigm. *Communication Monographs, 56,* 55–58.

Fitzpatrick, J. L., Sanders, J. R., & Worthen, B. R. (2003). *Program evaluation: Alternative approaches and practice guidelines* (3rd ed.). Boston: Allyn & Bacon.

Folger, J. P., & Jones, T. S. (Eds.). (1994). *New directions in mediation: Communication research and perspectives*. Thousand Oaks, CA: Sage.

Folger, J. P., Poole, M. S., & Stutman, R. K. (2005). *Working through conflict* (5th ed.). Boston: Allyn & Bacon.

French, R. P., & Raven, B. (1959). The bases of social power. In D. Cartwright (Ed.), *Studies in social power* (pp. 150–167). Ann Arbor: University of Michigan Press.

Frisch, M. H. (2005). Coaching caveats. *Human Resource Planning, 28*(3), 14–16.

Galbo, C. (1998). Helping adults learn. *Thrust for Educational Leadership, 27*(7), 13–17.

Gergen, K. J. (1999). *An invitation to social construction*. London: Sage.

Gleeson, J. P. (1990). Engaging students in practice evaluation: Defining and monitoring critical initial interview components. *Journal of Social Work Education, 26*(3), 295–309.

Goffman, E. (1955). On facework: An analysis of ritual elements in social interaction. *Psychiatry, 18*, 213–231.

Goffman, E. (1959). *The presentation of self in everyday life.* New York: Doubleday.

Goffman, E. (1967). *Interaction ritual: Essays on face-to-face behavior.* Garden City, NY: Doubleday.

Goldsmith, M. (2004). Changing leadership behavior. *Journal for Quality & Participation, 27*(4), 28–33.

Gottman, J. M. (1994). *What predicts divorce? The relationship between marital processes and marital outcomes.* Hillsdale, NJ: Lawrence Erlbaum.

Gottman, J. M., Katz, L. F., & Hooven, C. (1997). *Meta-emotion: How families communicate emotionally.* Mahwah, NJ: Lawrence Erlbaum.

Greenspan, S. I. (1997). *The growth of the mind and the endangered origins of intelligence.* Reading, MA: Addison-Wesley.

Griffin, E. (2006). *A first look at communication theory* (6th ed.). Boston: McGraw-Hill.

Grillo, E. (2005). Foreword. In E. Grillo (Ed.), *Power without domination: Dialogism and the empowering property of communication* (pp. vii–xvii). Amsterdam: John Benjamins.

Gudykunst, W. B., & Ting-Toomey, S. (1988). *Culture and interpersonal communication.* Newbury Park, CA: Sage.

Guttman, H. M. (2005). Conflict management as a core leadership competency. *Training, 42*(11), 34–39.

Hall, E. T. (1959). *The silent language.* Garden City, NY: Anchor/Doubleday.

Hall, E. T. (1966). *The hidden dimension.* Garden City, NY: Anchor/Doubleday.

Hall, E. T. (1976). *Beyond culture.* Garden City, NY: Anchor.

Hall, E. T., & Whyte, W. F. (1966). Intercultural communication: A guide to men of action. In A. G. Smith (Ed.), *Communication and culture* (pp. 567–575), New York: Holt, Rinehart, and Winston.

Hall, J. (1969). *Conflict management survey.* Conroe, TX: Teleometrics.

Hammond, S. A. (1996). *The thin book of appreciative inquiry* (2nd ed.). Bend, OR: Thin Book Publishing.

Hargie, O. (2006). Skill in theory: Communication as skilled performance. In O. Hargie (Ed.), *The handbook of communication skills* (3rd ed., pp. 7–36). New York: Routledge.

Harré, R., & van Langenhove, L. (1999). *Positioning theory.* Oxford, UK: Blackwell.

Harris, R. (2005). Unlocking the learning potential in peer mediation: An evaluation of peer mediation modeling and disputant learning. *Conflict Resolution Quarterly, 23*, 141–164.

Harrison, T. (2007). My professor is so unfair: Student attitudes and experiences of conflict with faculty. *Conflict Resolution Quarterly, 24*, 349–368.

Hatfield, E., Cacioppo, J. T., & Rapson, R. L. (1992). *Emotional contagion.* Paris: Cambridge University Press.

Havelock, R., & Havelock, M. (1973). *Training for change agents.* Ann Arbor: University of Michigan Press.

Hedeen, T. (2005). Dialogue and democracy, community and capacity: Lessons for conflict resolution education from Montessori, Dewey, and Freire. *Conflict Resolution Quarterly, 23*, 185–202.

Heilman, M. E. (1974). Threats and promises: Reputational consequences and the transfer of credibility. *Journal of Experimental Social Psychology, 10*, 310–324.

Hewitt, J. P. (2003). *Self and society: A symbolic interactionist social psychology* (9th ed.). Boston: Allyn & Bacon.

Hewitt, J. P., & Stokes, R. (1975). Disclaimers. *American Sociological Review, 40*, 1–11.

Hobbs, J. R., & Evans, D. A. (1980). Conversation as planned behavior. *Cognitive Science, 4*, 349–377.

Hofstede, G. (1980). *Culture's consequences: International differences in work related values.* Beverly Hills, CA: Sage.

Hofstede, G. (1983). Dimensions of national cultures in fifty countries and three regions. In J. Deregowski, S. Dziurawiec, & R. Annis (Eds.), *Explorations in cross cultural psychology* (pp. 335–355). Lisse, The Netherlands: Swets and Zeitlinger.

Hofstede, G. (1991). *Culture and organizations: Software of the mind.* London: McGraw-Hill.

Infante, D. A. (1987). Aggressiveness. In J. C. McCroskey, & J. A. Daly (Eds.), *Personality and interpersonal communication* (pp. 157–192). Newbury Park, CA: Sage.

Infante, D. A., & Rancer, A. S. (1993). Relations between argumentative motivation, and advocacy and refutation on controversial issues. *Communication Quarterly, 41,* 415–426.

Infante, D. A., & Wigley, C. J. (1986). Verbal aggressiveness: An interpersonal model and measure. *Communication Monographs, 53,* 61–69.

Infante, D. A., Anderson, C. M., Martin, M. M., Herington, A. D., & Kim, J. (1993). Subordinates' satisfaction and perceptions of superiors' compliance-gaining tactics, argumentativeness, verbal aggressiveness, and style. *Management Communication Quarterly, 6,* 307–326.

Izard, C. (1977). *Human emotions.* New York: Plenum.

Izard, C. (1993). Organizational and motivational functions of discrete emotions. In M. Lewis & J. M. Haviland (Eds.), *Handbook of emotions* (pp. 631–642). New York: Guilford Press.

Jameson, J. K. (1998). Diffusion of a campus innovation: Integration of a new student dispute resolution center into the university culture. *Mediation Quarterly, 16,* 129–146.

Jandt, F., & Pederson, P. (1994). Indigenous mediation strategies in the Asia-Pacific region. *Aspire Newsletter, 4*(1), 10–11.

Jones, S. E. (1994). *The right touch: Understanding and using the language of physical contact.* Cresskill, NJ: Hampton Press.

Jones, T. S. (1994). A dialectical reframing of mediation process. In J. Folger & T. Jones (Eds.), *New directions in mediation: Communication research and perspectives* (pp. 26–47). Thousand Oaks, CA: Sage.

Jones, T. S. (2000). Emotional communication and conflict: Essence and impact. In W. Eadie & P. Nelson (Eds.), *The language of conflict and resolution* (pp. 81–104). Thousand Oaks, CA: Sage.

Jones, T. S. (2005). Emotion in mediation: Implications, applications, opportunities and challenges. In M. Herrman (Ed.), *Blackwell handbook of mediation: Theory and practice* (pp. 277–306). New York: Blackwell.

Jones, T. S. (2006). The emperor's 'knew' clothes: What we don't know will hurt us. *Conflict Resolution Quarterly, 23,* 129–140.

Jones, T. S., & Bodtker, A. (2001). Mediating with heart in mind: Addressing emotion in mediation practice. *Negotiation Journal, 17,* 217–244.

Jones, T. S., & Compton, R. O. (2003). *Kids working it out: Stories and strategies for making peace in our schools.* San Francisco: Jossey-Bass.

Jones, T. S., Remland, M. S., & Sanford, R. (2007). *Interpersonal communication through the life span.* Boston: Allyn & Bacon.

Kampa-Kokesch, S. (2001). Executive coaching: A comprehensive review of the literature. *Consulting Psychology Journal: Practice and Research, 53*(4), 205–228.

Katz, R., & Kahn, D. (1976). *The social psychology of organizations.* New York: Wiley.

Keil, J. H. (2000). Coaching through conflict. *Dispute Resolution Journal, 55*(2), 65–69.

Kellett, P. M., & Dalton, D. G. (2001). *Managing conflict in a negotiated world: A narrative approach to achieving dialogue and change.* Thousand Oaks, CA: Sage.

Kemper, T. D. (1978). *A social interactional theory of emotions.* New York: Wiley.

Kets de Vries, M. F. R. (2005). Leadership group coaching in action: The zen of creating high performance teams. *Academy of Management Executive, 19*(1), 61–76.

Kiel, F., Rimmer, E., Williams, K., & Doyle, M. (1996). Coaching at the top. *Consulting Psychology Journal: Practice and Research, 48*(2), 67–77.

Kilburg, R. R. (2000). *Executive coaching: Developing managerial wisdom in a world of chaos.* Washington, DC: American Psychological Association.

Kilburg, R. R. (2004). Trudging toward Dodoville: Conceptual approaches and case studies in executive coaching. *Consulting Psychology Journal: Practice and Research, 56*(4), 203–213.

Kilmann, R., & Thomas, K. W. (1975). Interpersonal conflict handling behavior as reflections of Jungian personality dimensions. *Psychological Reports, 37,* 971–980.

King, A. (1987). *Power and communication.* Prospect Heights, IL: Waveland.

Kipnis, D. (1974). The powerholder. In J. T. Tedeschi (Ed.), *Perspectives on social power* (pp. 82–122). Chicago: Aldine.

Kipnis, D. S., Schmidt, S., & Wilkinson, I. (1980). Intraorganizational influence tactics: Explorations in getting one's way. *Journal of Applied Psychology, 65,* 440–452.

Kirkpatrick, D. L. (1976). Evaluation of training. In R. L. Craig (Ed.), *Training and development handbook: A guide to human resource development* (2nd ed., pp. 301–319). New York: McGraw-Hill.

Kitayama, S., & Markus, H. R. (Eds.) (1994). *Emotion and culture: Empirical studies of mutual influence.* Washington, DC: American Psychological Association.

Knapp, M. L., Putnam, L. L., & Davis, L. J. (1988). Measuring interpersonal conflict in organizations: Where do we go from here? *Management Communication Quarterly, 1,* 414–429.

Knowles, M. (1990). *The adult learner: A neglected species* (4th ed.) Houston, TX: Gulf Publishing.

Kottler, J. A. (1994). *Beyond blame: A new way of resolving conflicts in relationships.* San Francisco: Jossey-Bass.

Kressel, K. (1997). Practice-relevant research in mediation: Toward a reflective research paradigm. *Negotiation Journal, 13,* 143–160.

Laing, R. D. (1961). *The self and others, further studies in sanity and madness.* London: Tavistock.

Lang, M., & Taylor, A. (2000). *The making of a mediator: Artistry, reflection and interactive process.* San Francisco: Jossey-Bass.

Langellier, K. M. (1989). Personal narratives: Perspectives on theory and research. *Text and Performance Quarterly, 9,* 243–276.

Lax, D., & Sebenius, J. (1986). *The manager as negotiator: Bargaining for cooperation and competitive gain.* New York: Free Press.

Lazarus, R. S. (1991). *Emotion and adaptation.* New York: Oxford University Press.

LeBaron, M. (2002). *Bridging troubled waters: Conflict resolution from the heart.* San Francisco: Jossey-Bass.

Levine, T. R., & Boster, F. J. (2001). The effects of power and message variables on compliance. *Communication Monographs, 68,* 28–48.

Levinson, H. (1996). Executive coaching. *Consulting Psychology Journal: Practice and Research, 48*(2), 115–123.

Lewicki, R. (2002). New directions and issues in the teaching of conflict resolution. *Conflict Management in Higher Education Report, 2*(2) 1–4. Retrieved September 2, 2005, from www.campus-adr.org/CMHER/ReportArticles/Edition2_2/Lewicki2_2.html

Lewicki, R. J., Saunders, D. M., & Minton, J. W. (1999). *Negotiation* (3rd ed.). Boston: McGraw-Hill.

Lieberman, E., Foux-Levy, Y., & Segal, P. (2005). Beyond basic training: A model for developing mediator competence. *Conflict Resolution Quarterly, 23,* 237–257.

Lipsky, D. B., Seeber, R. L., & Fincher, R. D. (2003). *Emerging systems for managing workplace conflict: Lessons from American corporations for managers and dispute resolution professionals.* San Francisco: Jossey-Bass.

Locher, M. A. (2004). *Power and politeness in action: Disagreements in oral communication.* Berlin: Mouton de Gruyter.

Ludema, J. D. (1997). Narrative inquiry: Collective storytelling as a source of hope, knowledge, and action in organizational life. *Dissertation Abstracts International Section A: Humanities and Social Sciences, 58*(1-A), 0218.

Ludema, J. D. (2002). Appreciative storytelling: A narrative approach to organization development and change. In R. Fry, F. Barrett, J. Seiling, & D. Whitney (Eds.), *Appreciative inquiry and organizational transformation: Reports from the field* (pp. 239–261). Westport, CT: Quorum Books/Greenwood.

Lukes, S. (1974). *Power: A radical view.* London: Macmillan.

Lustig, M. W. & Koester, J. (2003). *Intercultural competence.* Boston: Allyn & Bacon.

Lutz, C. (1988). *Unnatural emotions: Everyday sentiments on a Micronesian atoll and their challenge to western theory.* Chicago: University of Chicago Press.

Lyon, M. L. (1995). Missing emotion: The limitations of cultural constructionism in the study of emotion. *Cultural Anthropology, 10,* 244–263.

Manstead, A. S. R. (1991). Emotion in social life. *Cognition and Emotion, 5*(5/6), 353–362.

Markus, H. R., & Kitayama, S. (1991). Culture and the self: Implications for cognition, emotion, and motivation. *Psychological Review, 98,* 224–253.

Marwell, G., & Schmidt, D. (1967). Compliance-gaining behavior: A synthesis and model. *Sociological Quarterly, 8,* 317–328.

McCorkle, S. (2005). The murky world of mediation ethics: Neutrality, impartiality, and conflict of interest in state codes of conduct. *Conflict Resolution Quarterly, 23,* 165–183.

McDavid, J. C., & Hawthorn, L. R. L. (2005). *Program evaluation and performance measurement: An introduction to practice.* Thousand Oaks, CA: Sage.

Moore, C. (2003). *The mediation process: Practical strategies for resolving conflict* (3rd ed.). San Francisco: Jossey-Bass.

Morgan, H., Harkins, P., & Goldsmith, M. (2005). *The art and practice of leadership coaching.* Hoboken, NJ: Wiley.

Morley, I., & Stephenson, G. (1977). *The social psychology of bargaining.* London: Allen and Unwin.

Morris, D. (1977). *Manwatching: A field guide to human behavior.* New York: Harry N. Abrams.

Morris, D. (1994). Bodytalk: The meaning of human gestures. New York: Crown.

Mosten, F. (2005). Establishing a mediation practice. In J. Folberg, A. L. Milne, & P. Salem (Eds.), *Divorce and family mediation: Models, techniques and applications* (pp. 544–565). New York: Guilford Press.

Mumby, D. K. (1988). *Communication and power in organizations: Discourse, ideology and domination.* Norwood, NJ: Ablex.

Murphy, S. (2005). Recourse to executive coaching: The mediating role of human resources. *International Journal of Police Science and Management, 7*(3), 175–186.

Natale, S. M., & Diamante, T. (2005). The five stages of executive coaching: Better process makes better practice. *Journal of Business Ethics, 59,* 361–374.

Nelson, D., & Wheeler, M. (2004). Rocks and hard places: Managing two tensions in negotiation. *Negotiation Journal, 20,* 113–128.

Neuliep, J. W. (2003). *Intercultural communication: A contextual approach.* Boston: Houghton Mifflin.

Newell, S. E, & Stutman, R. K. (1988). The social confrontation episode. *Communication Monographs, 55,* 266–285.

Ng, S. H., & Bradac, J. J. (1993). *Power in language: Verbal communication and social influence.* Newbury Park, CA: Sage.

NHS conflict coaching gets off to slow start. (2005, November 29). *Personnel Today,* 3.

Nichols, M. P. (1995). *The lost art of listening.* New York: Guilford Press.

Northouse, P. G. (2007). *Leadership: Theory and practice* (4th ed.). Thousand Oaks, CA: Sage.

Northrup, T. (1989). The dynamic of identity in personal and social conflict. In L. Kreisberg, T. Northrup, & S. Thorson (Eds.), *Intractable conflicts and their transformation* (pp. 55–82). Syracuse, NY: Syracuse University Press.

Ochs, E. (1997). *Discourse as structure and process.* Thousand Oaks, CA: Sage.

Ortony, A., Clore, G. L., & Collins, A. (1988). *The cognitive structure of emotions.* New York: Cambridge University Press.

Palmer, M. T. (1989). Controlling conversations: Turns, topics and interpersonal control. *Communication Monographs, 56,* 1–18.

Parkinson, B. (1995). *Ideas and realities of emotion.* New York: Routledge.

Pearce, W. B., & Cronen, V. E. (1980). *Communication, action and meaning.* New York: Praeger.

Pearce, W. B., & Littlejohn, S. W. (1997). *Moral conflict: When social worlds collide.* Thousand Oaks, CA: Sage.

Perry, B. D., Pollard, R., Blakely, T., Baker, W., & Vigilante, D. (1995). Childhood trauma, the neurobiology of adaptation and "use-dependent" development of the brain: How "states" become "traits." *Infant Mental Health Journal, 16*(4), 271–291.

Picard, C. A. (2003). Learning about learning: The value of "insight." *Conflict Resolution Quarterly, 20,* 477–484.

Pike, G. R., & Sillars, A. L. (1985). Reciprocity of marital communication. *Journal of Social and Personal Relationships, 2,* 303–324.

Pondy, L. P. (1967). Organizational conflict: Concepts and models. *Administrative Science Quarterly, 12*(2), 296–320.

Pruitt, D. G. (1983a). Integrative agreements: Nature and antecedents. In M. H. Bazerman & R. J. Lewicki (Eds.), *Negotiation in organizations* (pp. 35–50). Beverly Hills, CA: Sage.

Pruitt, D. G. (1983b). Strategic choice in negotiation. *American Behavioral Scientist, 27*(2), 167–194.

Putnam, L. L. (1988). Communication and interpersonal conflict in organizations. *Management Communication Quarterly, 1,* 293–301.

Putnam, L. L., & Poole, M. S. (1987). Conflict and negotiation. In F. M. Jablin, L. L. Putnam, K. H. Roberts, & L. W. Porter (Eds.), *Handbook of organizational communication: An interdisciplinary perspective* (pp. 549–599). Newbury Park, CA: Sage.

Putnam, L. L., & Wilson, C. (1982). Communicative strategies in organizational conflict: Reliability and validity of a measurement scale. In M. Burgoon (Ed.), *Communication yearbook 6* (pp. 629–652). Beverly Hills, CA: Sage.

Rahim, M. A. (1983). A measure of styles of handling interpersonal conflict. *Academy of Management Journal, 26,* 368–376.

Rahim, M. A., & Magner, N. R. (1995). Confirmatory factor analysis of the styles of handling interpersonal conflict: First order factor model and its invariance across groups. *Journal of Applied Psychology, 80,* 122–132.

Rancer, A. S., & Avtgis, T. A. (2006). *Argumentative and aggressive communication: Theory, research, and application.* Thousand Oaks, CA: Sage.

Raush, H. C., Barry, W. A., Hertel, R., & Swain, M. A. (1974). *Communication, conflict and marriage.* San Francisco: Jossey-Bass.

Reiter, H. I., Eva, K. W., Hatala, R. M., & Norman, G. R. (2002). Self and peer assessment in tutorials: Application of a relative ranking model. *Academic Medicine, 77,* 1134–1139.

Remland, M. S. (2004). *Nonverbal communication in everyday life* (2nd ed.). Boston: Houghton Mifflin.

Retzinger, S. (1993). *Violent emotions: Shame and rage in marital quarrels.* Newbury Park, CA: Sage.

Robbins, L. P., & Deane, W. B. (1986). The corporate ombuds: A new approach to conflict management. *Negotiation Journal, 2,* 195–205.

Ross, R., & DeWine, S. (1982, November). *Interpersonal conflict: Measurement and validation.* Paper presented at the Speech Communication Association convention, Louisville, KY.

Rowe, M. P. (1987). The corporate ombudsman: An overview and analysis. *Negotiation Journal, 3,* 127–140.

Rubin, J. Z. (1983). Negotiation: An introduction to some issues and themes. *American Behavioral Scientist, 27,* 135–147.

Rubin, J. Z., Pruitt, D., & Kim, S. L. (1994). *Social conflict: Escalation, stalemate and settlement* (2nd ed.). New York: McGraw-Hill.

Runde, C. E., & Flanagan, T. A. (2007). *Becoming a conflict competent leader: How you and your organization can manage conflict effectively.* San Francisco: Jossey-Bass.

Ryan, F. J., Soven, M., Smither, J., Sullivan, W. M., & Vanbuskirk, W. R. (1999). Appreciative inquiry: Using personal narratives for initiating school reform. *Clearing House, 72*(3), 164–168.

Saarni, C. (1999). *The development of emotional competence.* New York: Guilford Press.

Sander, F. E. A., & Goldberg, S. B. (1994). Fitting the forum to the fuss: A user-friendly guide to selecting an ADR procedure. *Negotiation Journal, 10,* 49–67.

Schenck-Hamlin, W. J., Wiseman, R. L., & Georgacarakos, G. N. (1982). A model of properties of compliance-gaining strategies. *Communication Quarterly, 30,* 92–100.

Schön, D. A. (1983). *The reflective practitioner: How professionals think in action.* San Francisco: Jossey-Bass.

Segrin, C., & Givertz, M. (2003). Methods of social skills training and development. In J. O. Greene & B. R. Burleson (Eds.), *Handbook of communication and social interaction skills* (pp. 135–176). Mahwah, NJ: Lawrence Erlbaum.

Senger, J. M. (2002). Tales of the bazaar: Interest-based negotiation across cultures. *Negotiation Journal, 18,* 233–250.

Shannon, S. (2003). Adult learning and CME. *Lancet, 361*(9353), 266.

Shapiro, D. L. (2002). Negotiating emotions. *Conflict Resolution Quarterly, 20,* 67–82.

Shapiro, D. L., & Kolb, D. M. (1994). Reducing the litigious mentality by increasing employees' desire to communicate grievances. In S. B. Sitkin & R. J. Bies (Eds.), *The legalistic organization* (pp. 303–326). Thousand Oaks, CA: Sage.

Shweder, R. A. (1993). The cultural psychology of the emotions. In M. Lewis & J. M. Haviland (Eds.), *Handbook of emotions* (pp. 417–434). New York: Guilford Press.

Sillars, A. L. (1980a). Attributions and communication in roommate conflicts. *Communication Monographs, 47,* 180–200.

Sillars, A. L. (1980b). The sequential and distributional structure of conflict interactions as a function of attributions concerning the locus of responsibility and stability of conflicts. In D. Nimmo (Ed.), *Communication yearbook 4* (pp. 217–235). New Brunswick, NJ: Transaction Press.

Sillars, A. L. (1980c). Stranger and spouse as target persons for compliance gaining strategies. *Human Communication Research, 6,* 265–279.

Sillars, A. L., & Parry, D. (1982). Stress, cognition and communication in interpersonal conflicts. *Communication Research, 9,* 201–226.

Slaikeu, K. A., & Hasson, R. H. (1998). *Controlling the costs of conflict: How to design a system for your orientation.* San Francisco: Jossey-Bass.

Spangle, M. L., & Isenhart, M. W. (2003). *Negotiation: Communication for diverse settings.* Thousand Oaks, CA: Sage.

Sperry, L. (2005). *Executive coaching: The essential guide for mental health professionals.* New York: Brunner-Routledge.

Spitzberg, B. H., & Cupach, W. R. (1984). *Interpersonal communication competence.* Beverly Hills, CA: Sage.

Spitzberg, B. H., & Cupach, W. R. (1989). *Handbook of interpersonal competence research.* New York: Springer-Verlag.

Stephenson, P. (2000). *Executive coaching.* Frenchs Forest, New South Wales, Australia: Pearson Education Australia.

Stern, L. (1994). Executive coaching: A working definition. *Consulting Psychology Journal: Practice and Research, 56*(3), 154–162.

Stokes, R., & Hewitt, J. P. (1976). Aligning actions. *American Sociological Review, 41,* 838–849.

Susskind, L. (2004, August). Negotiation training: Are you getting your money's worth? *Negotiation,* 3–5.

Tannen, D. (1994). *Gender and discourse.* New York: Oxford University Press.

Thomas, K. (1976). Conflict and conflict management. In M. D. Dunnette (Ed.), *Handbook of industrial and organizational psychology* (pp. 889–935). Chicago: Rand McNally.

Thomas, K. W., & Kilmann, R. H. (1974). *Thomas-Kilmann conflict mode instrument.* Tuxedo, NY: Xicom.

Tidwell, A. (1997). Problem solving for one. *Mediation Quarterly, 14,* 309–317.

Ting-Toomey, S. (1988). Intercultural conflict styles: A face-negotiation theory. In Y. Y. Kim & W. Gudykunst (Eds.), *Theories in intercultural communication* (pp. 213–235). Newbury Park, CA: Sage.

Ting-Toomey, S. (1997). Intercultural conflict competence. In W. R. Cupach & D. J. Canary (Eds.), *Competence in interpersonal conflict* (pp. 120–147). New York: McGraw-Hill.

Ting-Toomey, S. (2004). The matrix of face: An updated face-negotiation theory. In W. B. Gudykunst (Ed.), *Theorizing about intercultural communication* (pp. 71–92). Thousand Oaks, CA: Sage.

Ting-Toomey, S., & Kurogi, A. (1998). Facework competence in intercultural conflict: An updated face negotiation theory. *International Journal of Intercultural Relations, 22,* 187–225.

Ting-Toomey, S., & Oetzel, J. (2001). *Managing intercultural conflict effectively.* Thousand Oaks, CA: Sage.

Ting-Toomey, S., Oetzel, J., & Yee-Jung, K. (2002). Self-construal types and conflict management styles. *Communication Reports, 14,* 87–104.

Tjosvold, D. (1985). Power and social context in superior-subordinate interaction. *Organizational Behavior and Human Decision Processes, 35,* 281–293.

Tjosvold, D. (1990). The goal interdependence approach to communication in conflict: An organizational study. In M. A. Rahim (Ed.), *Theory and research in conflict management* (pp. 15–27). New York: Praeger.

Tobias, L. L. (1996). Coaching executives. *Consulting Psychology Journal: Practice and Research, 48*(2), 87–95.

Ury, W., L., Brett, J. M., & Goldberg, S. B. (1988). *Getting disputes resolved: Designing systems to cut the costs of conflict.* San Francisco: Jossey-Bass.

Uyesug, J. L., & Shipley, R. (2005). Visioning diversity: Planning Vancouver's multicultural communities. *International Planning Studies, 10*(3/4), 305–322.

Valerio, A. M., & Lee, R. J. (2005). *Executive coaching: A guide for the HR professional.* San Francisco: Pfeiffer.

Van Dijk, T. (1993). Principles of critical discourse analysis. *Discourse and Society, 4,* 249–283.

Van Oosten, E. B. (2006). Intentional change theory at the organizational level: A case study. *Journal of Management Development, 25,* 707–717.

Vaughn, L., Gonzalez del Rey, J., & Baker, R. (2001). Microburst teaching and learning. *Medical Teacher, 23*(1), 39–43.

Versfeld, N. L., & Dreschler, W. A. (2002). The relationship between the intelligibility of time-compressed speech and speech in noise in young and elderly listeners. *Journal of the Acoustical Society of America, 111,* 401–408.

Volkema, R. J., Bergmann, T. J., & Farquhar, K. (1997). Use and impact of informal third party discussions in interpersonal conflicts at work. *Management Communication Quarterly, 11,* 185–216.

Wade, R. K. (1984). What makes a difference in in-service teacher education? A meta-analysis of research. *Educational Leadership, 42*(4), 48–55.

Wagner, M. L. (2000). The organizational ombudsman as change agent. *Negotiation Journal, 16*, 99–114.

Walton, R. E., & McKersie, R. B. (1965). *A behavioral theory of labor negotiations: An analysis of a social interaction system.* New York: McGraw-Hill.

Warters, W. C. (2000). *Mediation in the campus community: Designing and managing effective programs.* San Francisco: Jossey-Bass.

Wasylyshyn, K. (2003). Executive coaching: An outcome study. *Consulting Psychology Journal: Practice and Research, 55*(2), 94–106.

Watkins, M. (1999). Negotiating in a complex world. *Negotiation Journal, 15*, 229–270.

Watkins, M. (2001). Principles of persuasion. *Negotiation Journal, 17*, 115–137.

Watson, O. M., & Graves, T. D. (1966). Quantitative research in proxemic behavior. *American Anthropologist, 68*, 971–985.

Watzlawick, P., Beavin, J. H., & Jackson, D. D. (1967). *Pragmatics of human communication: A study of interaction patterns, pathologies, and paradoxes.* New York: Norton.

Weick, K. E. (1979). *The social psychology of organizing* (2nd ed.). Reading, MA: Addison-Wesley.

Weiss, J., & Hughes, J. (2005). Want collaboration? Accept and actively manage conflict. *Harvard Business Review, 83*(3), 92–101.

Weller, K., & Weller, D. (2004). Coaching and performance: Substantiating the link. *LIA, 24*(2), 20–21.

Wexler, J. A. (2000). In-house resolution of employment disputes. *The CPA Journal, 70*(12), 62–63.

White, M., & Epston, D. (1990). *Narrative means to therapeutic ends.* New York: Norton.

Wholey, J. S., Hatry, H. P., & Newcomer, K. E. (2004). *Handbook of practical program evaluation* (Jossey-Bass Nonprofit and Public Management Series). San Francisco: Jossey-Bass.

Wilmot, W. W., & Hocker, J. L. (2007). *Interpersonal Conflict* (7th ed.). New York: McGraw-Hill.

Winslade, J., & Monk, G. (2000). *Narrative mediation: A new approach to conflict resolution.* San Francisco: Jossey-Bass.

Winslade, J., & Monk, G. (2005). Does the model overarch the narrative stream? In M. Herrman (Ed.), *Blackwell handbook of mediation: Theory and practice* (pp. 217–228). New York: Blackwell.

Winum, P. C. (2005). Effectiveness of a high-potential African American executive: The anatomy of a coaching engagement. *Consulting Psychology Journal: Practice & Research, 57*(1), 71–89.

Witherspoon, R., & White, R. P. (1996). Executive coaching: A continuum of roles. *Consulting Psychology Journal: Practice and Research, 48*(2), 124–133.

Witten, M. (1993). Narrative and the culture of obedience at the workplace. In D. K. Mumby (Ed.), *Narrative and social control: Critical perspectives* (pp. 97–118). Newbury Park, CA: Sage.

Womack, D. F. (1988). A review of conflict instruments in organizational settings. *Management Communication Quarterly, 1*, 437–445.

Index

About the Authors

Tricia S. Jones (PhD, Ohio State University, 1985) is a professor in the Department of Psychological Studies in the College of Education at Temple University in Philadelphia. She has published over 40 articles and book chapters on conflict and conflict resolution education and has coedited *New Directions in Mediation, Does It Work? The Case for Conflict Resolution Education in Our Nation's Schools*, and *Kids Working It Out: Stories and Strategies for Making Peace in Our Schools*. She has coauthored *Interpersonal Communication through the Life Span*. Her research has been funded by the William and Flora Hewlett Foundation, the Packard Foundation, the Surdna Foundation, the Pennsylvania Commission on Crime and Delinquency, the George Gund Foundation, the United States Information Agency, and the U.S. Department of Education. She is currently working with the Global Partnership for the Prevention of Violence and the United Nations to develop an action agenda for conflict resolution education and peace education, and she is a founding member of the International Network for Conflict Resolution Education and Peace Education. Dr. Jones is the past president (1996–97) of the International Association of Conflict Management. She served two terms (2001–07) as the editor-in-chief of *Conflict Resolution Quarterly*, the scholarly journal of the Association for Conflict Resolution. She is the recipient of the 2004 Jeffrey Z. Rubin Theory to Practice Award from the International Association for Conflict Management.

Ross Brinkert (PhD, Temple University, 2006) is an assistant professor of corporate communication in the Division of Arts and Humanities at The Pennsylvania State University, Abington College in Abington, Pennsylvania. He is also a consultant, training development professional, and coach with over 10 years of experience in the private and public sectors. Dr. Brinkert's research, teaching, and applied work focus on the communication processes that organizations and individuals use to clarify purpose, develop pathways to success, and achieve measurable results.

321

He is especially involved in conflict management as it relates to internal organizational strategy, effective self-presentation, and leadership development. Dr. Brinkert helped pioneer conflict coaching while completing graduate studies and co-leading the Conflict Education Resource Team at Temple University from 1998 through 2001. Dr. Brinkert is currently active in researching the application of conflict coaching in large organizations.

DATE DUE
